Sun Tunnels and Secrets

For my best friend Mick,
who is a partner in every aspect of my life.

Walnut Springs Press, LLC
110 South 800 West
Brigham City, Utah 84302
http://walnutspringspress.blogspot.com

ISBN: 978-1-935217-75-6

Sun Tunnels and Secrets

Carole Thayne Warburton

WALNUT SPRINGS PRESS

Acknowledgements

So many have helped me with this novel. Thanks to all the friends and family who have shared stories and images of Grouse Creek and the surrounding area that may, in some form, have found their way into the pages of this book. Thanks especially to my talented niece Emily Warburton Jensen, for her editing and shaping of this novel. Thanks to Linda Prince Mulleneaux for her vision of this book and to the team at Leatherwood Press.

Thanks to my good friend Diane Tanner, who first told me the true story that I stretched beyond recognition to create this novel. Thanks also to Delma and Verl Smith for answering questions about Naf and Grouse Creek. Thanks to Alan Smith for his enthusiasm and support. Also thanks to Verna and Marge.

My heartfelt gratitude to my writing friends, Anne Stark, Kathy Herbert, Julie Dymock, Josi S. Kilpack, Janet Kay Jensen, and Arianne B. Cope, for all their encouragement and expertise. Thanks also to LDStorymakers for their support, humor, and generosity. Last but not least, thanks to my family.

One

IT LOOKED LIKE A BODY.

The three elderly sisters had just turned off the lonely highway onto the even more desolate dirt road when Norma saw it. Her foot trembled as she pressed the brake pedal.

"Oh, are we here?" LaRue asked, looking up from her embroidery and squinting through her spectacles. "I can't see those sun pipes. I thought you said they were out past Lucin."

"What is that on the side of the road?" Mabel pointed from the back seat.

"I . . . I believe it's a dead man," Norma answered in a tiny voice she didn't recognize. She swallowed hard.

"I'm getting one of my bad feelings." LaRue strained to see around Norma, clutching her embroidery basket to her chest. Suddenly, LaRue yelped, "Goodness gracious! That man isn't wearing any clothes!"

Norma's eyes went wide as she realized the man was indeed naked. She drummed the steering wheel with her fingers and thought. "What should we do?"

"Nothing. It would be indecent to—"

"Remember the story of the Good Samaritan?" Mabel interrupted, opening her door. "The man by the side of the road was without his clothes as well."

As Norma and LaRue watched, their impulsive and somewhat arthritic sister carefully made her way over the gravel to the body, which lay face-up a few yards from the side of the road. Mabel leaned over him, hand on her back, and hollered, "If I fall over, you'll help me up now, won't you?"

Norma glanced at LaRue, who was as white as her lace collar. The light gray curls framing her pudgy face shook slightly as she stared out the window at Mabel. "It's unseemly to see her hovering over a man, a n–naked man, no less."

"I imagine she's making sure he's dead. If he's not, then we'll need to help him. Mabel is right about that."

Norma didn't think it was possible, but LaRue paled even more at this suggestion.

Mabel shouted, "You still have that umbrella in your car?"

"Yes," Norma said, reaching under the seat and handing the umbrella to Mabel, who had shuffled up to the car window.

Mabel walked over and poked the body with the tip of the umbrella. The man didn't move. "Bring over something to cover him with."

Norma searched under the seat again, then in the glove compartment, but found nothing suitable. She turned to LaRue. "What do you have in your basket?"

LaRue now sat with her eyes shut, as if she thought the dead body would disappear if she didn't look at it. Finally, she slowly opened one eye, then sighed and pushed her embroidery basket toward her dark-haired, green-eyed sister. Norma fumbled through the paraphernalia and grabbed a partially embroidered pillowcase. "This will work."

LaRue let out a gasp. "Over my dead body!"

"No, but maybe over someone else's." Norma brusquely opened her door, then walked over to Mabel and the body.

As Norma stared at the man, she suddenly felt nauseous. He looked no older than her grandson Zach, who was twenty years old. His sandy hair was matted to his head, and black bruises outlined his closed eyes. Blood had congealed in a gash on his forehead.

"He doesn't seem to be alive," Mabel said, shaking her head. "Poor, poor, boy. And would you look at that nasty sunburn? He's been here a good while—and it sure looks like someone has beaten him, doesn't it?"

Norma shuddered. The body was indeed scorched from lying in the desert sun, and the man had clearly been beaten. She wondered if the assailant was still around. She scanned the flat landscape and saw only small scrub bushes and gravel—nowhere to hide. She dabbed at her sweaty forehead with the back of her hand. "Well, should we go call the authorities?" She wished her cell phone had service out in the middle of this nowhere.

Then she looked back at LaRue and sighed. There was no way she and Mabel would get her to come out here again. Norma had been looking forward to this outing—her first time out of town since her husband had passed away several weeks earlier. She looked back at the body; it wasn't going anywhere.

Mabel put her hand on Norma's arm. "We can't really do anything for him now, dear."

"Yes, and I guess we can call the sheriff when we get back home, so . . ."

Norma felt a little guilty at the thought, but what was a little more time to the deceased? And they had already come so far. Besides she hoped to be able to visit with Mabel about the phone call she'd had from a young woman named Katie that morning.

"Is Mr. Wesley Weaver there?" the caller had asked. It had shocked Norma to hear someone ask for her husband, but then she remembered most of the bills were still in his name.

"May I ask who's calling?" Norma had asked.

"Just tell Hummer it's Katie."

This obviously isn't the gas company, and why did she refer to Wes as Hummer? "Katie who?"

"Just Katie. I need help."

Norma's mind raced with all the possible Katies she had ever known, but none had any sort of personal relationship with her husband. When she'd told the caller that Wes had passed on, there was silence, as if the young-sounding woman were processing the information. Finally, Norma heard a sob, and then the caller hung up.

The strange phone call worried Norma, and she couldn't stop wondering who Katie was—and what she'd wanted from Wes.

Now there was this dead man. Norma hugged herself and watched as Mabel leaned over the man once more and asked, "Are you dead?" She poked him again with the umbrella. Silence.

"Get me LaRue's bottle of water."

Thinking Mabel was thirsty, Norma made her way back to the passenger-side door. "Mabel needs your water."

LaRue harrumphed. "What'll I take my decongestant tablets with?"

"She won't drink all of it."

LaRue reached into her basket again and grumbled, but handed Norma the water.

Norma hurried back to Mabel and gave her the bottle. Then Mabel slowly knelt down, her blue skirt scooting up on her bare, wrinkled legs. She poured the water onto the pillowcase and wiped the blood from the man's forehead. Then she carefully laid the embroidered pillowcase where it would do him the most good. "There now, that's better. If it were me lying here dead, I wouldn't want to be exposing myself." She paused and looked at Norma. "Nor would I want to ruin anyone's excursion. So let's just go see those tunnels before we drive back to Grouse Creek and call the sheriff. I think in the long run this young man will feel better about that."

Norma smiled, glad Mabel thought it was all right to continue on. Mabel stayed on her knees half a minute longer, her soft, gray curls peeking out from beneath her baseball cap.

"I said a prayer for him. I can give him that much." Mabel straightened up again. Slowly she took off her cap and placed it over the man's face. Then she opened the umbrella and propped it up to shade his body. "To keep the sun from doing any more damage, and to slow down the poor boy's decomposition. Now give me a hand up, you hear?"

Norma held out her hand and tugged her eighty-two-year-old sister to her feet.

"Well?" LaRue said when they got back into the car.

"He's dead." Mabel handed her the nearly empty water bottle.

"Well, he certainly can't wear my embroidery. It's not finished."

Norma smiled slightly. "Well, LaRue dear, you're welcome to retrieve it." LaRue glanced past them at the body and a look of horror crossed her face. She remained rooted in her seat.

The sisters didn't speak the rest of the way to the *Sun Tunnels*—a land art project built in the 1970s in the remote desert west of the Great Salt Lake. Norma's red Subaru bumped over railroad tracks and down through gullies and swells. She recalled the hubbub about the Sun Tunnels when they were first built, but since then, few people other than locals even knew of their existence. And none of the three sisters had ever been to the tunnels. Recently, however, there had been renewed interest in the tunnels, and people from all over were making the trek to the isolated northwest corner of the state to see them. Rumors abounded that during the summer solstice, hippies, Druids, and tree-huggers—although there wasn't a single tree there to hug—converged on the property, danced naked beneath the lowering sun and rising moon, and smoked marijuana. Norma suspected the rumors were exaggerated and was sure LaRue had never heard them, since she had consented to the trip. Nevertheless, the sisters made certain their outing would happen the day *after* the solstice, just to be on the safe side. Norma didn't want to run into any nude dancers, pot-smoking or otherwise.

When they came to a fork in the road, Norma got out her map, crudely drawn by one of the teenagers in town. "Guess we go left." There weren't any signs to mark the way, and the landscape was flat, although still somewhat greenish from the spring runoff. To the east were the Salt Flats, white desolation that stretched as far as one could see. Heat rose up like steam in the windswept summer sky.

The farther they drove, the more Norma realized the potential danger of traveling so many miles off the main road. She tried to remember if she had told anyone where they were going. Her nerves were starting to get the best of her. What if whoever killed that young man was still out there somewhere?

Suddenly, Norma saw the four massive concrete pipes and breathed a sigh of relief. She drove to the north side of one pipe and stopped. The three sisters got out of the car and quietly approached the land art.

Each of the Sun Tunnels was about nine feet in circumference and about twelve feet long, and the four tunnels formed an "X." The waning light of the setting sun cast long shadows, and a diffused glow danced through the strategically placed holes that mirrored constellations in the tunnel walls. The light played on Mabel's face, emphasizing the creases in her tawny skin. Watching Mabel step into one of the tunnels, Norma thought she could hear their mother's voice: "Dear, you just can't leave a man out in the desert like that. He could die from exposure."

"Mabel, did you say something?" Norma wanted to argue with her mother and remind her the man already was dead.

"I said LaRue went back to the car because her sinuses were closing up."

"Oh." Norma watched the glow dim as the sun set.

"It's almost magical here, isn't it?" Mabel reached her arms as high as she could in an effort to touch the tunnel's ceiling. But since she had shrunk to under five feet two inches, the ceiling was a good foot above her outstretched fingertips.

The sisters walked out of the tunnels, then turned and watched the sun, which was just about to slip behind the mountain. The two circles aligned, one inside of the other, black silhouettes against the orange sky.

Mabel gasped. "It's beautiful."

Norma nodded, feeling tears well up in her eyes.

Mabel took her arm. "Sweetie, are you worried about that young man?"

"Not worried exactly. Just thinking maybe we should pray or something, so we know what to do."

"Don't have to pray to know what to do, Norma," Mabel said. "We were raised in a good home, weren't we? I think it's high time we head back to attend to what has to be attended to."

As they slowly walked toward the car, Mabel sighed quietly. "What kind of a person would beat someone up and abandon him clear out in the middle of nowhere, more than thirty miles from the nearest town? Maybe he's dead because he tried to stop something bad from happening."

Norma shuddered. She thought of how much she missed Wes, and that reminded her of the phone call. "I had a strange phone call this morning. A young woman named Katie asked for Wes."

"What did she want?" Mabel pulled out a handkerchief to wipe her dusty face.

"She said she needed help, but she didn't say what kind of help. Who do you think she is? I don't remember Wes knowing anyone named Katie. Do you?"

"You didn't ask LaRue, did you?" Mabel stuffed her handkerchief back into her shirt pocket.

"Heavens, no. She would jump to the wrong conclusion."

"Hmm. Maybe Katie will call back again."

Norma sighed. It was silly, but she'd hoped somehow Mabel would know exactly who the desperate-sounding woman was. Norma opened the car door and helped Mabel into the back seat.

"It's getting dark, so it's about time you got back," LaRue said. "Just a bunch of old pipes anyway. Besides, don't you think we ought to call someone about that body we found?"

When the sisters drove to where they had seen the body, Norma slowed the car to a crawl. Mabel peered out the side window, prepared to tell her when to stop. In the dusk, the land all looked the same, with a few scraggly plants struggling for life, and the only distinguishing feature would be the body itself.

The three sisters strained their eyes, looking for the body. "What happened to him?" Mabel wondered aloud. "Surely we would've seen him by now. Dead men can't walk! See, we're almost back to the highway."

"I'm going to turn around and retrace our path. We missed him somehow." Even as Norma said it, she found it hard to believe. He'd been lying close to the road, his bare belly shining in the sun like some sort of beached fish. Even in the fading light they couldn't have missed him. Norma turned the car around and drove back toward the tunnels. A little way past the spot where she was certain the body had lain, she turned the car around again and backtracked, slowing the car to a mere five miles per hour. But there was no sign of Mabel's hat, her umbrella, or LaRue's embroidery.

And there was no body.

Two

Hi, Sam!

Remember the cabin Stacey lived in before you married her? That's right, I managed to get the same place here in Grouse Creek for my summer job! Not that there was anything else available in a town of 100 people, but still I was thrilled that it was available, especially after all the nice things you said about Herman and Maggie. And my big brother was right again—Herman and Maggie are every bit as wonderful as you said. Even though Herman must be around 85 years old, he still manages to do much of the work on his ranch.

So much has happened since I managed to get away from the polygamist cult, even though it was less than a year ago. Can you believe it? I know you thought I should continue in counseling to deal with Mom and Dad's death and keep going in for evaluations after the cult, but I seriously think a summer out in the fresh, open air doing research on the sage grouse is just the thing. After one week of smelling sagebrush, I feel almost whole. Besides driving over a hundred miles every week to meet with a counselor is way too much of a hassle.

You won't believe this. Remember Tony? Yep, you're right again. He got a job here for the summer too, working on the Box C Ranch. He's such a great friend to hang out with. Things could not be better. Tell your awesome wife I said hi, and email me back soon.

Love, Kelli

TONY WAS A COWBOY, BUT HE WORE HIS BLOND HAIR shaggy, a few inches over his ears, had both hard-rock and country tunes on his mp3 player, and had only recently traded in his baggy pants for boot-cut jeans.

He also loved skateboarding and had been known to break a few rules in both high school and college as he boarded in the no-skateboarding zones around campus. But in Grouse Creek, the only asphalt surrounded the church building, and the parking lot got boring really fast. So it was a good thing his new love of horseback riding mostly satisfied his need for thrills. Tony believed skateboarding and horseback riding required similar skills: balance, patience, passion, and guts. In college, Tony had discovered his natural flair with horses when he'd signed up for Horse Training 1010. By the second week of the course, he'd changed his major from engineering to agribusiness. And by the end of his sophomore year, he was somewhat assimilated into the cowboy culture, with a few snap shirts in his wardrobe. He even pulled out his old acoustic guitar his senior year, and he actually enjoyed playing it more than his electric guitar.

Tony knew he still had a lot to learn about ranching, but he hoped to prove to Jay, his boss at the Box C, that when it came to horses he had what it took. But the real reason he'd taken the job at the Box C Ranch in the tiny northwestern Utah town of Grouse Creek was to be closer to his soul mate, Kelli Carson. This beautiful redhead didn't know she was Tony's perfect match, but he hoped she'd figure it out by the end of the summer.

Today, Jay had sent Tony to the other end of the valley to check out a green-broke Quarter Horse gelding. Before leaving the bunkhouse, Tony had tossed his saddle and bridle into the back of the pickup. His goal was to take the horse out for a test ride to check its soundness and temperament.

Tony found the horse corralled and waiting for him ten miles east of Grouse Creek, next to a dilapidated pioneer settlement house, right off the main road. The neglected gelding looked gaunt and had overgrown hooves, but Tony liked the way the horse was built. And more importantly, Tony recognized something in the animal's eyes: a spark of spirit. It took Tony most of the afternoon to earn the horse's trust enough to get a blanket on its back. An hour later, Tony had saddled the horse. As he worked with the animal, the sun lowered in the sky, casting an orange glow across the Grouse Creek Valley.

Finally, Tony eased onto the horse. The horse bucked a little so Tony spoke calmly to him and stroked his neck. Just then, a bright pink car rolled up by the old house and stopped. Tony figured it must be James, the horse's owner, so he waited for James to come speak with him. But even as he tried to stay calm so the horse would continue to settle down, Tony saw a stranger get out of the car. Tony watched him as he quickly walked up to the fence.

"Hey, I was wondering if I could borrow some clothes."

When Tony looked up again, he saw that the man wore only a baseball cap and some kind of cloth wrapped around his midsection. Tony laughed, thinking it must be some kind of a joke.

"It's not funny. I need clothes. In fact, I have a gun."

A gun? This can't be for real. Tony tensed and the horse reared. Unable to keep his balance, Tony hit the ground hard. Pain jolted through him and he curled into a ball, then rolled away from the nervous animal's hooves.

With a groan, Tony looked back at the man, whose bruised face was etched with panic. His eyes darted wildly from the horse to Tony.

"Give me your clothes," the man demanded, pointing a gun at Tony.

"Say what?" Tony stood up and brushed the dirt off his jeans.

"Look, I've got to have some clothes."

"No way, man. What is this, some kind of joke?"

"This isn't a joke. Just do what I say!" The thin, sunburned man held onto the top of what Tony now could see was a pillowcase. He motioned for Tony to follow him, so Tony climbed over the cedar-pole fence. As they walked toward the house, the man got behind him and poked him in the back with the gun barrel.

"I don't live here," Tony said shakily. "I don't even know if it's open." But as Tony pushed hard on the door, it swung wide.

A putrid smell of mice droppings and mold caused Tony to pause and shield his nose. The man nudged Tony forward. Empty beer cans littered the small kitchen, and a dirty pan sat on the stove. In the next room, an army cot and a bed with a bare mattress were the only furniture. "You want me to keep going?" Tony asked.

"Yeah."

Surprisingly, Tony felt a strange calm replace his initial fear. He opened the closet at the back of the room. A pile of filthy, greasy overalls lay in the corner of the otherwise bare closet.

"Looks like you're going to have to take off your clothes."

"What?"

"Well, there's no way I'm wearing those things," the man said nervously, "and I gotta get out of here."

Tony thought quickly. If he gave him his clothes, the man would hopefully go without any trouble. If he argued—well, the man might use the gun on him. Tony sighed as he slipped off his jeans, keeping his belt, and then unsnapped his western shirt.

"Keep your underwear, but I want the boots." The man fumbled to dress single-handedly while keeping the gun aimed in Tony's direction.

Tony pulled off his boots one by one and tossed them over, wondering if he should try hitting the man with the hard leather heel. He loved those boots. They were at the perfect stage, softened by wear enough that they molded to his feet, yet they still had a generous heel. He'd religiously rubbed them with mink oil to keep the leather conditioned. "I'm keeping the belt," Tony said. The buckle had been a Christmas present from Kelli.

"No, you aren't. It's worth money, isn't it?"

"Well . . ." Tony hesitated, knowing a silver buckle this size had to be worth close to a hundred dollars. "You'd have a hard time selling it at a pawn shop. It's a one-of-a-kind so it'd be easy to trace."

"Okay man, you can keep that, but I'll need the hat."

"No way!" Tony's hand reached up to his new brown felt

hat. He silently cursed himself for not wearing his old straw hat, which actually worked better at keeping the sun out of his eyes.

"I gotta have it." The man struggled to pull the boots on. "Give it to me or I'll—I'll shoot." He took off his baseball cap and tossed it on the floor.

"All right, all right, hold your horses." Tony pulled off the hat and handed it over. *This guy must be crazy.*

"Okay, now give me the keys to your truck," the thief demanded. "I'll trade you." He handed Tony a set of keys dangling from a miniature cowboy boot.

"What? You've already got a car. Why do you need mine?"

"The cops can spot that thing from miles away. And it's about out of gas."

Now Tony thought about Kelli again. He hadn't set anything definite, but he'd promised to stop by after work.

"Got any cash?" the man interrupted his thoughts.

"Not on me." With dread, Tony realized his wallet was in his pickup.

The guy started to leave the room and then stopped. "Almost forgot. Guess I'd better tie you up before I leave."

"Oh, shoot," Tony muttered under his breath.

"Did you just tell me to shoot?"

"No! That's not what I meant. But hey, you don't need to tie me up. I don't have a phone here, so I can't call the police, and you said yourself the car is about out of gas."

"I'm not dumb. You're a cowboy—you could ride your horse. Besides I can't afford to take any chances. I need to get somewhere." The man looked around, and Tony guessed he was searching for something to use to tie him up. "Come on, we're going outside."

Tony thought for a second. The young man didn't seem to be very bright and was built similar to Tony. Maybe Tony could overpower him before he could fire a shot. Then Tony thought again. *Kelli.* Before Kelli came into his life he would've taken the chance, but now he had a lot to live for. He followed the man out the front door.

"Lay down on the ground, and put your hands behind your back."

Tony knelt and then dropped to his stomach in the dust. Fear crept back into his mind, and he felt his heart quicken and sweat form on his forehead. Tony wondered if the man's odd behavior had anything to do with the gashes on his face.

The man grabbed a rope that hung on the corral fence, then fumbled as he tied Tony's hands together and then his feet. The rope cut into Tony's wrists as the rope was cinched.

"Anything I need to know about the truck?"

Tony shook his head.

"Just remembered something else." The man unknotted the silk scarf around Tony's neck, then tied it around Tony's mouth. Then he put the pillowcase over Tony's head. After a few moments of silence, Tony heard his truck roar to life and rumble down the road.

Now what? Tony couldn't see or speak, and he could barely move. As the night darkened, all he could do was listen to the crickets chirp, the horse snort, and the coyotes howl.

Three

"CRAP!"

"Norma, you shouldn't use such language!" LaRue scolded as they turned back onto a paved road.

"Well, this is all very upsetting. First we find a dead man, and then he disappears. People are going to wonder what happened. They'll ask why we didn't bring him with us, or why we left him to go to the Sun Tunnels. Won't that make us look heartless? It might even be illegal, as far as I know."

"No, sweetie, it's not illegal to leave a dead person. It's illegal to move one, though." Mabel put her hand on Norma's shoulder. "For what it looked like, it very well could have been a crime scene. I know this because at the Cowboy Grill in Montello, someone died in a fight and they had to leave him right in the middle of the floor until the police came out and investigated. It was business as usual with a dead man on the floor. By the time the police arrived, people were laughing, eating, and drinking, without giving him another thought. My friend LaVell said the whole incident was rather disturbing."

LaRue huffed. "I couldn't eat with a dead man on the floor."

Norma silently agreed. Yet, while Mabel's story sounded awful, it also was rather comforting. In all of her seventy-nine years she'd never done anything that gave the police—or anyone for that matter—cause for concern, and she really didn't want to start now.

"I think we should chalk the whole thing up to a desert mirage. I mean, did you actually feel his body, or did you just think you saw him?"

"We all saw him—even you, LaRue—and that man was real enough an hour ago. I put your embroidery on—"

"Please don't!" LaRue let out a panicked squeak.

"Well, dear, if it was a mirage, then you'd still have your embroidery," Norma said. "Do you have it?"

LaRue rummaged through her hand basket. "No, it's not here."

With no other options, they headed toward the highway. At the crossroads, Norma looked for Mabel's car.

"Oh, no!"

"What?" LaRue looked around wildly.

"Don't panic, Mabel, but your Lincoln is missing," Norma said.

Mabel caught her breath as Norma slowed the car. The bright pink color of her car always struck Norma as odd, but Mabel said the best thing about being older is that it allowed you to do things considered socially unacceptable in the younger crowd. She said the garish car added to her "image." This image also included baseball caps. And that wouldn't have been so unusual if she'd worn trousers with them, but Mabel always wore long, button-down skirts, white ankle socks folded over just once, and Nike sneakers. She preferred the Nike brand because she liked the "swish" logo on the sides.

"Holy Hannah, doesn't that beat all?" LaRue turned up the automatic fan she wore around her neck for, as she described it, "cooling down and ridding my personal space of contaminants."

Almost before Norma stopped the car, Mabel opened her door and hurried over to the spot where she'd parked her Continental. She walked in a circle, studying the ground for a moment before returning to the Subaru. As she got back in, she announced, "They headed toward Grouse Creek, so I'll need to go with you and see if we can't find my car. Maybe Deloy drove it home."

Norma nodded. She could just barely make out the tire marks crossing the sand and heading to town.

"Why would Deloy take it? He lives in Park Valley, and you said they drove toward Grouse Creek." LaRue strained her neck to see.

Norma nodded again. Their baby brother had no reason to take Mabel's car.

"Why does he keep chocolate bars under his bed?" Mabel asked. "Deloy just does what Deloy does."

"I didn't know Deloy kept chocolate under his bed," Norma mused as she started down the road toward Grouse Creek.

They had gone a few miles when Mabel shouted, "Wait! Let's go check out the Riggs' house."

"Why? The house is dark," Norma said. "No one is living there these days."

"Let's just check," Mabel insisted.

Norma didn't want to stop, but Mabel's instincts were usually spot on. The Riggs had moved away in 1978, and now seasonal workers hired by the local ranchers occasionally used the abandoned place. It was a ramshackle, pieced-together home with additions protruding in every direction.

While Mabel and Norma knocked on the weathered door, LaRue waited in the car to try to catch a few winks.

"No one's home," Mabel said.

Norma heard a shuffling noise. "What's that?" She peered around in the dark. Then she heard a thumping sound that seemed to come from the corral.

"Oh, it must be this horse makin' a racket," Mabel said, watching the bay paw at the ground.

"That's strange. No one's home, but someone left their horse saddled." Norma frowned. Then she heard the noise again, and it didn't sound anything like a horse. It was more like something dragging across dirt.

The hair on the back of Norma's neck stood up and she could feel goose bumps rising on her arms. In the dark and with no one living within a ten-mile radius, she knew three elderly women would be a pretty easy mark for a criminal. "Mabel, get in the car," she ordered, trying not to attract attention. But Mabel walked toward the other side of the house.

"Mabel, come on!"

"Lookie here," Mabel said.

The shuffling got louder and louder. Norma ran to her car, jumped in, and started the engine.

"Oh, my!" In the headlights, she saw Mabel tugging on the door handle of her pink car. Norma rolled down the window and shouted, "Mabel Hansey McDonald, get in this car this instant!"

"Good gracious, however do you think my car got to be here?" Mabel turned back, her face triumphant.

"Someone drove it here, obviously," Norma said frantically, "and whoever drove it is a thief and could very well be insane. Let's get out of here!"

"What is going on?" LaRue yawned. "Are we home yet?"

Mabel walked back to Norma's car and got in the back seat. "The keys weren't in it. I always leave them hanging on the mirror so I'll be sure to find them when I need them."

"And so that every Tom, Dick, and Harry can steal your car?" LaRue asked incredulously.

"I always figure if someone needs a car badly enough to take it, then I might as well make it as easy as possible for them."

Mabel's good nature and obvious trust in mankind had always irritated LaRue, but even the normally pleasant Norma found it remarkable in today's age.

As they backed out the driveway, something caught Norma's attention and she stopped the car. A form moved beneath the pole fence, and Norma's heart began to beat wildly again.

LaRue screamed, "That thing is wearing my embroidered pillowcase!"

Four

NORMA CLUTCHED AT HER HEART. SHE SLAMMED HER foot on the gas, backed the car out of the driveway, and barreled toward Grouse Creek.

The three women sat in shocked silence, broken only when Mabel piped up from the back, "There's a chance I left an extra set of keys in the glove box of my car. Let's go back and see."

"Mercy, Mabel! We aren't going back there. Hasn't it dawned on you that the man scooting on the ground—if it even was a man—had to be the one who robbed you in the first place?" LaRue said in a squeaky voice. Then, after a few composing breaths, she added, "Besides, who does he think he is, wearing my pillowcase on his head, of all places? The unseemly manners of folks today is lacking beyond belief. He's bound to be a murderer or worse."

Norma wondered what could be worse than a murderer. "It must be the man we thought was dead. He . . . must . . ." But she couldn't think how he could've gotten there.

Mabel sighed. "Dears, obviously that isn't the poor boy we left in the desert. If it was him, why on earth did he put LaRue's half-finished pillowcase on his head? Besides, LaRue, didn't you want to finish that pillowcase for Heather's wedding in August? We've got to go back and get it."

LaRue gasped. "I can't finish it now! Do you expect me to just forget where it has been? The pillowcase is completely ruined!"

Norma pulled the car to the edge of the washboard road so she could think. Mabel had made a good point. Why would the dead man put the pillowcase on his own head? He wouldn't. Whoever it was crawling on the ground might need their help. With a deep breath, she turned the car around.

LaRue gasped again. "What are you doing?" She looked at Norma like she was crazy. "You don't honestly think we should . . . no! Turn back around."

She continued to rant and rave, but Norma ignored her. In truth, Norma wanted to turn around, get home, and just forget the whole incident. But she knew Mabel was right.

Soon they were back at the Riggs' place, and Norma stopped the car partway up the drive. "Should we plan some kind of action just in case?"

"I'm not getting out of this car." LaRue shook her head. "I'm much too old to be consorting with murderers and their ilk."

"There are three of us," Mabel said, "and one of him. He's on the ground. Surely, three silly old women can take on one man if need be. Besides he doesn't have a weapon."

LaRue drew a sharp breath. "Who are you calling silly? I've never been silly in my life."

Mabel rolled her eyes. "Truer words were never spoken. Now come on."

"Okay, but how do you know he doesn't have a weapon on him?" Norma asked.

"He wouldn't be sitting on the ground with a pillowcase on his head," Mabel answered matter-of-factly. "If he had a gun, he would've shot the guy before he could put that on his head."

When Norma pulled further up the driveway, she noticed the man had managed to get closer to the main road. Now she could see his feet were tied up, and she felt confident he couldn't hurt them even if he wanted to. Mabel got out of the car and Norma followed. LaRue stayed put, gasping for breath. Norma could hear the whir of her battery-operated fan.

As Norma approached the man, a horrific odor reached her nostrils. She glanced around and saw a couple of abandoned pigpens. She was afraid to get close to the man, but she knew if he could move much, he would have done so by now. As Norma and Mabel hunched down to look at him, the smell intensified. Norma turned her head away and buried her nose in her blouse, then snatched off the pillowcase and handed it to Mabel. Now they could plainly see a young, handsome man, bound, gagged, and wearing tattered grimy coveralls.

"See, he isn't the man we left in the desert," Mabel said, her arthritic fingers struggling to remove the tight gag from the man's mouth. Norma joined in the effort, but they couldn't loosen the fabric. The man looked to be in his twenties. He had blond, wavy hair and blue-green eyes, and he was clean shaven. Norma thought it odd that such a pleasant-looking young man could smell so bad.

Norma remembered LaRue's hand basket and figured she would have a pair of scissors. She hurried over and knocked on LaRue's window, but LaRue held the whirring fan closer to her face and ignored Norma's pounding.

"LaRue, do you have a pair of scissors in your basket?" Norma shouted through the closed window. LaRue looked up at Norma, then with a grimace reached into her basket and pulled out a tiny pair of scissors made for snipping thread. She unrolled the window a crack and pushed them out. "Don't know what you'd need scissors for at this time of night," she griped before quickly rolling up the window.

The scissors fell to the ground, so Norma grunted and knelt to find them. She looked up and saw Mabel trying to untie the man's wrists and feet. "Don't do that. If he's riding in our car, you've got to leave him tied!"

Once she located the scissors, Norma went over and started snipping at the gag. The man's eyes widened and he jumped and made a sound. Realizing she must have poked him with the sharp points, Norma tried to be more careful. Finally, the scarf loosened and fell away from the man's face.

"Thanks," he said in a raspy, breathless voice. Then he gulped the dry air several times. "Water?"

"Get LaRue out here. We've got to help this young man to his feet."

This time Mabel knocked on the car window. "LaRue, dear, you know I don't ask for much, but we really need your help."

LaRue looked horrified. Mabel tugged on the door handle, but it was locked. Mabel folded her arms and waited, staring at her sister with her best you-better-open-this-up-if-you-know-what's-good-for-you look. After a few moments LaRue got out of the car, and the three struggled to pull the man to his feet.

"I'm sure glad you came along, but couldn't you just untie me?" he asked. "It'd sure be easier that way."

"I'm so sorry, sir, but not knowing you or your intentions, we can't do that," Norma felt a bit embarrassed, since the man looked nice enough. Still, he was a man, and looks could be deceiving.

"You could conk us on the head or steal our car—*again,* I might add—or worse," LaRue put in.

The young man leaned against a fence post for balance. Then the three sisters helped him hop over to Norma's car.

LaRue reached frantically for her battery-operated fan. She

switched it on and held it in front of her face. "The odor emanating from that pigsty is simply ghastly!"

Norma wondered why LaRue didn't just say the place stank, but she always seemed to be overly dramatic with language.

Mabel opened the back door of the Subaru.

"Wait," LaRue said. "Maybe it would be better for all of us if we had him ride in the cargo space. That way—"

"Certainly not," Mabel interrupted. "We aren't heathens. Where are your manners, LaRue? I've a good mind to put him in the front seat. He's our guest."

"No, no, I'm just grateful for the ride, but if you don't mind I really don't want to ride in the back." The man backed into the rear seat, bumped his head on the top of the doorframe, and groaned.

Norma helped Mabel into the other side of the back seat, while LaRue got in the front, doing everything she could to fan the scent away. Norma settled into the driver's seat and pulled back out onto the road.

"I hope it's not putting you out too much to ask for a ride to the Box C Ranch," the young man said. "It's about twelve miles ahead."

"Oh, my goodness, I should've known! You must be Tony Stratton, the new hired hand for the summer." Norma was pleased to have sorted things out in her mind. "We should have untied you."

"Well, I doubt those scissors could have done the job," Tony said with a chuckle.

LaRue harrumphed.

"On second thought," Tony said, "as late as it is, please just drop me off at Herman Anders' place. It's closer and I'm late."

"You know Herman?"

"Yeah. Actually, I'm a friend of Kelli, who rents—"

"Why didn't you tell us you were Kelli Carson's boyfriend?" Norma exclaimed. "Why, isn't she just the cutest thing? I met her just the other day at the post office."

"Well, she's great, but we're just friends. I met her in Montana."

"Then I guess you already know about her past," LaRue interjected.

"Past?"

"I heard she was one of a dozen wives." LaRue stared back at Tony. "She's cute, but do you really want to tie yourself to one of those people?"

"It wasn't like that. Kelli was duped. And she showed a lot of courage in escaping from that awful cult."

"LaRue! Good gravy, what a thing to say! Forgive us, Tony." Mabel frowned. "LaRue, apologize right now."

LaRue turned her face to the door. "I'm sorry that Kelli—"

Norma couldn't believe that this young man, clearly interested in Kelli, would visit the pretty girl in such a state of disarray. She cracked the window an inch. Kelli didn't seem like the type to get involved with a polygamist group. There must be more to it than LaRue had heard.

"Um . . . could I get some water?" the young man spoke up.

"Oh, I'm sorry, dear." Norma had forgotten. "LaRue, your water."

"My goodness. What if I need it to take more medication?" LaRue complained, then turned and handed the water bottle to Tony. But since his hands were tied, the bottle fell to the floor.

Mabel picked it up and tried to untie Tony, but she couldn't even loosen the ropes. "I'm sorry, I just can't do it." Awkwardly, she helped him gulp down the remaining water in the bottle.

The car rumbled over a cattle guard. Now Norma could see the lights of town.

"Herman will have something to cut these ropes."

"Sweetie, where'd you say you were from?" Mabel asked, scooting away from Tony and his overpowering odor. LaRue had her fan going full blast now as she held it under her nose.

"Bozeman, Montana."

"Good heavens, how can you people even talk with the air so putrid?" LaRue asked in a high-pitched tone. "What is that ghastly odor that has been with us ever since—"

"That'd be me." Tony sighed. "My clean clothes were . . . you're not going to believe this . . . stolen by a man with a gun. These are—"

"Was it a pearl-handled .32 Special?" Mabel interrupted.

"Um, yeah, I think so."

"Oh, sweetie, that thing doesn't even work. I just carry it with me just in case I run into trouble."

"I don't get it," Tony said. "How did the guy have your gun?"

"I imagine he found it in the glove box of my car."

"Your car? The pink one we left at the house?"

"Actually, dear, it's magenta."

"Mabel, what about your car?" Norma asked as they drove down the last hill into Grouse Creek.

"Oh, it's in a fine place tonight. We'll get Deloy to come and tow it out of there tomorrow."

"Actually, I have the keys to your car in the pocket of these coveralls, although the guy said it was almost out of gas."

"Thank you." Mabel smiled sweetly. "You can give them to me when we get to Herman's place."

When they arrived in Grouse Creek, Norma considered taking LaRue and Mabel to her house on the north side of town, but decided they shouldn't waste any time before reporting everything to the police. Unfortunately, dropping by a police station wasn't an option, as the nearest one was well over a hundred miles away.

As they neared Herman's house, Norma thought about what had happened. The man in the desert must not have been dead at all and must've walked to the crossroads where Mabel had met them after visiting Deloy in Park Valley. It had seemed to be a fair distance, but they had been driving so slowly it might've only been a mile. Instead of a death in the desert, they had a crime to report, although Norma wasn't sure what kind of a crime. Then a thought struck her. "Tony, did you have a vehicle out at the Riggs' place, or did you come on your horse?"

"I had a truck, but the crook took off with it."

"Just to be sure, was the man wearing a red and white baseball cap embroidered with 'Cowboy Grill'?" Mabel asked.

"Yeah, and he didn't have any clothes except for an embroidered pillowcase, which he kindly gave to me," Tony replied sarcastically.

"Did it ever occur to you while you were frolicking around in the dirt, that the exquisite embroidery would be ruined?"

Mabel ignored LaRue. "Hmm. The dead man would've needed something with more gas in it. I only had enough to get back home."

"Dead man?" Tony asked.

"Well, he was dead, or we thought he was," Norma explained as she turned into Herman's drive. "But he must've come back to life or awakened from a deep sleep or something, walked to the crossroads, took Mabel's car, got to the Riggs' house, robbed you with Mabel's gun—even though he clearly couldn't have killed you with it—then stole your truck and vanished."

LaRue shook her head. "There is no appreciation for handiwork these days. Young folks today think nothing about sticking their heads in fine embroidery. I just don't understand it."

"We can still go back and get that pillowcase tomorrow," Norma offered. "With a little washing and stitching, it'll be fine."

"No, no."

"I'm sure sorry," Tony said. "I'll try and make it up to you somehow."

Norma got out and knocked on the door. It was after ten o'clock and the house was dark. Herman and Maggie must've gone to bed. Norma pounded on the door again and waited. Herman was older than Mabel but still spry for his age, and since he had married Maggie, he seemed even more vital than ever.

When the door finally opened, Norma stared into the barrel of a rifle. She automatically threw her hands in front of her face.

"Herman Anders, it's me, Norma! Put that gun away!"

Herman chuckled and opened the door wide. He wore a pair of pajamas, and his disheveled gray hair sprung from his head in all directions. "Look what the cat done drug in."

"Herman, hush now and listen. We've got Tony Stratton and he needs help."

Herman rubbed his chin. "Well, I'll be! Send him on in."

"He's tied up."

"He's too busy to come in?"

Norma grimaced. "No, he's tied up with ropes."

Herman disappeared for a minute and came back wearing a pair of jeans with his pajama top. He ambled down the porch steps and out to the car, with Norma trailing behind. He opened Tony's side of the car and began untying him. "What's the trouble?"

"Has Kelli been asking for me? I told her I'd stop by."

"Well, you ain't gonna see her while you're smellin' like a dead pig." Herman fished out a pocketknife and cut away Tony's rope. "Come in, all of you. You got some explainin' to do."

Norma sighed as she and her sisters followed Tony and Herman up the steps. As they entered the living room, a bleary-eyed Maggie emerged from the bedroom, a red satin robe wrapped tightly around her. Her salt-and-pepper hair just reached her shoulders, and even though she was in her late seventies, she was still an attractive woman. She and Herman had been married for a few years now.

When Maggie saw Tony, her face broke into a smile and she approached him for a handshake, but then she stopped short, her eyes wide. "What happened to you?"

"Sorry. I know I stink. After I call the police, I'll just step out to the cabin and say hi to Kelli before heading home to shower." He grinned at Maggie. "Um, mind if I use your phone?"

"It's right through there." Maggie pointed to the kitchen.

"You'll be killin' any chance for lovin' with the girl if you head over like that. She'll mistake you for a skunk." Herman chuckled. "We'll round you up some clothes, and you'd better be showerin' here 'fore you go anywhere."

Tony's face went red. "Well, you know, Kelli and I are just friends."

Herman nodded. "That's right, and that's all you'll be forever more if she gets a whiff of you."

"Okay, thanks." Tony grinned. "A shower would be great." With that, he disappeared into the kitchen.

When Tony returned to the living room, he found everyone listening as Mabel told about finding the dead man, exploring the Sun Tunnels, and coming across Tony with a pillowcase over his head. Herman laughed so hard that Tony wondered if his heart could take it.

"Well, I called the police," Tony said. "They'll keep an eye out for the guy."

"Oh, dear, Tony, your ordeal must've been awful!" Maggie handed him a stack of clean clothes.

"Thanks."

"And there's a burn barrel out back. Just take those overalls out right away."

Tony glanced around the room. "Well, thanks for everything. I'd still be out there if you hadn't come along. I'll get Kelli to take me back to the Box C, so I won't trouble you ladies anymore."

After a long, hot shower, Tony stepped out the back door of the house into the black night. In the glow of the back porch light, he saw a rusty metal barrel a few yards from the steps. He dropped the overalls into the barrel, and the acrid smell of ashes assailed his nose.

As Tony made his way to Kelli's cabin, he thought back to the first time he saw her. She was running up the steps at his apartment building in Montana, her red hair streaming behind her. Tony had never believed in love at first sight until that moment.

Common sense should've told him that a girl running from the police was trouble, but Tony had been immediately drawn to Kelli. Soon he learned she'd gotten involved with a fundamentalist group that had used false pretenses to persuade her to join. When she realized what the group was really about, she tried to leave but was held against her will. Finally, she escaped. She'd run from the police, unsure whom she could trust at the time.

Tony liked to think he had been the answer to Kelli's prayers, or maybe vice versa. Why else had he been home playing his guitar when she needed help? He had rarely stayed home in the evenings, but on that particular night, he felt he should.

Kelli's cabin was dark. Tony stood on the porch and raised

his hand to knock on the door, but then decided not to wake her. He'd just ask Herman to drive him to the ranch.

"Good night," he whispered before he left.

Five

EARLY THE NEXT MORNING, TONY RETURNED TO work. His first chore, hauling a load of hay to the north pastures of the Box C Ranch, took him past Herman and Maggie's house. When Tony craned his neck to get a glimpse of Kelli's cabin, he spotted his own stolen truck, parked right next to the tiny cabin.

He slammed on the brakes, and before the truck came to a complete stop, he jammed it into PARK, jumped out, and ran to the cabin. The door was unlocked and he flung it open to see Kelli lying still on the floor, her red hair surrounding her head like a halo.

He knelt beside her and put his ear to her mouth; she was breathing. He rushed out the door to find help and saw Norma driving down the road. He waved frantically and she stopped the vehicle, jumping out of the car without turning off the ignition.

"Something's happened to Kelli. Did you see anyone running from here?"

"No, I didn't. Oh dear, oh dear!" Norma said, then followed Tony inside. After taking one look at Kelli, she rushed to the sink and grabbed a washrag, moistened it with cold water, and laid it on Kelli's ashen forehead. "What on earth happened?"

Suddenly, Kelli whimpered. Tony took her in his arms, his heart feeling like lead in his chest. "Kelli, wake up, please!"

Her eyes slowly opened. "I . . . he was wearing your clothes, Tony," Kelli whispered. Tony lifted her head and Norma gave her several sips of water. Kelli continued softly, "I heard you coming—your truck. I must've jumped up too fast. Last thing I remember . . . a man . . . wearing your clothes." Kelli shivered as Tony slowly helped her to her feet.

"Shh. You're safe now." Tony guided her to a kitchen chair and then turned to Norma. "Kelli sometimes faints when she stands up too fast. She thinks it's no big deal, but she does have a large bump on the back of her head." He turned back to Kelli. "You're sure he didn't hit you?"

"I don't remember for sure." Kelli reached around to feel the lump. "He said he wanted to talk."

"I'll run over to Herman's and call the police. The guy probably bolted after Kelli fell, and he won't get too far on foot. Norma, you'll stay with her, won't you?"

"Oh, my goodness, of course."

Tony stepped onto the front porch. "Norma, your car's gone!"

Norma jumped up and looked out the door. Her hand flew to her mouth. "He's struck again! There goes my car now!"

Tony saw a plume of dust rising over the hill.

"Doesn't this make three stolen vehicles?" Norma asked. "And terrifying this young woman half to death? It never ends."

Tony shook his head, then jogged to Herman's back door and banged on it. When no one came to the door, he went in and called the police. A few minutes later, he was back in Kelli's cabin.

"The police will be out in a while to check for evidence, fingerprints—that sort of thing," he explained.

“There won’t be any fingerprints.” Kelli sighed. “He was wearing your work gloves.”

Tony stood next to Kelli as she sat at the small kitchen table. He knelt next to her chair and embraced her. “It sure scared me to see you lying on the floor. I thought for a second you were dead.”

Kelli leaned into Tony, her eyes filling with tears.

Norma cleared her throat. “I’ll walk on home and wait for the police in case they need to question me. You two don’t need me anymore.”

“Thanks for everything,” Tony said. Then he turned his attention back to Kelli. “Don’t worry—we’ll find him.”

The face of the crazy man came into Tony’s mind and he felt his anger surge. That psychopath! The sooner the cops found him and put him behind bars, the better. Tony would do everything he could to make sure that happened. Now he wished he’d listened to his instincts the night before and warned Kelli there was a criminal in the area. He could’ve even stayed nearby to keep her safe.

With relief, Tony noticed Kelli’s color was improving. He pulled her trembling body close again, and soon her tears soaked the front of his shirt.

When Kelli was young, both of her parents were killed in a car accident. Then, just one year ago, members of a fanatical religious group had nearly killed her when she escaped. Tony knew that since Kelli’s ordeal with the male-dominated cult, she was fearful of men, even those she knew. How could Tony help her feel safe now?

“I’m okay,” Kelli said, then took a few deep breaths. “It’s just that when I saw him wearing your clothes, I thought he . . .” Kelli put her hand over her face and gulped. “I thought he might’ve hurt you.”

“Shh.” Gently, Tony pushed Kelli far enough away that

he could see her face. "Can I get you something to drink?" he asked her.

"Water would be great, thanks."

Tony found a cup in the small cupboard above the sink, filled it with water, and handed it to Kelli. Her hand shook as she held the cup to her lips. When Tony reached to steady the cup, his hand brushed hers. How he wanted to hold her hand in his! But they were just friends. And even though they'd hugged a few times before, he felt certain it was with the same affection she'd show Sam, her brother and hero. Tony knew from his friendship with Kelli in Montana that the sun set and rose with her brother, so when she told Tony she loved him like her brother, he was flattered but also hurt. From that day forward, he had tried to relinquish any hope he and Kelli could be more than good friends.

It would take at least three hours before the police would converge on the small town, since they had to travel all the way from Brigham City. That was plenty of time for the perpetrator to disappear on one of the lonely roads out of town, or to hole up in a hidden canyon.

"Come on, let's get out of here. It'll take all morning for the cops to get here. Do you mind coming with me while I do my chores? I need to take this hay out and then pick up a horse. I was on my way when I saw my truck."

"Sure. I can't just sit here, and I don't feel like working alone."

Tony held his hand out to pull Kelli up. "Milady." She managed a weak smile.

In less than an hour, they arrived at the Riggs place, where just the night before Tony had been held up with a worthless gun. He shook his head in disgust.

With Kelli's help, they coaxed the horse into the trailer. Tony paused before closing the door behind the animal. "There's something I've wanted to tell you." He took a deep breath.

"Yeah?" Kelli looked at him anxiously.

"I'm really hoping you'll help me out with something I've been trying to get the nerve up to do." Tony ran his fingers through his unruly blond hair, and then opened the truck door for Kelli. "You know Buck Branson?"

"Well, not personally, but yeah, of course. Buck Branson, who in your opinion is the greatest country-western singer on the face of the planet? Buck Branson, whose goal is to put fidelity back in marriage? Buck Branson, the guy whose pictures you have on your wall like a schoolgirl with a crush? I have to tell you, Tony, I've always thought that was a little nerdy. I mean, you're twenty-six years old."

"Just hear me out." Tony laughed as he walked to the driver's side and got in. He glanced down the road to make sure no cars were coming before he pulled out. "Anyway, he'll be in Salt Lake next month."

"And you've got tickets?"

"Yeah. Front row."

Kelli squealed. "How did you manage that?"

"Let's just say my mom knows the guy."

"You never told me that. I didn't think you even talked to your mother. It drives me crazy when people have parents and don't get along with them. I'd give anything to have my mom around."

"I wish Mom and I were close, but it's her choosing. She puts on a good show, but that's all it is. She showed me years ago I didn't mean all that much to her." Tony thought about his mother's late nights singing at night clubs, which meant she had rarely attended his soccer and little-league games, missed his birthdays, and forgot about promises she'd made to him. "It's complicated."

"Still, she got you tickets—that's all I'm saying."

Tony turned away from Kelli's gaze and watched the road. "She owed me a favor. But there's more." Tony couldn't help smiling.

Kelli laughed and pushed her hair behind her ears. "Don't tell me you managed backstage passes."

"More than that."

"More? What? Tell me, tell me."

Tony took another deep breath and felt his heart race. When he was twelve years old, his mother had bought him his first electric guitar, and she had told him that if he got really good, maybe he could play in a band someday. He'd always imagined it would be a rock band, but lately it was more, well, country.

"I have an audition to try out for the band."

"What?" Kelli screamed. She unfastened her seat belt and jumped over next to Tony, grabbed his face, and planted a kiss on his cheek. "I can't believe this. That's huge."

"Whoa, I'm trying to drive here! And I'm not in the band yet."

"Still, I want to be the first to say I once knew Tony Stratton, the best guitar player ever."

"So will you come?"

"You want me to come with you? You have just two tickets and you want to take me?"

"Of course. Who else would I take?" Tony looked at her seriously.

"This is your chance to impress some hot babe."

"You're the hottest babe I know."

Kelli laughed. "Then I feel sorry for you."

"So you'll go with me?"

"I can't wait."

"I'm going to be practicing every night, so I might not be able to spend as much time, you know, taking walks and stuff."

Tony drove under the archway to the Box C Ranch and parked next to the corral.

"Can't I just hang with you while you practice and 'ooh' and 'ahh' in all the right places?"

"Sure, if you want to." Tony undid the trailer latch, opened the door, and released the horse into the corral. When Tony glanced back at Kelli, he saw her wipe her eyes. He tossed some hay over the fence. "Let's go see if the police are here yet."

As they approached Kelli's cabin, Tony noticed yellow crime-scene tape strung around the small building. Two cars from the sheriff's department were parked at Norma's house. Knowing the officers would want to talk to him and Kelli, Tony parked behind one of the vehicles.

Norma and her sisters stood on the lawn under a box elder tree, pointing and gesturing with their hands in an animated fashion. Two deputy sheriffs stood near the elderly women, nodding and writing in pocket-sized notebooks.

Before he got out of the truck, Tony noticed Kelli's face had turned white. He reached over and touched her arm. "It'll be okay, Kelli. You just need to tell them what happened."

"Oh, it's not that. Every once in a while when I see police cars . . . it's hard to explain, but it feels like my heart jumps in my chest, and I feel like I'm fourteen again, and I'm at the accident that killed my parents."

"I'm so sorry. "

"Yeah." Kelli hesitated, then forced a smile. "We've both got some reporting to do, so let's go." She opened the door and jumped out before Tony could say anything else.

As Tony and Kelli approached her, LaRue pointed at him. "And here's the young man who wore my pillowcase on his head. He'll tell you all about it, officer." LaRue glanced up at the sun. "Oh, my! I'm very late for my appointment."

"You can get your hair done another day," Mabel said pointedly. "The world won't come to an end if you miss it."

"An appointment is an appointment. I'll frighten folks if I don't have my hair curled every week." LaRue stared at her sisters as if assessing their looks, then clucked her tongue.

"Tony, dear, we were just telling these men that we didn't actually see the color of the perp's eyes," Norma said. "His eyes were closed when we saw him."

"'Perp' is short for 'perpetrator,' if you don't know," Mabel interrupted.

"Oh, honey, I'm sure he knows that." LaRue rolled her eyes. "I mean, he's probably known at least a few perps in his time, or maybe even been—"

"LaRue," Mabel said sharply, "all young people are not criminals."

"It's okay." Tony tried to remember the color of the thief's eyes. "They weren't closed while he outfitted himself with my clothes, but I didn't notice his eye color. Guess I was too busy noticing the gun he was shoving in my back."

"And I only got a glimpse of him before I passed out, but I did think it was peculiar . . ." Kelli started.

"What was peculiar?"

"That he was wearing Tony's clothes and they fit him so well. His hair was blond like Tony's, and except for the fact that he hadn't shaved in a while, he kind of looked like him." Kelli sighed. "His eyes were swollen and bruised, but I'm pretty sure they were the same color as Tony's, blue green."

"Okay, let me see if I've got this straight." Sheriff Williams, a middle-aged man with graying blond hair, looked over his notes. "He stole Mrs. Mabel McDonald's car from the highway crossroads and drove toward Grouse Creek, stopping at that abandoned house ten miles out of town, where he encountered

Tony. There, the perpetrator stole Tony's clothes at gunpoint, tied him up, and stole his truck. He then drove it here this morning, frightened Kelli Carson, and took off with Norma Weaver's car." He grunted. "I think we have a professional criminal on our hands."

"And I'm sure he'd rather have a nearly new car than that junker Tony drives," Kelli said. "I mean, I can see what he was thinking. Besides, the more times you change cars, the harder to follow the trail, right?"

"Just to make sure—none of you had ever seen him before this happened?" the sheriff asked. "Can you venture a guess as to why he would go to Miss Carson's place?" He turned to Kelli. "Did he even know you?"

"He has my wallet—" Tony kept a picture of Kelli in it, though she didn't know about that. He'd taken it the year before, while she was working at the café in Trout Haven, Montana. But how would a picture in his wallet send the thief to Kelli's cabin?

Tony glanced at Kelli. "Well, I had a photo of Kelli in my wallet. Maybe—"

"You think he was looking for Kelli, then?"

"I don't know." Tony shuddered at the idea. The man whom he'd mistaken as harmless might be after Kelli. He felt a knot tighten in his gut.

Six

An Eventful Week

by Grouse Creek Correspondent
Norma Weaver

Herman and Maggie Anders had company this extended weekend from Bountiful, as Maggie's granddaughter Jana Erickson and her friend Ashley were here. Herman taught them to ride horses, rope steers, and pluck chickens. Jana said she didn't know people still lived like pioneers. She was surprised the Anderses even owned a telephone, since they didn't have a cellular one. At first Jana was distressed by not being able to text message any of her friends for an entire weekend, but

```
soon she found out how much fun the
real world is. She can't wait to
get home and tell her city friends
about life on the ranch.
```

USUALLY NORMA HAD TO STRUGGLE TO COME UP with something to write about this sleepy town to send in for the rural route column of *The Tremonton Leader*. But this week she had more information than she could put in one article.

While she thought about the strange events of the last few days, Norma stood and picked up the photo of Wes from her dresser. She thought of her husband almost every minute of every day, and she often wondered if she would ever get through a day without feeling the agony of losing him. In the photo she now gazed at, he wore his army uniform, and he looked so handsome. To her, he had changed so little over the years. Of course he had aged, but he'd stayed almost as slender as the day they'd married, and he wore the same serious expression. Norma carried the photo to her computer desk, placed it where she could look at it, and went back to writing her article.

```
   The Hansey sisters had an
unusually wild week as their trip
to the Sun Tunnels proved more
eventful than planned. They came
across what they thought was a dead
man, and the experience became even
more horrifying when they realized
he wasn't wearing anything at
all—that is, until LaRue kindly
supplied him with an embroidered
pillowcase she'd been working on
```

for a granddaughter's wedding. LaRue is at a loss as to what she'll give the couple now, saying, "The remaining pillowcase simply will not do." Happily, the man wasn't dead after all, but unhappily, he ended up stealing Mabel's Lincoln Continental. Then he found Tony Stratton from the Box C Ranch. The perp used Mabel's gun to hold Tony hostage. The gun doesn't work, so I doubt she needs a permit to keep it, but you know how it is when you get to be in your eighties, and who knows what kind of crazies you'll meet up with? Take our young perp, for example. At any rate, the man wearing only LaRue's pillowcase held Tony up with Mabel's gun and stole not only the clothes he was wearing, but also his truck, although fortunately for Tony and the Box C it was an old truck with lots of miles on it and a few dents besides.

The next day, Tony and Norma found an unconscious victim, perhaps knocked on the head by the before-mentioned criminal. As they helped her, Norma's nearly new Subaru Outback was stolen. She is still looking for it, so if anyone sees a red Subaru, please call Norma Weaver in Grouse Creek.

On a happier note, the Grouse Creek Supply is featuring hand-crocheted hangers for sale at $3.50 each. They are made by Grouse Creek's own talented Jean Brooks. Also, she wants everyone to know that she will start knitting dishcloths again if anyone is interested. Lots of folks tell her they work like a charm. This particular correspondent finds them better than an S.O.S pad at really getting the gunk off your dishes, and they won't harm fine china.

Everyone is bustling with plans for the upcoming Fourth of July celebration, and many look forward to having a house full during the festivities. More on this next week.

When Norma finished her article, she read over it and changed "was stolen" to "went missing." She tried to keep current on trends in journalism, and these days things weren't actually stolen, and people didn't vanish and weren't kidnapped. Instead, they all seemed to have mysteriously gone missing as if things just happened without cause. Norma didn't like this fad, but she also didn't want to be considered an amateur. She submitted the article via e-mail, congratulating herself for staying up to date on technology."

After such a harrowing week, Norma had asked Mabel to stay with her a while, to help her cope with her loneliness. "But who will run things in Montello?" Mabel had asked, but after one look at Norma's anguished face, she had consented.

"Where is Mabel?" Norma wondered out loud. She looked out the back door, but no Mabel. Norma decided her sister must've walked down to the co-op to pick up some cheese, since they'd run out.

Norma stepped outside and began to pull a few weeds around her rosebush. She'd planted eight rosebushes right after she and Wesley were married, and all but one had died within a year. The surviving bush had deep pink blossoms and it smelled heavenly. Norma breathed in the aroma, and with some effort she got down on her knees and tugged at a stubborn mallow weed. When she was a child she'd eaten the little "cheesettes," as they'd called them. Norma's daughter Marianne used to gather them up in her wagon and try to sell them to the other children in town. Of course no one ever bought them. Norma told her it was because folks could pick them themselves. Things had to be rare to be valuable, and there wasn't anything unusual about mallow. Later in the summer, Marianne found an authentic Indian arrowhead. Grouse Creek residents often found arrowheads, but this one was especially nice, perfectly formed from obsidian. Herman Anders gave her five dollars for it. Marianne felt so encouraged by her good fortune that she'd spent the rest of the summer looking for more, but never found another one.

"Beautiful day, isn't it?"

Norma didn't hear Mabel come up behind her, so she jumped at the sound of her voice. "I was just thinking about Wes, remembering the day he brought those rosebushes home for me. They were just bare sticks, and I teased him about planting twigs in the ground and expecting something to grow."

Mabel's laugh rumbled from her chest and then broke through in hearty snorts. "LaRue thought your husband was plum crazy when she saw them, and said those twigs won't grow a lick. But look at that one—it's beautiful, isn't it? A reminder of his love for you, dear."

Norma closed her eyes to think. "Let me ask you something that's been bothering me. That girl who called asked for Mr. Wesley Weaver, and then she called him 'Hummer.' Didn't LaRue write to a soldier named Hummer?"

"I believe so, but . . ."

"But LaRue's soldier was killed in the war, right?" Norma asked. Since the Grouse Creek school didn't accept students past tenth grade, LaRue had boarded with their cousins in Brigham City to finish high school. She seldom made the trip home, but Norma remembered LaRue writing to a soldier.

"She met him at a dance in Naf before he shipped out," Mabel replied. "I doubt she ever got over the fact that he never returned from the war. She did call him Hummer, though. I'm sure of it."

Norma straightened up and stared at Mabel, who put her arm around Norma and said sympathetically, "Oh, sweetie, it doesn't matter, not now."

Of course, Hummer might be a common nickname. The mallow dangled from Norma's hand. She'd been unable to pull the root, so the pernicious weed would sprout again in a week or two. She shook the dirt off and tossed the weed onto the sidewalk.

Mabel looked away from Norma and sighed, then focused on a knot in the maple tree. "No. LaRue jilted her soldier, but I'm not sure when. It was either during the war or after. He was from Garland, I believe, just like your Wes."

Norma felt a tingle go through her. "What . . . are you saying that Wes was—"

"Some things are best left alone," Mabel interjected, her eyes glistening with moisture.

"But if LaRue rejected Wes, then why did I always get the feeling that she resented me?" Norma's mouth was moving faster than her brain, but she didn't care. "You knew, didn't you?"

"I've never been sure and never asked. But it's possible. And as for LaRue's resentment, well, I remember telling Mama that I was too old for dolls, so she shouldn't give me one for Christmas. But then when you and LaRue got your porcelain dolls with jet-black ringlets on Christmas morning, I went upstairs and cried my eyes out. We never really know what we want until someone else gets it. I imagine if LaRue's soldier was your Wes, she probably felt a little like that."

The ringing of the phone jolted Norma back to the present. She wiped her dirty hands on her gardening smock and went to answer the phone. It rang nearly a dozen times before she managed to make it inside.

"Hello." She tried to catch her breath.

"Hi, is this Norma?" a young man's voice asked.

"Yes, it is."

"Hi, again. This is Tony."

"Oh, yes. How is Kelli?"

"She's fine. Listen, I heard from him."

"Him?"

"The man who stole your car."

Norma squinted her eyes in confusion, her mind pondering the possibility that her husband and LaRue's soldier had been one and the same. "Oh, gracious. Is he there? Did he bring the car back? Is it okay?"

"Oh, I'm sorry," Tony said. "I shouldn't have worded it quite that way. I didn't actually hear from him. He tried to use a credit card of mine—you know, from my wallet. After it was rejected, the credit card company gave me a call. Anyway, it looks like he's been in the Burley area. My card was used at one of those quickie auto paint job places—"

"He painted my car?" Norma was horrified. "What color?"

"They're trying to pull the records up on it so they can tell us that," Tony explained. "They said they remember the man, and his description matches the thief. He even had bruises around his eyes. Truth is, he looks like me, so he was able to use my driver's license for I.D."

"Have you called the police?" Norma felt her hand tremble on the receiver.

"Yeah."

Norma's mind raced. "I certainly hope he has good taste and didn't go with something too outlandish, like that horrendous school-bus yellow that's become so popular. I would hate to drive something like that around. Or that nearly fluorescent green. I so very much dislike that color. Now a nice sky blue wouldn't be bad, or a forest green."

"Sure. Well, I'll let you know when they call me back about the color."

"Thank you. I'll need to know what color my car is," Norma said. "Do you think he paid any attention to the interior? It's tan and red. Certainly he has enough sense to realize that some colors would clash. I'm very conscious of my surroundings and would hate to drive in clashing colors."

Norma could tell Tony was trying not to laugh when he replied, "Well, a lot of us guys are sort of color blind or something. I probably walk around all the time with clashing colors. Can you imagine the horror of mucking out a horse stall wearing mismatched clothes?"

Now he was making fun of her, Norma decided, but she would take it graciously and say nothing.

"All right then, Norma. You tell Mabel hello and that I loved her cookies."

Norma put her hand over the mouthpiece. "Tony loves your cookies, Mabel,"

Mabel came over. "Let me talk with the boy."

Norma handed the phone to Mabel.

"Well, sweetie, get over here and get some cookies then. I'll start making them right now for lunch tomorrow around noon. And bring that adorable Kelli, if she'll have you. Norma picked a bunch of asparagus and she makes a mighty tasty soup with it."

Tony laughed. "That's sounds great. Thanks, Mabel. I gotta get going."

"Bye, hon." After Mabel hung up the phone, she started pulling bowls from cupboards and utensils from drawers. "I invited Tony over and that girl he's so sweet on for lunch," she said without looking up.

"I heard. That will be nice. I think I'll call and invite LaRue. Maybe she'd even drive herself from north Grouse Creek for your cookies."

"Anyone would." Mabel tied on an apron.

Norma picked up the phone. She needed to have a serious conversation with her sister the next day at lunch. A conversation about Hummer.

Seven

Sam,

No! You do not need to come over here! You are such an amazing brother, but seriously, between Tony, the sisters, Bishop Watkins, Herman, and Maggie, the guy would be insane to try anything again. Besides, I don't think he meant to hurt me. It was probably just the shock of seeing a stranger wearing Tony's clothes that caused me to faint. Guess I was just in the wrong place at the wrong time. I have to admit it scared the daylights out of me. Tony is picking me up in a few minutes. He is almost as amazing as you are. ☺ I don't know why he's so good to me. I know what you're thinking, and he's just a very good friend.

Love, Kelli

P.S. Tell Stacey that we need to get together for some serious shopping. I need some new jeans.

TONY HAD ONE MORE CHORE TO DO BEFORE HE could call it a day. Jay had asked him to check on the cattle out on the range near the Raft River. The sun was beginning to set and Tony hoped Kelli had finished work for the day. At the present time, she worked on a project for the Department of Wildlife and Natural Resources, counting sage grouse to see how the diminishing sagebrush was affecting their population.

As he parked in front of Kelli's cabin, she stepped out onto the porch as if she'd been watching for him. Her face broke into a smile when she saw him and she hurried toward him.

"I was hoping you'd stop by. You're finished for the day, aren't you?"

"Just got one more chore," Tony said. "Want to come along for the ride?"

"I don't know. I need to check my day planner."

Tony laughed at their standing joke.

"Actually, I was on my way to the post office to check my mail," Kelli explained. "Can we stop there first?"

Realizing she hadn't been waiting for him after all, Tony sighed and opened the passenger door of his truck. "Sure, hop in."

They backtracked a block to the new post office—a 12-by-12-foot white clapboard building set on a hill off the town's only through street. While Kelli checked her post office box, Tony checked his. He seldom received any mail since he hadn't lived in the area long, and he hadn't checked his box in days. He flipped through the stack, mostly junk by the looks of it. It seemed the postmaster simply put the previous owner's mail in his box. After he tossed the junk mail into the recycling container, he held a single letter in his hand. "Tony Stratton" was handwritten in block letters.

Tony put the letter into his front pocket; it could wait. He and Kelli climbed back into the truck and soon headed for the upper range.

The heavy snows of winter and a wet spring had curtailed the long drought. Even though the Grouse Creek area had a lot less foliage compared to southwestern Montana, local ranchers thought it would be a good year. And a good year to the ranchers meant Tony would have plenty of work all summer.

As he drove, Tony admired the grass that grew high beneath the tall sagebrush. Multi-hued cliffs surrounded both sides of the road, dropping into the Raft River Valley, where a swollen creek rushed over the rust-colored stone slabs. Then the rock disappeared in a slow-moving pool. Tony stopped the truck next to the stream.

Then he remembered. "Mabel asked the two of us over for lunch tomorrow. Can you come?"

"That'd be awesome. I usually just pack a light lunch for my fieldwork, but going there would be a nice break."

Tony opened his door. "The cattle on both sides of the road belong to the Box C. I'm just going to check on them."

"I'll just stretch my legs some," Kelli said as she climbed out of the truck.

A few minutes later as Tony walked back though the cattle, he noticed Kelli crouched down by the pink blossoms on a cactus plant, the sunlight highlighting her auburn hair. Then he watched her pick up a flat piece of shale and skip it across the water, bouncing it twice before it hit onto the bank on the opposite side.

Suddenly, he heard a bellow from the direction of the brush willows. He paused long enough to hear it a second time before shouting, "Run, Kelli!"

A cow moose crashed through the brush and headed straight for Kelli, not slowed one bit by the swollen stream. Tony ran toward Kelli as she scrambled up the talus slope. He grabbed her hand and together they ran to the truck and leapt into the back.

The moose slammed into the truck, bellowed again, then did an about-face and ambled back toward the stream. It was then that Tony saw a calf on the bank near Kelli's cactus. The moose went to her calf and licked it, then nudged it gently. The calf struggled to stand up and soon frolicked around his mother, who continued to eye the truck. "There's the reason she charged. I imagine she's even more scared of us than we are of her."

"I don't think so. Look." Kelli showed him her trembling hand.

Tony took her hand and held it between both of his. "Let's just watch for a minute. I can never get over quite how much they look like horses—awkward, gangly horses."

The mother crossed the stream and waited for the calf to follow. He hesitated midstream with the rushing water swirling around his chest, and then galloped to his mother. The pair disappeared into the brush.

"Moose are pretty rare through here, aren't they?" Tony asked. "I mean, in Montana we saw them all the time. I think we were lucky to see them here today." Tony reluctantly released Kelli's hand, then hopped out of the truck and held his hand out to help her down.

"Lucky? It could've trampled us!"

"But we weren't trampled, so we were lucky."

"Always the optimist. Wow! Here I was looking at a cactus flower when a newborn moose was inches away from me."

"Yeah, I didn't see it either. Sometimes we don't see what's right in front of us. If that cow moose hadn't come barreling through, I doubt we would've ever noticed it. Anyway, I'm almost done here. I just need to check on the grass. Jay wants me to report on how much longer these cattle can feed here before we'll need to move them to another range."

When Tony got back into the truck he started humming "On the Road Again," then turned on the radio. "Gotta get home and practice my guitar. Working sunup to sundown, it's hard to find the time."

"Maybe you'd better start canceling your social engagements—your lunch appointments with your old lady admirers and such. And, as much as I hate to say it, hanging out with me so much."

"Yeah, I'm afraid so. I've got to be ready for the audition. So after this one lunch engagement, it's time to buckle down."

Kelli laughed and opened another envelope from her stack of mail: "Great! My last paycheck from the Lazy Moose Café: $27. I'll treat you to dinner in Burley sometime."

"You're on." Tony reached into his shirt pocket and pulled out his letter. "That reminds me. Since I'm driving, read this to me before it gets too dark."

"Interesting." Kelli turned the envelope over. "No return address."

"Maybe if I'm really lucky there'll be a check for me, too."

Kelli opened the letter and a ten-dollar bill fluttered out from the envelope. "Close, it's cash." She picked it up and handed the money to Tony. "Dear Tony," she read, "sorry to have to use your cash and credit. I'll pay you back when I can. You seem like a pretty cool dude and—"

"What in the world—who's it from?" Tony interrupted.

"It doesn't say, but there's more."

"Okay, keep going."

"—I can explain it all to you, so you know why I had to do what I did. First of all, I'm sorry I did what I did. It doesn't explain everything. I'll do that in person, but I have a condition that I'm on medication for. When I got beaten and robbed out at the Sun Tunnels, well, as you can guess, my medication was taken too. My thinking gets way off, when I'm off my meds, so all I knew was I needed to get away. I know you'll understand because I saw the picture in your wallet of the pretty girl that fainted when I stopped by her place. It was easy to find out where she lived, because the first person I saw knew her."

Kelli stopped reading and looked wide-eyed at Tony. "It's him!"

Tony felt his face flush at the mention of his photo of Kelli. After all, she wasn't his girlfriend. But she was his best friend, and why did it hurt to carry a picture of his best friend?

"Tony, I didn't know you had a picture of me in your wallet."

"I know and I'm sorry, but I can't do anything about it now, so keep reading."

Kelli sighed and turned back to the letter. "Anyway, I figured she's your girlfriend. So you must know what it's like to be in love and—"

"You've got to be kidding." Tony said, punching the dashboard. "That is this guy's lame excuse for stealing three cars, leaving me tied up and gagged, and knocking you out? He's an idiot. He wants me to understand? Well, I don't!"

"Are you through? He said he has a condition. Obviously he's trying to make things right. Besides, he said I'm pretty."

Tony only grunted.

"Anyway, it says, 'If you are in love even a tenth of what I feel for my girlfriend, you'll know how desperate I am to find her. Maybe you won't think I can be trusted, but I hope that you will give me a chance. Tell the old ladies that I'll try to return their car when this is all over, but meanwhile it's been a nice car to drive. It gets good gas mileage, which I'm sure you'll appreciate since I've been using your American Express card for gas, doctor visits, and some cash—'"

"What? I cancelled my VISA when he used it to paint the car, but I forgot about my American Express card. I haven't used it in months!"

Kelli put her hand on Tony's knee. "Stop interrupting me. This is turning out to be a very sweet letter!" She continued reading, "'I need to figure out a way to contact you and find out if you can be trusted. It's important—trust me on this—that we get together without the cops involved. I'd like to meet on Saturday at 7:00 p.m. at Price's Café in Burley. I ate there when the car was being painted. Bring your girlfriend too—she seems cool. I'm really, really sorry I scared her.'"

"'Bring your girlfriend?' Is this guy out to lunch or what?" Tony shook his head and muttered, "Never trust a criminal, a thug, especially a dumb one like this guy."

"Well, he does think I'm your girlfriend. See, that's just one of the reasons you shouldn't have my picture in your wallet, but I really don't think he's dumb. There isn't one misspelled word in this letter. Besides, you of all people should understand mental illness."

"What? He could've killed you. Yeah, I'll meet him and when I do—"

Kelli went quiet and looked away.

Tony stopped, realizing she must've been talking about herself. She'd had some depression that had required counseling—maybe even medication—to get over. He hadn't meant to be insensitive. But Kelli hadn't ever hurt anyone, so she wasn't anything like this guy.

"Don't forget, he could've killed you, Tony, but he didn't. I mean, I'm not saying I want to get involved, but on the other hand he might be telling the truth. What has happened in his life that made him so desperate? Obviously a woman is involved—one who he's in love with, I might add."

Tony wasn't convinced. Who in his right mind would agree to meet with the criminal who'd robbed him, tied him up, stolen his vehicle, stolen two of his friends' vehicles, and messed with the woman he loved? Logically, Tony knew the only place he should see this guy's face was in court, when Tony testified against him. The perp had tried to excuse away his illegal behavior by saying he had a medical "condition," but his very desire to make excuses revealed that he knew what he was doing was wrong. Therefore, he was responsible for his crimes. Besides, in Tony's mind, no "condition" could explain away the perp's actions—they were still wrong and they were still illegal. Taking all this into account, Tony decided he should meet with the guy, but just to make sure he didn't get away with his crimes.

Soon they reached the top of the mountain. Cotton Thomas Basin, its meandering stream banked with clumps of willows, lay far below them.

"This is where I spend a lot of time counting and banding grouse. There's some prime grouse habitat here," Kelli explained. Then, as if she could read Tony's thoughts, she reached over and touched his arm. "If you do decide to meet him, I'm coming with you. Price's Café is right on the main street in Burley, and it's very public. I'll have my cell phone just in case we need to call the police."

Tony considered the idea as they drove down the mountain. Finally, he sighed. "Yeah, I guess we can at least listen to him, but we're calling the police no matter what." He made the turn into Grouse Creek, glancing at the large sign that read A Place Like No Other. Despite Tony's dark mood he smiled at the moniker, which now seemed more appropriate than ever.

Eight

NORMA KNOCKED AGAIN BUT THERE WAS NO ANSWER. Anxious to talk to LaRue about Wes, Norma had decided to invite LaRue to lunch in person.

Norma knocked again and then pushed the door open. "Hello! LaRue, it's just me. It's Norma."

LaRue sat in front of her console television with her legs stretched out in front of her, swaying her arms over her head in imitation of the woman on the screen. Without turning to face Norma, LaRue said, "Go get a chair from the kitchen and watch *Sit and Be Fit* with me. Mary Ann was just telling me that bananas are high in potassium. Did you know that?"

"My daughter Marianne?"

"No, silly. The woman on the program," LaRue corrected, her ample thighs hanging over the sides of the vinyl chair. "She's *Mary Ann*, not Marianne."

Norma glanced around the room. Dolls with elaborately crocheted dresses lined the dark walnut shelves. "When are you going to give the dolls to your grandchildren, LaRue?"

"What's that?"

"Your dolls." Norma went into the kitchen and pulled another chair into the living room so she could sit next to LaRue. Mary Ann's outstretched arms now turned in slow circles. LaRue's arms rested on her lap, but she moved her hands in a circular movement. "I'm giving all my dolls to my granddaughters."

"Oh, good." *It's about time*, Norma thought.

"In my will."

Norma rolled her eyes. "Your granddaughters are having babies of their own."

"That's right," LaRue said. "Say, does Mabel still chew with her mouth open?"

"I hadn't noticed."

"You haven't noticed? She's been doing that ever since she was ten, I imagine."

Norma circled her arms in large motions, feeling like a bumblebee trying to take flight. She thought about the possibility of Wes and LaRue together—tried to imagine Wesley courting LaRue—but it didn't seem possible. She decided to jump right in. "LaRue, did you love Vernon?"

"Why do you ask such a ridiculous question?"

"I've just been thinking. I remembered that you were writing to a soldier during the war."

LaRue shot Norma a disapproving look and turned back to the television. Mary Ann touched her toes and clapped to polka music, whereupon LaRue touched her calves and clapped three times. "I never wrote to any soldier. Must've been Mabel you're thinking about."

"Mabel married Myron before the war and had a baby by then, remember? Myron was 4-F on account of a rheumatic fever that left him with a heart murmur. She didn't write to any soldier." Norma didn't want to be insensitive, but she just had to know the truth. "If I remember right, you wrote to a soldier you called Hummer."

Now LaRue lifted her feet slightly off the floor in tiny increments. "I can't really remember. I might've written to someone called Hummer for a while. But why do you want to know anyway?"

"Mabel and I were just talking about it." ·

"Mabel is a nosy busybody and a darn fool who strung men along like pearls on a necklace, never wanting to cut any loose."

Norma gasped. "You know that isn't true." Even for LaRue, the comment was more than a little mean-spirited.

Norma dragged her chair back to the kitchen and opened a cupboard, looking for a glass. A clean jelly jar sat next to a row of china cups, so she grabbed it. Her hand trembled while she held the jar under a stream of cool water from the faucet. As she stood near the kitchen doorway, she could clearly see LaRue's every exercise move.

The more Norma thought about it, the more she realized it was pretty unlikely that two men in the small community of Garland would share a very uncommon nickname. She sipped her water and wondered how she would get LaRue to open up.

LaRue rocked in her chair as TV Mary Ann cooed encouragement. Norma shook her head and wondered if the woman on the set was more real to LaRue than she was. LaRue often talked about the people on television as if they were friends or family. She particularly fancied TV weatherman Mark Eubank, his hair as tidy as a ladybug's, and had been so disappointed when he retired. LaRue didn't care for any of the anchors on the Fox channel—they were too casual—and she especially didn't approve of their hairstyles. "They look like a hurricane touched down." "Tornado," Norma had wanted to tell her. "They look like a *tornado* touched down." Hurricanes did not happen in Utah. Norma returned to the sink, rinsed out the glass, dried it with a cotton towel, and set it back in the cupboard where she'd found it.

"I just came by to invite you to lunch tomorrow. Tony Stratton and Kelli will be coming, and Mabel's making her cookies right now. Can you come?"

"You know, don't you, that Mabel was probably having an affair with what's-his-name in Montello even before her husband died, don't you?"

Norma clenched her jaw. Then with as much sweetness as she could muster, she said, "Anyway, dear, do you want to bring something? Some hot rolls would be good."

"I'll think about it, but don't expect me to be nice after the things you've accused me of, Norma."

"How could I possibly ever expect you to be nice?" Norma stormed toward the door, then paused before walking out the door. "Interesting that Wes's nickname was Hummer, isn't it?" Norma saw LaRue's head snap toward the door, her eyes wide, before Norma slammed the door behind her.

Norma fumed as she drove back home. It was true that Mabel had numerous suitors before she married. Boys flocked around her like bees to a hive, even though she didn't pay them any mind.

Mabel was Norma's hero and she hated to hear anyone put her down. She remembered throwing a rock at Dale Simpson in the fourth grade because he said something unrepeatable about Mabel. The rock made a three-inch gash across his forehead and sent him into Burley for stitches. Even though Norma hadn't known what the word meant, she knew it wasn't nice because of the sneer on his face when he said it. As punishment Norma had to sit in a corner during recess for weeks, but she never regretted throwing the rock.

To help take Norma's mind off things, she and Mabel spent the next morning rearranging the furniture in the living room. The sofa was too heavy for the two women to move, but they slid the rocking chair from one corner to the other and then put the captain's chairs in the vacated spot. By the time they finished, the living room looked almost exactly as it had before.

At precisely 11:30 a.m., Norma drove Mabel's car to LaRue's, parked out front, and laid on the horn. She didn't care if everyone in Grouse Creek heard the blaring noise. *I will not be nice to her!* she thought. But as she watched LaRue come out, carrying her roll basket in one hand and her black purse in the other, trying to balance herself with the handrail, Norma forgot her resolve and jumped out of the car.

"Thank you dear," LaRue said. "Mabel come?"

"She's out picking some flowers for the centerpiece."

"Now that is nice of her, isn't it?"

Norma couldn't imagine what had gotten into LaRue. "Are you feeling all right, LaRue?"

"Quite."

"Your sinuses aren't closing up today?"

"Clear as a bell."

They drove in silence and soon arrived at Norma's house. She followed LaRue inside.

"So you aren't angry with me?" Norma said as she saw Tony's truck pull up out front.

"What's that? Angry? Why?"

Norma decided to drop it. She hurriedly placed LaRue's delicious-smelling rolls in the middle of the table. Tony and Kelli came in laughing and Mabel soon joined them, her arms filled with wildflowers. Norma smiled as Tony took off his baseball cap and placed it on the rack. *What a nice young man.*

Tony and Kelli listened to Mabel tell a colorful story about when she had first met Myron. "And he thought I had the prettiest buns in the whole county!"

LaRue looked horrified. "Mabel!"

"Well, it must be time to eat," Norma said, then quickly sat.

They gathered in the kitchen and sat down to eat the rolls, salad, and asparagus soup. Tony complimented LaRue on the rolls, and Kelli gushed to Norma about her place settings.

After a few minutes, Mabel put down her fork. "Tony, I'm sure you've heard something about our dead man by now, haven't you?"

"Uh, well . . ." He looked at Kelli.

"Let's tell them," she said. Then she turned to the three sisters. "He wrote Tony a letter. He's got a condition, probably mental—although he didn't say. He was out of his medication and needed to get into town for help. I guess that's why he felt the need to steal—"

"It doesn't matter what was wrong with him," Norma said. "It doesn't give him the right. Besides, why didn't he just ask for a ride?"

"Exactly what I thought, but in his letter, he said he's enjoying your car, thinks it gets great gas mileage, and wanted Tony to tell you he's sorry about taking it."

"My goodness, that's mighty nervy of him, isn't it? So he's bringing it back?" Norma stood and walked to the sink to refill the water pitcher. *How could a young man just take a car from three elderly women and leave them stranded?* she wondered. What's more, Mabel didn't seem to be taking the situation seriously at all.

"No, he didn't say anything about bringing it back." Tony shook his head. "But he does want to talk to me soon."

Mabel clapped her hands excitedly. "Maybe we can get this whole thing straightened out by the Fourth of July."

"So did he say what color he painted my car?" Norma asked.

Tony swallowed a spoonful of soup. "The painting company called out to the Box C. Said they painted it green."

"Green? Well, that doesn't tell me anything. Did they specify the type of green? Grass, teal, forest, pea, avocado, jade, olive, emerald, lime, chartreuse? I hope it's not that horrific neon green that seems so popular today." Norma closed her eyes.

"Mabel, you certainly aren't going to invite that criminal to our Fourth celebration," LaRue put in. "You know as well as I do, he's armed and extremely dangerous. He could take us and . . . well, I just shudder to think of all the possibilities. If I've said it once I've said it a thousand times. The youth of today are going to heck in a hand basket."

Norma glanced at the table, her eyes settling on the hand basket full of rolls. "I don't think that's what Mabel meant, LaRue. I think she was thinking that I might have my car back by then."

"And Mabel, while we are on the subject of you and your endless muddles, why did you and Norma discuss the soldier I wrote to during the war?"

Norma tensed at this abrupt change of topic, but Mabel simply walked to the freezer and removed a carton of vanilla ice cream. She hummed as she pulled bowls out of the cupboard and scooped up the ice cream. Norma thought maybe she hadn't heard LaRue, but as she opened the cookie jar, she said, "LaRue, dear, it's nothing to be ashamed about. If you and Wes were a couple before Norma came along, it certainly doesn't matter now. I'm sure you had your reasons for not saying anything about it." Mabel put two cookies in each bowl on top of the ice cream and started carting them over to the table.

LaRue's mouth dropped open and she started to tremble. "I

can't believe this—my own two sisters prying into what's none of their business. It's just unthinkable. Unthinkable and simply unseemly, that's what it is! Norma, dear, could you please pass me a bowl of ice cream?"

"No," Norma said, glancing over at Kelli and Tony. The two of them looked nervously at each other and fiddled with their spoons. Norma knew her guests must be horrified at the sisters' arguing.

"Well," Tony said, standing up. "It's getting late and I've gotta get back to work."

"Yes, thanks so much for everything." Kelli said, pushing a whole cookie into her mouth.

"Oh, no, dears. You haven't finished your dessert. Please stay." Mabel seemed oblivious of their discomfort.

Kelli glanced at Tony and grabbed his hand to pull him back into his seat. Uncomfortable silence followed.

"Well, I couldn't be with a man who had fathered a child out of wedlock. It would be more than unseemly." LaRue paused, looking straight at Norma. "Absolutely unthinkable! How could he profess his love for me after another woman had borne him a child?"

"What?" Norma gasped.

LaRue stood up, trembling, her face as red as a radish. "Oh, dear. Oh, I didn't mean to bring up something that's long since water over the bridge."

"Under," Norma whispered. She felt hot, then sick. She thought she might faint. She pushed the ice cream away and watched the blob begin to melt.

No one said anything for at least a minute. Kelli looked ashen, and Tony's eyes were fixed on the table.

Mabel ate her bowl of ice cream as if nothing was wrong, then finally looked up at LaRue. "Norma is different than you.

She loved Wes, warts and all. Isn't that right, Norma dear?"

Norma felt like a rock had lodged in her throat. She stood up and held onto the table, her tears falling without warning. The abandoned spoons on the table jangled as Norma's trembling body shook the table. *Is this true? Why didn't he tell me? Why didn't he give me the chance to understand?* "I . . . I didn't know," Norma eventually managed to say. "He never said anything about this. He never even told me he courted LaRue. He certainly didn't tell me about any baby."

"Goodness," Mabel mumbled.

Suddenly feeling dizzy, Norma put her hands over her eyes. Tony jumped up and led her into the living room, where he helped her sit on the sofa. Mabel grabbed the afghan LaRue had crocheted for Norma three Christmases ago, and even though the summer air was stifling, she covered her older sister with it.

Norma's brain buzzed until she thought it would explode. *When did this happen? Who is the mother of the child? Where is the child? Why didn't Wes trust me? How could he die without saying anything?*

Norma forgot her guests and her manners, weeping with great sobs as the world closed in around her.

Nine

Sam,

A new colt! Congratulations, although I have to admit I was kind of hoping for another kind of arrival. ☺ I hope Stacey isn't too disappointed. It will happen soon, I'm sure. Things are getting weirder and weirder around here. Tony got a letter from the guy who stole his truck, and he wants to meet us! How bizarre can things get? Who would have thought so much could happen clear out here in the middle of nowhere? Remember I told you I was sort of disappointed that Grouse Creek was nothing like Montana? Well, surprise . . . a moose charged us. Crazy! No one around here remembers seeing any moose out of the Sawtooths.

Oh, I almost forgot the most awesome news of all. Tony has an audition with Buck Branson.

I miss seeing him since he's practicing most of the time. (Seriously, he's practicing every minute he's not working.) He is an amazing guitarist, as you know. But he's even better than the last time you heard him in Montana. I get to be his adoring audience and ooh *and* ah *for him—which isn't hard at all, if you know what I mean. And tell Stacey anytime next week for jeans shopping. I'm expecting her to know where the best deals are in all of Burley, since it's been a while.*

Love, Kelli

AFTER WORK THE NEXT EVENING, TONY KNOCKED on Kelli's door with his guitar in hand. He stood there for almost a minute but she didn't answer. He could see a light on in the cabin, so he knocked again.

A cold fear stole over him, and images flashed through his mind—images of Kelli lying unconscious on the floor of the cabin. He propped his guitar against the log wall and knocked harder. "Kelli!" he shouted. "You in there?"

When he found the door was unlocked, he pushed it open. "Kelli?" he called, but there was no response. Then Tony heard something behind him and spun around.

"Tony?" Kelli stood there smiling at him. "I thought I heard something. I'm visiting at Herman's. Come on over and bring your guitar. I was just telling Herman and Maggie about your audition with Buck Branson."

"Oh?" Tony tried to calm his racing heart.

"It was all right to tell them, wasn't it? I'm just so excited for you."

"I guess so." Tony shrugged and picked up his guitar case.

He hadn't really wanted anyone to know. It made him even more nervous to think a lot of people would find out and expect great things to happen. And while some days he knew he could do it, other days he was sure he would blow it.

"You okay?" Kelli asked.

"Yeah, sorry. It just worried me when you weren't here."

"Don't worry." Kelli smiled. "Tomorrow we'll be able to hear firsthand what the thief has to say, but until then we'll just try to forget everything that happened."

"You still plan to come to Burley with me to meet this crazy guy?" Tony followed Kelli toward Herman and Maggie's house.

"Of course. If you're going, then I'm going."

"I'll put the police on speed dial for tomorrow, just in case," Tony said as they stepped through the Anderses' back door.

"Well, howdy do, Tony." Herman stood in the kitchen at the back window. "I was just purt-near ready to call out a posse to see what was takin' you two. Come on in and take a load off. Maggie's dished up some vanilla ice cream with fudge sauce."

"Thanks." Tony grinned. "You didn't need to go to any trouble."

"No trouble," Maggie said from behind Herman. "You know Herman would never forgive me if I didn't offer ice cream to the next superstar to hit the music scene." Maggie motioned for them to follow her and they all went into the living room. Tony set his guitar down, and when Kelli patted the sofa cushion next to her, he sat down, careful not to sit too close.

"It's just an audition," Tony said. "I doubt it will amount to anything."

"Nonsense. Of course it will. By the looks of it, you got everythin' you need—a guitar and good looks to boot. At least I think you're good lookin'," Herman drawled. "It's hard to tell with all that hair in your face."

"Uh, thanks." Tony pushed his hair out of his eyes. "Been meaning to get a haircut, but we've been so busy working."

Maggie handed Tony a dish of ice cream. "Don't listen to him, Tony. I think your hair looks fine. Besides you can't be a rock-and-roll star without long hair, and you're only halfway there."

"Actually, Buck Branson is country western," Kelli explained. "But that's one thing I like about Tony. He's a cowboy—at least for now—but he looks more like a skater with Wranglers. But he's not a skater either. He's indefinable and one of a kind."

In his embarrassment, all Tony heard was that Kelli liked his hair.

"We heard you two had a visit with the Hansey girls," Herman said. "How was your visit? Get Norma's vehicular back yet?"

Kelli squinted. "Hansey girls? Oh, Norma and her sisters. It was interesting. And no, the Subaru is still missing."

"Didn't I tell you those sisters, bless their little hearts, were an odd bunch?" Herman asked, rocking in his big oak chair.

"They are a little different," Kelli admitted.

"Different? Odd as a blue moon, 'specially that middle gal, the one that drives that doggone pink-colored car. Known her my whole life—good ol' Mabel."

Tony took a bite of his ice cream. "Sure is good chocolate sauce. Did you make it yourself, Mrs. Anders?"

"Why, thank you, Tony. Yes, I did make it."

"Tell me, Herman, is Mabel starting to be forgetful?" Kelli asked delicately.

"All those sisters are eccentric, like I said, but there's nothing wrong up here." Herman tapped his head. "Mabel's sharp as a farrier's file. Hope I'm as sharp when I'm as old as they are."

"You're older than all of them, dear." Maggie patted Herman's hand.

"Not if you count the difference between you and me and subtract it. That's how it works, don't it?" The old man smiled and winked at Maggie, who laughed good-naturedly.

"Anyways, ol' Wes, bless him, went on to greener pastures no more than a month or so ago. Was out moving some sprinkler pipes and keeled over—his heart o' gold gave out quick as a lightning bolt. Just goes to show that we never know when our time will be, don't it? Who woulda thought Wes would go before this old geezer? Not me, that's for darn sure." Herman leaned back on his kitchen chair and gazed out the window.

Kelli finished her ice cream and stood to gather the bowls. She seemed right at home with the Anderses, and Tony was happy about that.

"Did you know anything about Norma's husband?" Tony asked Herman and Maggie. "Did he once date the oldest sister, LaRue?"

"No, but if it were true, he was a heap lot better off with Norma. Norma is as sweet as a cherry pie on a summer afternoon, but LaRue always seemed to have a bee in her bonnet about somethin' or other."

Tony handed his empty bowl to Kelli and wiped his mouth with his napkin. "Thanks, Kelli." He winked at her and stood up to go.

"Oh, no, you don't. That was just to give you some energy so you could play your guitar for us." Kelli pushed him back down, so he reluctantly reached for his guitar.

Maggie took the dishes from Kelli and put them in the kitchen. When she returned, she said, "I don't know about the rest of you, but I can't think of anything I'd enjoy more than a live concert. Tony, whenever you're ready."

Tony had played in front of crowds before, especially since last summer when he'd joined the Cattle Rustlers and had gigs all over Montana. He always played a few solo numbers during those gigs, but this was something different. After checking the guitar to make sure it was still in tune, he began.

First, he sang a familiar Buck Branson tune, and then he played one of the Rustlers' originals. Next, he sang one of his own. His style had evolved from copying and mixing oldies to writing his own country songs. Sometimes he even shook things up and played rock. It all depended on his mood. If he felt sad, he wrote sad songs; if he wanted to celebrate, he wrote happy songs. Today he felt content. His eyes closed partway, shutting out his fear, and he envisioned a beautiful meadow with a river running through it. The meadow brimmed with lupine, columbine, and Indian paintbrush. And the only person he could see was Kelli.

The room was quiet as he sang, and the only thing he could hear besides his own voice and strumming was the occasional squeak of Herman's rocker.

After he finished with a ballad about horseback riding, Tony heard Kelli gasp. "Oh, Tony! You've gotten even better than the last time I heard you. You're going to make it. I just know it."

Maggie applauded and Herman roused as if he'd been sleeping, his head jerking to attention. "What in tarnation?"

"It's nothing, dear," Maggie said loudly. "Tony's been singing. It was wonderful, absolutely wonderful. Please come back soon and play us some more tunes."

Tony glanced at the clock on the mantle and realized he'd been playing for over an hour. He wondered if he should have taken so much time. But they did seem to enjoy it, at least the women. Herman always nodded off, so you couldn't tell by him.

After saying goodbye to Herman and Maggie, Tony walked Kelli back to her cabin. He longed for things to be different between them. The moonlight played on her face and he wanted to kiss her. Instead he pulled her in for a friendly hug. "Thanks for listening."

"Listen, tomorrow night we've got dinner with our mysterious stranger and I was hoping to stop by my brother's place, so why don't I drive?" Kelli looked up at him. "I want to get my tires rotated anyway."

Tony scratched his head. "Okay, but I'm sure the boss will want me to pick up some grain or something. 'Never waste a trip' is a mantra we live by at the Box C."

"All right. I'll pick you up tomorrow at 5:30. Love ya." With that, Kelli turned and disappeared inside the cabin.

Tony watched her until she shut the door and wondered if she had any idea how much she was torturing him.

Ten

NORMA LOOKED AT THE OLD CHEST WHERE WES HAD kept his medals, photos, letters, and other mementos from before she knew him. If she was going to find anything about Wes's past in this house, it would be in this chest.

She carried the chest up from the basement and set it on the floor in the bedroom, then unsnapped the hinges. She waited until her hand stopped trembling before lifting the lid. When she did, she was surprised by the amount of papers, photos, and other things stuffed inside. The smell of old paper and dust tickled her nose. First, she picked up the medals. There were three, each individually encased in a satin-lined box. Norma picked up one of the medals, a star hanging on a striped ribbon.

She fingered the star's edges and remembered sitting with Wes under a black walnut tree on the campus of Utah State University a few months before they married. He had cracked each walnut open with two rocks, then placed half of the nutmeat into her hand. This went on for several minutes until he stopped abruptly, rolling a walnut in his hand. Then he told Norma about the hundreds of emaciated bodies piled high in a trench in a German concentration camp that he and others had liberated—too late for most of the victims. He'd told her about survivors who looked more like skeletons than humans.

"Have you ever seen walking death?" Wes had asked before his voice caught and he turned away from her. Norma remembered hugging him and crying with him. "I'll never stop seeing that image in my mind," he had explained. "And even then there were Americans who didn't believe what Hitler was doing. Heck, if I hadn't seen it, if the memory wasn't burned in my mind, I wouldn't have believed it either."

He had shaken his head. "You'd think meeting someone as beautiful as you are would erase that awful memory, but it's still there."

After that conversation, Wes had occasionally shared bits and pieces of his war memories with Norma. She knew it was hard for him to talk about, so as the years went on she never pushed him. Now, thinking again about that day when he first broke down, Norma tried to stifle her own tears.

When she finished admiring the medals, she placed them back in the chest. Next, she pulled out a photo album, a palm-sized leather book with one snapshot glued on each black page. Wes must have put the album together in his teens. Many pictures were of him as a boy, but on the last page, he stood next to a girl with his arm around her. His head was cocked back, and a cigarette dangled from his lips. Norma had forgotten he'd ever smoked, since he had quit before she met him. In this photograph, he wore a felt fedora, jeans, and a white T-shirt. The girl wore a fitted polka-dot dress that showed off her tiny waist. She wore high heels and gazed intently at Wes, who looked proud and defiant. Norma stared at the girl's face. At first glance, she thought she was looking at a photo of herself, but then she realized it was LaRue.

On the photo's white border, someone had written, "LaRue Hansey, girl of Wesley's dreams—engaged August 1943."

Engaged? Wes had been engaged to LaRue? Norma couldn't believe it! It must have happened days after his high school graduation—right before he shipped out. She slammed the book closed, then shuffled through the newspapers and other memorabilia. There was no other sign of LaRue.

Finally, in the bottom of the suitcase, Norma found a photograph of herself, held in a stiff black folder with gold edges. Norma remembered having the photo taken in a portrait studio and giving it to Wes before they married. Her wavy blond hair was shoulder length and she wore a black dress and a string of pearls.

Norma picked up the photograph and then grabbed the photo album to thumb back to the photo of LaRue. Comparing the two, she was shocked to see how much she had resembled her sister back then. When they were younger, everyone had always said they looked alike, but somehow she had failed to see it, always thinking LaRue was so much prettier. Now she could see that she had been every bit as pretty as LaRue. Norma slipped the photograph of herself into the book of snapshots and set it on top of the bed. Then she pushed the chest under the four-poster bed.

She took the photo album downstairs and set it on the coffee table. Mabel had gone to Montello for the day and wasn't sure when she would return. Norma felt compelled to get some housekeeping done in her absence, but she couldn't stop thinking about the photos. Mabel had been wrong. Wes hadn't chosen her because he loved her; he'd chosen her because the one he loved wouldn't have him. He had still found a way to marry the girl of his dreams, since Norma had looked practically the same as LaRue. They even lived in the same town. How convenient for him! Norma and LaRue's personalities were as different as oil and water, but what difference would that make to a man in love? A man's attraction was always based on the physical at first.

Now, at age seventy-nine, Norma realized in horror what the problem had been—the problem that had never gone away, the reason Wes had seldom smiled. She'd always thought memories of the war had haunted him, but now she suspected it was more than that. Worse than the fact that he'd had a child with another woman, he might have secretly been in love with her sister LaRue for all those years. Norma hated to even form the words in her mind—to acknowledge what he had kept from her for so many years.

The tears welled up in Norma's eyes, but this time she refused to give in. She got the mop out of the closet, filled the mop bucket with water, poured ammonia on the floor, and swirled the string mop around the linoleum kitchen floor. Afterwards, she dried the floor, spread on plenty of wax, and buffed the linoleum until it shone. By the time she finished, two hours had passed, and she slumped into an overstuffed chair in the living room and flipped on the television. She picked up her husband's book on horses and was leafing through the book when Mabel walked through the door, humming as usual.

Mabel wore her straw cowboy hat, a tan skirt, a man's short-sleeved shirt with a blue silk scarf around her neck, and brand-new Nikes. Norma hadn't noticed until now that although Mabel often wore Nikes, the shoes never looked old. Norma wondered now how many pair Mabel owned and how often she bought new ones. Maybe she could endorse the brand and become a spokesperson for the company. In spite of Norma's dreary mood, she laughed aloud at the image.

Mabel dragged in an oversized brown suitcase. "Figured since I decided to stay on here, I ought to have a few more of my things. My, the house sure looks nice, dear. You've been busy."

"I went through some of Wes's things. Found out he was engaged to LaRue."

"Oh, sweetie, why don't you just let things be?"

"But when was it? Why didn't we know?"

Mabel pulled her suitcase into the bedroom where she stayed. When she came back in she was in mid-sentence, ". . . wasn't really official, I don't imagine. We knew she planned to marry her soldier, Hummer—it's just that we didn't know Hummer was Wes. But goodness, it doesn't matter now. You've certainly heard the story of how she met her soldier. We don't need to rehash it now."

Norma pulled the photo of LaRue and Wes from the album and held it where she could see it. "Actually, I haven't heard how they met. Please tell me."

Mabel looked skeptical. "Well, let's see. She met Hummer in Naf at a dance. My, they were just kids. You know how all the boys and girls liked to meet up there. Carloads of young people drove in from as far away as Brigham and Burley. It was a great place in its heyday, remember? Once, LaRue and I sat together, squeezed onto the back seat of Deloy's sedan in between Ralph Brown and Vern Tettleson from Almo. I wore a black satin dress that I was more than pleased to wear. Felt as pretty as a picture—thought it made me look like one of those Parisian models. But by the time the car rumbled forty plus miles over dirt roads, sucking in dust like a Hoover, that black dress was completely gray. It never did look the same."

Norma had only been to Naf a few times, but she remembered the dance hall crowded with young people all dressed in their Sunday best, except some ruffian cowboys who liked to keep things in a dither.

Mabel sat down on the sofa and refolded her ankle socks. "LaRue met Hummer just months before he signed up for the service. Way I heard it, LaRue was standing next to Adele Brown, and Hummer eyed her from all the way across the hall. Then the couples separated, opening up a conduit that led right to her. And with smoke hovering in the room, it looked mystical as if a spotlight was shining directly on her. He swore he'd seen a vision, and the vision was our LaRue. He hurried over to her and asked her to dance. They met there every Saturday night for the summer until he went off to war. I guess right before he left they promised to marry each other. 'Course that was long before he met you." Mabel pulled a magazine off the table.

Norma sighed. "I didn't think LaRue even went to those dances. She always said something about that place being a 'workshop of the devil, a place for drinkers and carousers.'"

"That was after the war. But before the war, entire families would attend those dances. Little children slept on blankets and benches."

"Where was I?"

"Well, you were so much younger."

"But why wouldn't I have heard that LaRue got engaged? That was certainly big news." Norma looked down at her hands.

"He was going off to war. Who knew if he'd return? Since it wasn't official, LaRue likely wanted to keep it a secret until after he returned."

"But you knew."

"I knew she'd met someone, but I never met him. I'd just gotten married myself."

Norma pulled herself up. Already she could feel her muscles stiffening from the day's work, but she hoped to muster enough energy to dust the living room. In the hall closet, she found a rag. As she ran the cloth across the television console, all she could think about was LaRue standing at the end of a heavenly path of light, with her Wesley gazing at her. In Norma's mind,

LaRue wore a white, frilly dress, the kind an attractive woman wears in the movies as she walks down the beach holding the hand of a handsome man. But the man was Wes, decked out in his army uniform. "Do you think I look like LaRue?" Norma asked.

Mabel squinted as if in thought. "Not so much anymore, but you certainly did when you were young."

"Goodness gracious, I'm sure beat," Mabel said suddenly. "We sure could use some rain to settle the dust on the roads." She slumped into her chair.

"Do you think Wes . . ." Norma started, but then her voice trailed off. She wanted to say, "would rather have married LaRue," but she couldn't allow herself to voice the terrible thought out loud.

"Goodness, Norma! I hope you aren't thinking what I think you're thinking."

"It's obvious, isn't it?" Norma grabbed the photo of LaRue off the coffee table, then grabbed her own photo. She held both portraits in front of Mabel's face.

"You think because you look like LaRue that he married you because he couldn't have her. That's what you think, isn't it?" Mabel shook her head.

"He didn't marry me—he married her, vicariously. I'm just more or less a stand-in for the girl of his dreams." Norma shut the photo album and went back to dusting.

"Horse feathers."

"Give me one shred of evidence that what I said isn't true."

"I don't have any, but I know you're wrong. Should we go over to LaRue's and ask her? I'm sure she can straighten this thing out for you. She knows the truth."

Norma closed her eyes. Did she really want to confront LaRue again? Who knew what hurtful things her sister would say this time around? But Mabel was right; LaRue was the only one living who knew the truth.

"Fine, let's go."

Norma abandoned the rag on the coffee table, snatched LaRue's photograph and the photograph of herself, and marched out to the pink Continental. Mabel traipsed right behind her, neither speaking another word. Within minutes they pulled up in front of LaRue's house.

Eleven

THE MAN STOOD UP WHEN KELLI AND TONY WALKED into Price's café. He wore sunglasses, probably to hide the bruises on his face. "If you brought cops this meeting is over."

"Settle down," Tony said, noticing the man was still wearing the cowboy hat he'd stolen from Tony. "We didn't bring cops. I thought you needed our help. But we can just walk right back out." Tony shook his head. *What a jerk!*

"I just need to be sure."

"Take a look outside. We came alone," Tony said.

Then Tony noticed the guy's new clothes. *Shoot, he probably got them before I cancelled the American Express.* "Did I pay for those clothes?"

"Yeah. They look good on me, don't they?" The guy sneered but then his face softened. "Look, dude, I really need your help. And like I said in the letter, I'm embarrassed to talk about it, but without my meds I become a little, I don't know—impulsive. Scout's honor." Instead of making the Scouts sign, the young man's fingers were spread in a peace sign.

"That's obvious," Kelli asked as she looked over the menu above the counter.

A waitress came and stood beside the booth. She wore a gold uniform and had short blond hair. "Did you get a chance to read the special? Hot roast beef sandwich, comes with your choice of potato and either broccoli or green beans."

"Uh, sure. Bring us three specials. That okay with you?" Tony asked the man.

"Yeah—can I have fries with mine and skip the vegetable?" the man said.

"And I'd like mashed potatoes and broccoli," Kelli added.

"Same," Tony said.

The waitress nodded and hurried away.

"If we help out, it has to be on our terms." Kelly looked the man in the eyes. "First off, what's your name?"

The man hesitated, looking away as if he had to think about it. "Kevin."

"Last name?" Tony asked.

"Just Kevin."

"You said you were in love," Kelli prompted.

"Yeah, you two should understand that part."

Tony glanced at Kelli to see if she caught Kevin's meaning. She smiled and tucked her hair behind her ears.

"We're not together—not really," Tony began. *Even total strangers can see we're meant to be together.*

"Not that it's any of your business," Kelli said. "But Tony's more like a brother to me—a friend."

Tony cringed at hearing Kelli describe their relationship, but he had more urgent things to worry about. "This isn't about us. So why don't you start with telling us why you stole my stuff and what you were doing without any clothes out near the Sun Tunnels. And what'd you go to Kelli's house for? You hurt her!"

The young man gazed out the window, fidgeting with the napkin dispenser. "A group of us were headed out for the solstice. We heard it's a real good time. We got lit up pretty good, danced around, and I remember getting into an argument. After that is a total blank, but when I came to, the guy had stolen everything, even my clothes. When I woke up, it was daylight and everyone was gone, including my girl. Thing is, I'd only known these dudes for a day or two. Met them in Reno. And they were all real cool, we thought. So we hitched with them to see these tunnels. My girlfriend—Cadence—she said the tunnels were in Utah, where she hoped to find some relatives to help us out. I know Cadence wouldn't have left me there. Something's happened to her, man. I can't call the police or anything because, you know, they might be looking for me. And Cadence left home when she was eighteen. She's twenty-two, but still I worry about her. I don't know if the others can be trusted. For one thing they left me to die. Didn't even leave me water. By the time I dragged myself to the highway . . . I mean, if that car hadn't been there, I might not have made it."

"What makes you worried about her?" Tony asked. "You passed out, and she probably went with the others willingly."

"I didn't pass out. I was knocked out. The thing is, she's pregnant. Even if she is hanging with one of those losers, she was only about a month away from having the baby."

"So you were drinking, doing drugs, probably, and all this with a pregnant girl?" Tony's voice rose in accusation. He knew what drugs did to people, and he had little tolerance for it. Early in Tony's life, his mother had used drugs as an escape. It took her years to break out of the addiction, but the damage to their relationship had been irreparable.

"Look, before I came along, she was so strung out all the time, she couldn't see straight. I found her living on the streets in L.A., doing tricks for a living. I tried to get her to get in touch with her family, just so they'd know she was alive, ya know—maybe even tell them she's pregnant."

Tony could feel the heat rising in his chest. He didn't believe you could trust a drug addict, and now he figured this guy was one as well. "So you want some reward for taking a runaway in, knocking her up, and keeping her clean for a few months before introducing her to the guys who kidnapped her. Did I get that I right?"

"Shh," Kelli warned as the waitress placed a plate of food in front of each person.

"Now save room for dessert," the waitress said as she sauntered off.

"Look, dude, you've got it all wrong." Kevin pointed his finger at Tony. "That's not even my kid she's having. Happened before I met her. When the father found out, he beat her up. One night about two in the morning, I walked out of this joint I was working at, ya know. And I saw this girl curled up in a ball lying next to a stinking garbage can. After getting beat up, she took some oxies—those are pain pills , ya know. I hauled her to my place and brought her back to life. She was checking out, dude. Another couple of hours on the street and she would have been dead."

"Did you take her to a hospital?" Kelli asked between bites of potatoes.

"A hospital?" Kevin laughed. "Hospitals are for people like you. People with credit cards in their wallets, people with trust funds and houses, people with families and jobs and—"

"And for pregnant girls who overdose and need medical attention," Tony interrupted.

"Man, you don't get it at all. If I'd taken her to a hospital, they would've dried her up first then hauled her butt to jail for, at the very least, drug use. Eventually she would've ended up in a chick's facility with a bunch of fat drug addicts, pushers, and prostitutes, and her kid would've been born in prison."

"Okay—so you did what you thought was right," Kelli said, clearly trying to calm him down.

"I'm starting to think I was wrong about you. If you aren't going to help me, I'm outta here." The perp shoved another French fry into his mouth. "I didn't do what I thought was right. I did what was right. I'm responsible, man—give me some credit."

"You mean you're responsible when you're on your meds." As soon as he said the words, Tony felt a sharp kick from Kelli beneath the table.

Tony understood all too well the kind of world Kevin had grown up in, but could see all kinds of holes in his philosophy. Still, he sensed Kevin's concern for Cadence. "Okay, what is it you want us to do?"

"I just want to find her. I love her. She's most likely looking for me, too, but she doesn't know where to look. I've contacted all the dudes I was living with back in L.A., and none of them have heard from her. Thing is, like I said before, she was trying to find some help. She wouldn't just vanish."

"Maybe she found help," Kelli said.

"No, she wouldn't leave me. I just need someone with resources to help me find her."

"So why do you think we have resources?" Tony asked.

"I went to the library and Googled your name, you know, since I'd borrowed your identity for a bit. Don't worry, I'll pay you back."

Tony knew he'd never see his money again, and he figured he should just call the police. But for some reason he felt torn. Maybe it was because Kelli seemed to want to help Kevin.

"Anyway," Kevin said, "you're one famous dude. Besides being in a country band, I found some newspaper articles about you saving some brainwashed women from drinking the suicidal punch."

Kelli cut him off. "It wasn't like that, not exactly."

Kevin's eyes widened. "Oh, so you were the woman! That polygamy stuff is weird. I don't get how some of those men get even one woman to marry them. I mean, they're such geeks."

"Some of the women don't know any different, and then some of them are like I was. They have low self-esteem and they're vulnerable, ready to try anything that makes them feel less guilty."

Tony noticed her emphasis on the word *was*, and hoped she truly had put all that behind her.

Kevin nodded. "Anyway, it made it sound like you were some kind of hero. I figured I needed a hero to help me out. It was kind of funny that I tied up the very dude who could help me." Kevin took a bite of beef and chewed it with his mouth open. "You know, don't ya, that I'll pay you back when I can. And as far as me taking the old woman's car, it seemed like a miracle. The keys were in the ignition, like I was being thrown a bone, so I took it. 'Course I still hadn't gotten my meds then. So whadaya think?" Kevin gulped his drink.

Tony didn't think the man's "condition" could so easily explain his crimes. He was clearly sane, and any mental issue he had wasn't serious enough to make him incompetent to stand trial. Tony wiped his mouth with his napkin. "It kind of weird that you ask the very people you stole from for help. And terrorizing Kelli—you still didn't tell us what that was about. And to think you'd do this all for a girl who was carrying someone else's baby. No one is that much of a saint."

"I know. I'm really sorry about hurting Kelli. At the time, I was just looking for someone to help me, and I saw her picture in your wallet. She had such a kind face. I thought maybe she'd help me, but I didn't think it through very well. I made a mistake." Kevin wrapped a piece of meat around his French fry and ate it in two bites.

"Big mistake." Tony folded his arms and sat back.

Kelli placed her hand on his arm. "I'm okay."

Tony thought for a minute. "Well, first you will return the car to Norma Weaver in Grouse Creek. Then we'll give you a head start out of town before we call the police. Tomorrow is a big celebration for the Fourth. Lots of people will be in Grouse Creek, including a few who will arrest you if you try anything."

Kevin grunted.

Tony continued, "Just drop the car off in front of Norma's house—you'll find it around the corner from the little store called Grouse Creek Supply. Norma's house is at the top of the hill. It's a white two-story with trees around it. And don't even think about bothering the ladies who live there. Just drop off the car and then blend yourself into the festivities. I'll find you there."

"We'll find you there," Kelli corrected. "Agreed?"

Kevin nodded. "Agreed."

They had all finished their food, so Tony pulled his new wallet from his back pocket and started fishing out some cash.

"No, I'll get this." Kevin pulled Tony's old wallet out of his back pocket and took out thirty dollars.

"How did you manage to get cash?"

"American Express and ATM machines. You know you left your PIN in your wallet." Kevin grinned, holding up the wallet. "I'm just kidding you. Here."

Tony grabbed his old wallet. "Here's fifty bucks. That's going to have to do."

"Look, Kevin," Kelli said, "you were right to pick us out as people who would understand what it's like to have someone you love missing, but you need to understand why we're so apprehensive." Kelli glanced at Tony, and while she was trying hard to act tough, he could hear the tremor in her voice. "I—I mean we—never want to be hurt again. Still, my gut instinct tells me you're in need of our help. But you'll have to understand if we do some things to protect ourselves. Tony is going to walk out to the car with you and get the gun you took. Also, know that in spite of Tony's crooked grin and his innocent little boy look, if needed, he won't hesitate to kill you."

Tony suppressed a laugh. He knew the only time he could possibly ever kill anyone was if he thought they'd harm Kelli. But he went along with the bluff, nodding in agreement.

After paying for the meal, the three walked to the parking lot. Tony smiled when he saw that the Subaru had been painted a dark green. He couldn't wait to tell Norma it wasn't neon or lime green.

"Tell the old lady that this color was cheaper than the metallic green I wanted—plus it looked good with the upholstery," Kevin said, searching the cargo area. Finally, he turned and looked at Tony. "I can't find the gun."

"What do you mean you can't find it?"

"Well, to be honest, I haven't seen it since I tied you up and borrowed your truck."

"Stole my truck, you mean," Tony said irritatedly. "Are you saying you might have left it in my truck?"

"I guess it's possible." Kevin hung his head. "Look, man, I'm sorry. I really am going to try to make things up to you. I could work for you, maybe. Even though I did a stint in jail for petty theft, I never steal from my employers."

Tony laughed. "I'll have to think about that. We'll see you tomorrow in Grouse Creek."

Kevin nodded, flashed the peace sign again, then jumped in Norma's car and drove away.

Twelve

"LARUE HAS COMPANY," NORMA NOTED AS SHE AND Mabel pulled up at their sister's home in Mabel's Continental.

"From the look of that silver sports car, it must be Patty."

Mabel was right. They found LaRue and her daughter Patty in the kitchen, cutting up fresh fruit.

Patty did not take after her mother. A free spirit, she had left Grouse Creek for California after high school and had done just about everything imaginable for a living, including working on fishing boats in Alaska, mining coal in the Appalachian Mountains, acting in a play off Broadway, and more. Occasionally, Patty wrote letters to Norma telling of her latest adventures, and once in a while she found her way back to Grouse Creek to visit her mother.

Norma looked at Patty, who was over fifty but still single and as beautiful as ever.

"Patty, you darling girl. So good to see you!" Mabel held her arms out for a hug.

When they parted, Norma hugged Patty as well, noting that she was still muscular and fit.

"She's just back from the coast," LaRue said. "I've been telling her about our disastrous adventure and how we were nearly killed by that young rapscallion."

"You don't mean Tony, do you?" Norma frowned. "He was a perfect gentleman."

LaRue rolled her eyes. "No, not him. The scoundrel. The one who wasn't wearing any clothes."

"Well, dear, how could he have nearly killed us?" Mabel asked. "He was all but dead himself. Besides, how could a man who so obviously wasn't carrying a weapon murder us? He would've had to strangle us one at a time."

Patty laughed. "What a grand adventure you three had! I wish I could have been there. Oh, and it's been ages since I've seen the Sun Tunnels myself. I know Mom doesn't want to see them again, but what about you two? Are you up for another trip to the tunnels, maybe Sunday afternoon?" Patty dried her hands on a towel and turned to face her aunts. Her blondish gray hair was pulled up in an untidy knot on top of her head. Her leathery skin was tan, and her blue eyes revealed her mischievous nature.

Norma hated to disappoint Patty, but another trip was the furthest thing from her mind. "Well, dear, you know I don't have a decent car anymore for those rough roads, and I doubt your car could do it. We have to dip down in quite a wash, and your little sports car would probably bottom out in the loose gravel." The image of the man's beaten body stretched out near the road flashed in Norma's mind, and she couldn't suppress a shudder.

"We can borrow a truck, can't we? The old Grouse Creek code still applies, doesn't it? What's mine is yours and what's yours is mine?"

"I've never heard of such a code," LaRue broke in.

"Oh, LaRue, Norma's right. Just about everyone and their dog begs, borrows, or steals whatever they need." Mabel chuckled.

"Long as it gets back to the right owner." Once again, Norma wished the thief had given her car back.

Mabel sighed. "I met her, you know, the artist who created the Sun Tunnels. Her name is Nancy Holt, and oh, she was great. She must be in her seventies by now. Remember that summer before I left home, when they installed those tunnels? I'd head out there with Robert Watkins, and that's when I met her. Nancy was still grieving the death of her husband. He's the one who created the Spiral Getty in the Great Salt Lake. He was killed in a plane crash, if I remember right."

For some reason, Norma had never even thought about an actual person, an artist, creating the Sun Tunnels. But it saddened her to learn that the artist's husband had died at such a young age.

"I don't know why anyone would want to go out there to those doggone ugly pipes. Hunks of concrete strewn on a flat, good-for-nothing, desolate land. If I never see them again it'll be too soon." LaRue scooped the seeds out of a cantaloupe and dropped them into the sink.

"Oh, Mom. Why should art just be on walls in galleries for pretentious snobs to impress their socialite friends with? What better place than out in the middle of nowhere? You literally have to use all your senses to enjoy the piece. And I've always believed, although she never told me this, that Nancy designed it as a memorial to her husband. It's a spiritual place."

"Spiritual?" LaRue scoffed. "All I felt was my sinuses closing in."

"I agree with Patty," Mabel said. "I did feel something spiritual there. It was . . . I don't know how to describe it."

"See, Mother? You just need to let yourself be more in tune with your surroundings." Patty popped a grape into her mouth. "You know it was there I decided to leave home. Robert and

I stood in one of the tunnels watching the sunset. And while the tunnels captured the lowering sun, we kissed long into the night."

"Oh, good heavens, Patty," LaRue exclaimed. "Haven't you ever gotten over wanting to shock me? You're over fifty, and that's the most unseemly thing I've ever heard."

"I truly doubt that." Patty took a few pieces of fruit from the bowl and arranged them on a plate. "You two sit down and we'll eat."

"That melon is for tomorrow," LaRue warned.

Patty ignored her mother and ate a piece of honeydew. The aunts joined her at the table and Norma reached for a strawberry. "Whatever happened to Robert, anyway? He disappeared from home shortly after you did."

"He came after me." Patty laughed. "We were together for several years—before Vietnam. He was drafted and I never saw him again. Didn't he come back here after the war?"

"Not that I ever heard," Mabel said. "Oh, he was such a sweet boy. You should've married him."

"What makes you think I didn't?" Patty laughed again.

"Oh, you! Always a tease," Norma said.

"Patty, behave yourself in front of our guests." LaRue glared at her daughter.

"Since when are Aunt Mabel and Aunt Norma guests, Mom?"

"Just don't go airing your dirty laundry in public."

"Mom, that's where you and I don't see eye to eye. What you consider dirty laundry, I consider more like, uh, paper towels. You use them until they're no longer useful and then you toss them in the garbage. But I see no reason to hide the truth."

Mabel chuckled. "I hope you don't think of Robert as a paper towel."

"No, but I don't think of our relationship as dirty laundry, either."

LaRue seemed upset, but she controlled her temper somehow. She and Patty used to fight like cats and dogs. Norma had stopped in once when they were having an argument. Patty, only thirteen at the time, was throwing popcorn at LaRue as she stood in front of the television to block some show she didn't want Patty to see.

Today, Norma assumed LaRue was so thrilled to have Patty home that she didn't dare speak too harshly.

"Speaking of airing dirty laundry," Norma broke in, "we came to clear something up." At first she'd hesitated to bring up the question while Patty was home, but then she realized it might be the perfect time to do so, since LaRue was desperately trying to be civil around her daughter.

"What's that?" LaRue asked, putting a plastic lid on a bowl of fruit before placing it in the fridge. Then she stooped lower, as if searching for something on the bottom shelf.

"Were you actually engaged to Wes?"

"Why can't you just let dead dogs die?" LaRue said, standing up quickly and turning to face Norma.

"Lie, let dead dogs *lie,"* Norma corrected. "Because I buried a man last month that might've wanted to be married to you all along and settled for me instead."

"And what's wrong with that?" LaRue washed her hands in the sink.

"Mom, you never told me that Uncle Wes had the hots for you," Patty said.

"Patty, that is a crude expression and I won't tolerate that kind of talk in this house." LaRue stared her daughter down.

Reeling at LaRue's callous attitude, Norma felt tears form in her eyes, so she turned and gazed out the kitchen window.

"What's wrong with it is that I was second choice. Don't you see how disturbing that is?"

"I can't imagine why," LaRue replied.

"Wait a minute here," Patty said. "Why does Aunt Norma suddenly think Uncle Wes had a thing for you, Mom?"

"Because I broke things off with him before the war."

Patty put her hands on her hips. "Really?"

Mabel moved to Norma and put her arm around her. "Now, the only thing we really know for sure is that Wes loved Norma very much and they had a happy marriage. Even though he may have been interested in you, LaRue, for a short time, I have no doubt that he married Norma because he wholeheartedly wanted to—to marry her, not you."

"I'm sure you're right." LaRue turned to face Norma. "After I jilted him, I'm sure he got over me. He never let on otherwise, and I know I certainly never had any lingering thoughts about him."

Mabel crossed the room and stood by the door with her hand on the knob. "There now, dears. This is settled. Let's go on back now, Norma. I've got cookies to bake for tomorrow."

"We're not leaving yet, Mabel. As far as I'm concerned, nothing is settled." Norma wiped her eyes. Then she pulled the photo of herself from her purse and placed it in front of Patty. "Patty, who is this a picture of?"

"I would imagine that it's either you or Mom. I was never able to tell early pictures of you apart."

"Well, it's me," Norma said. "The point is, I believe Wes probably married me because LaRue wouldn't have him and he saw little difference between us."

LaRue's eyes went wide. "What a thing to say! Besides, we both ended up happily married, so what difference does it all make now? As I said before its water over the bridge."

"Under," Patty and Mabel said in unison.

"And just because Wes wasn't good enough—I mean, wasn't right for me—is no reason why you should suddenly wonder now if he wasn't a good husband. He provided well for you, didn't he?" LaRue's voice rose and she slammed the drawer shut she'd been fishing through.

"Can I ask again what all of this is about?" Patty asked, pulling up the lid on the fruit bowl and shoving a piece of cantaloupe into her mouth. "I mean, Dad was no saint, and Uncle Wes was better looking."

"Looks have nothing whatsoever to do with morals." LaRue picked up the fruit bowl and set it where she probably thought it would be out of reach. "And I never said your dad was a saint, but he never tossed his oats around before marriage."

"So what you're saying is that it's true you broke things off with Wes because you found out that he'd fathered a child?" Norma tried to control the tremor in her voice.

"Yes, that's what I'm saying." LaRue untied her apron. "But I never would have told you if you hadn't come snooping around."

Norma tried to ignore the sting of her sister's words as she poured herself a glass of water.

"So, I have a cousin I never knew about. Where?" Patty asked.

"I certainly don't know where," LaRue said testily. "I never wanted to know."

When Norma tried to grab the bowl of fruit, LaRue pushed her hand away and put the bowl back in the fridge.

"Well, dears. I hardly think the word 'child' applies here," Mabel put in. "I mean, he or she would be older than Patty. Good gracious, he or she would be over sixty years old! If that doesn't make one suddenly feel ancient, I don't know what does."

Norma felt her face turn red. How could the people she loved the most keep such big secrets from her? Even worse, how could they be so unfeeling now that she'd discovered the truth? She felt like screaming, but her overwhelming sense of curiosity held her back.

What about that child? The man she had married, loved, and had children with may have another branch of family through the child he had kept secret. She felt compelled to know. Maybe if she found this child, she would find the missing piece in her life and in her marriage.

"LaRue, how do you know the child actually existed? Did you ever see it?" Norma placed her hands on the cool Formica tabletop and fingered the metal edge.

"No, I never saw the baby." LaRue's voice grew softer, but she looked Norma square in the face. "Never wanted to, as I said. But when Wes came home from the war, we met in Brigham City at the Idle Isle. He told me about the war and then he got real quiet and confessed that he'd gotten involved with a girl in high school, before he even met me. He didn't love the girl and she didn't love him. It was just one of those teenager flings, he said. I was horrified." LaRue sat down on a vinyl-covered kitchen chair, then shut her eyes for a few seconds. When she opened them, she said, "I didn't know how fathering a child could possibly be just 'one of those things.' I told him I never wanted to see him again. Of course I saw him at your wedding, and that was the most humiliating experience of my life. But I vowed to put it behind me, and especially to never reveal it to you, and I never did." LaRue had hardly taken a breath during her speech.

"But Mother, if he really loved you, why couldn't you forgive him?"

"It wasn't a matter of forgiveness. It was a matter of right and wrong. It was a matter of principle, of time and circumstance. How could I look people in the face?"

"No one would have thought any less of you, dear, but if you think you did right in giving him up, we can't judge that," Mabel said and then sighed. "I'm just sorry that you didn't keep this in a vault and throw away the key."

As girls the sisters had whispered secrets to one another, promising to lock them in a vault and throw away the key. Norma wondered how many of those secrets had been kept over the years. "I believe all secrets come out eventually and usually for a reason. I'm going to find that child. Was it a boy or a girl?"

"I don't recall if he ever told me." LaRue shrugged indifferently.

How can LaRue just not care? Norma thought, unsure as to whom she was angrier at, her husband or LaRue. "Fine. I'm leaving now. Mabel, are you coming with me?"

Mabel moved away from the door. "You go on ahead. I'll stay and help LaRue with a few things for a while. Go ahead and take my car."

Norma stormed out and got in the Continental. She pulled away from the house and drove to the cemetery.

No one was there and she saw that Wes's grave was still piled with fresh dirt. Some plastic red tulips stuck out of the mound. Norma pulled the flowers out and tossed them across the fence. At this moment, she didn't think Wes deserved flowers on his grave, even plastic ones.

Then she tore up the photo of LaRue and Wes, letting the tiny pieces flutter over the dirt like snowflakes. "There! You wanted her. Now you can have her." Norma whispered the words. Then, feeling foolish, she glanced around to make sure no one had heard her. The silence of the hills surrounding the cemetery consumed her and she sat down on a nearby headstone. It belonged to a cousin who had died years earlier. Wes's marker hadn't arrived yet.

Tears stung Norma's eyes and she wiped at them with the back of her hand. "Why didn't you tell me? Surely in fifty years of marriage you could've found a chance to mention a child you fathered, and that you were engaged to my sister." The sun dipped behind the darkening clouds and the air grew chilly. Norma cried as she sat on the stone, the cold seeping into her legs. She wished she could wrap up in her favorite quilt, the hand-stitched one given to her and Wes as a wedding present from his mother. It featured a wedding-ring design symbolizing eternal love, and sleeping beneath the quilt with Wes had been a nightly reminder that they belonged to each other.

Norma had conceived and nursed each of their children under the warmth of the quilt. And while she was still not certain that Wes had loved her for who she was at first, she suddenly felt confident that he had, in time, returned her love. It may not have been ideal, but it was enough. She needed to find his lost offspring; she could do that for the man she loved.

Norma's legs felt stiff, and she knew if she didn't move soon, someone would have to come find her. She took one last look at Wes's grave and determined to bring some roses over after the Fourth of July. With a groan she stood up, then walked back to Mabel's car and drove home.

Thirteen

Sam,

You're in so much trouble—Stacey was looking through the maternity rack at JCPenneys! Did she tell you I practically kissed her, I was so excited? I'm secretly hoping for a girl so she'll take after that gorgeous wife of yours. J/k. You aren't so bad yourself, now that you shaved that goatee.☺

Gotta run, Kelli

P.S. Can I tell everyone yet?

WHEN TONY BEGAN WORKING AT THE RANCH, HIS boss said, "Animals gotta be fed, come rain, snow, or holiday."

So before Tony went to bed the night before the Fourth of July celebration, he set his alarm for 5:00 a.m. so he'd have time to feed the stock before meeting Kelli at the celebration. Although Tony had never been in Grouse Creek for the holiday, he'd heard the celebration was the event of the year.

Tony also had a part in a program so he practiced the song in his head as he fed and watered the herd. By the time he drove in from the Box C, the parade had just started. To avoid being part of the procession, which came down the small town's main street, he parked north of the church and walked toward the school. An imposing structure built with gray sandstone, it stood in the center of town, across from the church. The grass and trees surrounding the school made up the largest expanse of green for miles, like a bright square in a dull quilt. On that bright square, Tony saw Kelli standing beneath a box elder tree apart from the other spectators. She spotted him and waved him over.

The first float was decorated with red, white, and blue crepe paper. In the middle of the float on a large, antique rocker sat an older man dressed in red, white, and blue, with a tall top hat. "Look, it's Herman as Uncle Sam!" Kelli said to Tony. Then she waved and shouted, "Hey, Herman."

"I want you!" Herman pointed at Tony with a serious frown, and then broke out into a chuckle.

Tony scanned the crowd for Kevin. With most of Grouse Creek's one hundred residents participating in the parade, there would've been more people in the parade than those watching, if many of their out-of-town friends and relatives hadn't shown up. Still, if Kevin were here, he shouldn't be hard to spot. Tony turned back to the parade to watch a fire engine topped with children of all ages, hurling salt-water taffy into the street. Tony picked up a few pieces and handed them to a little boy who was sobbing and clinging to his mother's legs.

Next came a float with a piano on it, played by a diminutive, silver-haired woman, and an elderly man dressed in new jeans, shirt, and suspenders, playing a fiddle. Some of the crowd began dancing to the music.

Kelli grabbed Tony's arm and pulled him down under the box elder tree. "I'm tired of standing in the sun. Let's sit down to watch the rest."

"I can see the last entry pulling out of the church parking lot now, so it's almost over," Tony said. A group of children rode by on decorated, prancing horses, followed by another half dozen horses ridden by older cowboys. A sign announced the second group as the Grouse Creek Posse.

"Hey, there's Mabel!"

Mabel sat on a hay wagon that was pulled by a four-wheeled ATV. A sign tacked to the side proclaimed her The Grand Marshal. She threw Tootsie Rolls, and one of them hit Tony in the face.

"Ouch!" Tony laughed. "Watch your aim, Mabel!"

"Oops, sorry sweetie," she called, tossing another piece that landed in his lap.

"I thought grand marshals *led* the parade!"

"This is Grouse Creek, Tony. They do things their own way." Mabel winked.

"Oh, my gosh! Take a look at the driver!" Kelli said.

Tony unwrapped the Tootsie Roll, slipped it into his mouth, and squinted. "What the heck? It's Kevin, and he's still wearing my hat."

"The sun is shining. He needs something to shield his eyes, doesn't he?" Kelli teased. "I can't imagine what he thinks he's doing."

"Kevin," Tony shouted. Kevin ignored the shout at first, but then turned in Tony's direction and waved happily.

"He's really getting into this whole thing. You'd think he was an actual Grouse Creek resident."

"Hey, dude," Kevin yelled. "Meet me at Norma's after the parade."

"What did he say?" Kelli asked.

"Something about Norma's." Tony felt his anger rising. He'd distinctly told Kevin to drop the car off and had warned him to stay away from the sisters.

After about ten minutes, Kelli and Tony made their way to Norma's house. The sun was hot on Tony's back and sweat surrounded his hatband. He took off the ball cap and wiped his brow, then smoothed his unruly hair. As they approached Norma's they heard a cacophony of voices and saw people of all ages enjoying a picnic on her front lawn. The newly painted green Subaru Outback was parked in the driveway right behind the pink Continental. Tony scanned the faces and saw Kevin eating a piece of fried chicken and engaged in lively conversation with a middle-aged man.

"Hey, Tony and Kelli, grab yourselves a plate," Norma said. "There's plenty."

They filled their plates with fried chicken, corn, watermelon, and baked beans, then sat down on some folding lawn chairs across from Norma. She pointed at her car. "Don't you think my car looks nice?" Norma asked. "Kevin has promised to make everything up to us too. Certainly it must've taken courage for him to come and ask for forgiveness."

Tony glanced at the Subaru. It was evident the coat of green paint was a quick spray job, and it wouldn't last long in the harsh climate.

"Kevin told us all about his awful ordeal in the desert," Mabel said. "And, my goodness, if we hadn't left my vehicle at the crossroads for him to take, he would most certainly have perished from exposure. I think it was providential to have left my keys hanging from the mirror."

"Providential, my foot. Being stranded in the desert would've served him right. Naked as the day he was born." LaRue waved her hand in the air to ward off the flies.

"Shh." Norma poked LaRue with her spoon. "We don't want Kevin to know that we had already come across him earlier."

LaRue huffed.

"But what a nice young man he's turned out to be. You just never know, do you? If it'd been up to me, I would've hung his sorry behind out to dry, but Mabel insisted we hear his story." Norma dabbed at the corners of her eyes, which seemed to have suddenly misted up.

"Hey, Kevin," Tony shouted in the thief's direction. Kevin didn't respond but continued his conversation.

Tony shook his head in disgust. It was hard for an outsider to be accepted in the small town, yet it seemed this punk had already wormed his way into everyone's good graces. Well, the sisters and the whole town might be ready to forgive, but Tony wasn't, and he would never trust Kevin.

Just then, Mabel rose from the head table, tapping a spoon and trying to get everyone's attention. She wore a blouse adorned with U.S. flags, and a matching baseball cap. "I wanted to welcome everyone on this Independence Day and to introduce our guests. Kevin, Tony, and Kelli, could you all please stand up so everyone can see you?"

Kelli and Tony stood, and Tony watched as the thief hesitated before pushing himself partway out of his seat. Then he waved to the crowd before slumping back down into the lawn chair.

Mabel cleared her throat and continued, "We met Kevin when he brought Norma's car back, and Tony when we found him tied and gagged. Tony found out about Grouse Creek through Kelli, who is here working on research for the summer. Friends just seem to keep turning up, like lucky pennies. You never know when and where, but we're mightily blessed by our good fortune."

LaRue grumbled, looking as if she wanted to burst from her chair, but Norma kept a firm grip on her elder sister's forearm. Mabel continued naming the collection of people, even a toddler underneath the table, for the benefit of the guests, as Mabel referred to them.

"Kevin, would you mind telling everyone a little about yourself? Then Kelli and Tony? We'd so love to know more about you. What brings you out to the desert, and who your kin are and so forth?"

Kevin held a napkin and wiped his face with it. He glanced sidelong at Tony again, and Tony noticed he'd ripped the sleeves out of the blue denim shirt he'd used Tony's credit card to purchase.

"Well, ya know, I met these extremely kind ladies recently due to a . . . a . . . somewhat freaky thing. I, uh, was beat up, and all my belongings were stolen. And to make matters worse, I was left to die stranded in the desert, with nothing but an umbrella to shield me from the sun. After dragging myself to the road, I came across this car that turned out to be Mabel's there. Stealing isn't in my nature, but, honest, dudes, if it wasn't for that car, I would've never seen another sunrise for sure. Then once again I found myself in a position where I needed to borrow another car. I tried to repay the women by having their other car painted for them, so anyway, today I brought that car out here to apologize and then met the sisters and you all." He tipped his hat awkwardly.

LaRue rolled her eyes, but Mabel clapped her hands together and encouraged him to go on. "Kevin has the most romantic story to tell."

"Uh, no. Another time maybe." He waved his hand in the air in protest.

"Nonsense," Mabel said, pointing at him with her spoon as if conducting a choir.

LaRue squirmed again and finally shot to her feet. "If that doesn't uncurl a pig's tail, then I don't know what does. You all believe this scallywag's lies, don't you? He's nothing but a crook, murderer probably, or even worse." Norma yanked LaRue back into her seat.

Tony had considered LaRue a bit ornery, but at least she was the only one in the group who saw Kevin for what he really was.

"Nonsense," Mabel said again. "Well, perhaps another time."

"I can't just sit idly by, watching my whole family get entangled in this man's web of lies, can I?" LaRue asked. "Naked as the day he was born."

"Shh!" Norma whispered to LaRue. "We don't want him to know we left him."

"Served him right."

Tony nodded.

"Tony, what about you?" Mabel pointed her spoon at him.

Tony wasn't sure how to introduce himself. Exactly what *was* he doing in Grouse Creek? He knew he wanted to be close to Kelli, but he could hardly say that. And as far as who his kin were, well, he wasn't ready to give out that information yet either. Finally, he stood and cleared his throat and adjusted his hat. "I'm Tony Stratton from up around Bozeman, Montana. I'm interested in ranching, so I jumped at the chance to work for the summer with the Tanners on the Box C. I guess most of you know my friend Kelli Carson from Burley."

As Kelli waved, Tony noticed the sun catching her long, auburn hair. "And you all have seen me around town. I'm here for the summer doing research on the grouse, counting them and checking habitat."

"Bet our tax dollars are paying for that," LaRue said under her breath. "Is that anything like counting sheep?"

Kelli laughed. "Not nearly as boring as all that. Actually, I really like this job and feel lucky to have gotten it, especially since I had very little training in this field of study. I mean, it doesn't pay all that much, but I get to be outside and do something really important."

Tony watched Kevin's every move and wondered when he could get him alone. By the time Tony had finished eating, Kevin had meandered away from the table and lay down under a sycamore tree. He slid the cowboy hat down over his eyes. Tony whispered to Kelli that he'd be back in a few minutes and then hurried over to Kevin. He sat down next to the young man, and then glanced up to see Kelli had followed him.

"Howdy, Kevin," Tony began, "if that's even your real name. Remember the deal we made in Burley?"

"Listen, dudes." He removed the hat and squinted as if the light was too bright even in the shade of the tree. "I tried leaving the car here and then blending in just like you said. But the old women were all outside when I pulled up. One of them—Mabel, I think—jogged over like I was her grandson or something. By the time I got out my apology, she had invited me to be in the parade. She insisted."

Tony pondered this. "What about that malarkey about borrowing the car to have it painted? You're acting like you didn't really steal the car at all, but actually did them a favor. And with my money! No one seems to remember that you didn't even pay for the paint job yourself."

Kevin dropped his head. "Yeah, well, like I said, when I'm back on my feet, I'll make it up to you. I just need to get things settled and find my girlfriend." He pointed at Mabel. "Thing is, I started to explain the way things went down, but Mabel squealed and said, 'I just knew you wouldn't really steal that car.' Said something about my honest face. How could I deny it, man? When someone believes in you like that, it almost seems like I could be the kind of guy she thinks I am." He smiled ruefully.

Kelli nodded. "It's funny, but I know what you mean. I've been lucky to find a few Mabels in my life. Remember Don Quixote, and how he treated the peasant Dulcinea? Tony is my Don Quixote."

"Don't know anything about him," Kevin admitted.

Tony felt himself blush. He certainly didn't feel he deserved to be on such a high pedestal.

"Well, Don Quixote refused to believe the world to be full of dreary events and dreary people. He saw the best in people and imagined a beautiful world in which he was a gallant knight. At first, those around him laughed and mocked him, but eventually they wanted to be just as wonderful and kind as Don Quixote imagined them to be. It's such a wonderful story. You have to read it sometime."

Kevin listened intently. "Yeah, you get it. Exactly. Mabel and her sister Norma make me want to be better. LaRue doesn't seem to like me much, but I could win her over in time."

"I don't think there will ever be enough time for that," Tony put in. But then he wondered, *Should I help Kevin?* He could be just unlucky and a bad thief, or he could be dangerous. "So, what's the romantic story they're talking about?"

"You've heard most of it, but it's the truth, Scout's honor." Again Kevin flipped Tony a peace sign.

"You weren't ever a Boy Scout, were you?"

"Not technically, but I always wanted to be one. I grew up on the other side of the tracks, so to speak. Boy Scout troops, Little League, and having a PTA parent weren't exactly part of my upbringing. I was a latchkey kid—know what I mean?"

"Yeah, okay. But just so you know, you've been giving me a peace sign, or a victory sign, depending on the era. Scout's honor is like this." Tony straightened three fingers on his right hand, holding them together with his thumb and pinkie, then held up his hand with his palm facing out.

"Man, I've been doing that wrong all these years. But, anyway, this is what happened—Scout's honor. I'd been drifting, you know. One job after the other, that is, until I met Cadence. Cadence gave me a real reason to get up in the morning—a real reason to get my act together so I could help her get clean. I never got into the drug scene myself, but still I had some habits that weren't all that great. And like I already told you, she was carrying life. I thought, wow, this is supremely sacred! Life. Ever hear of the Big Bang Theory?" Kevin looked at Tony.

"Sure—the scientific theory that the universe had a rather explosive beginning, that there isn't a God."

"That's it. Well, I believed that. You know, my mom raised me, and she was a devout Lutheran, but our life was revolting. We lived worse than rats in a sewer, and I just couldn't believe that the loving God my mom prayed to every night, if He existed, would leave us in such a mess. So when I learned about the Big Bang Theory, I thought, 'Yeah, man, this explains it. No one made this pigsty. It just happened—no wonder the world sucks.' But now Kelli tells me about this Don—what's his name again?"

"Quixote," Kelli said.

"Yeah, him. Maybe I've been looking at it wrong."

Tony nodded, remembering that he too had once questioned a loving God's existence. He had wondered how God would allow tragedies to occur.

Tony remembered waking up one morning at age ten. His mother stood over him, pink foam curlers in her hair. Tears streamed down her face. She sat on the edge of Tony's bed and stroked his hair. "Tony" —her voice broke— "Davy Walker died last night. He and his brother Vernon were swimming in the river, but Davy, he drowned."

Tony turned away from his mother so she wouldn't see him cry. "It's okay to cry, baby." Tony turned back, sat up in bed, and fell into his mother's arms. He let her hug him tighter than he had in years. He never told his mother that the three of them had been spending their hot afternoons jumping into the Gallatin River. They did cannonballs off the embankment and tried to see who could make the biggest splash, and who made it out the farthest. Tony had the record for going the farthest, but Vernon, ten pounds overweight, made the biggest splash.

"Why?" Tony had finally asked his mother.

"Maybe God needed him more than we did."

Her words haunted him. How could God need a 10-year-old if He was so all-powerful? And not just any 10-year-old, but the nicest boy Tony knew? Tony remembered thinking that maybe if Tony wasn't as nice as Davy, God wouldn't need him so much.

Tony's mind jolted back to the present.

"And Cadence," Kevin continued, "I'm her Don Quixote, aren't I? Man, I just got that. Pretty cool. And I was drawn to her—she wasn't pretty, not then, but I wanted to help her out. See? Just like Quixote and the peasant chick."

Kevin's face lit up as he talked about Cadence. "She was puking all the time and pale, but I just thought it was drug withdrawals, so when she started getting fat and we could feel that baby kicking, it somehow changed the way I started to think. I thought maybe all of this didn't just happen because planets collided. Even though I think in lots of ways God messed up big time, He must've known what he was doing to create life like that."

Tony understood Kevin better than he wanted to. Until he'd joined the LDS Church and turned his own life around, he hadn't been all that different from this troubled young man.

Kevin went on. "And I wanted to do something about these feelings I was having. So I married Cadence, so we could be a real family. I never knew my dad, and I thought it'd be cool to be one. But it went wrong—I lost her. See why I have to find her?"

Tony hadn't known his father, either. He felt a little sympathy for Kevin now. Tony glanced over to the tables to make sure Norma had enough help putting things away, then turned back to Kevin. Even though the story sounded convincing, Tony wondered now if he'd just thrown in the marriage detail to impress him. "So even though you knew you weren't the father, you still married her. So when did that happen? Because until now, you've been calling her your girl."

"Oh, we got married, all right." Kevin pulled at some long grass around the trunk of the sycamore. He held a blade of grass out to an ant and watched it crawl along the edge.

"Anyway, when we got out to the Sun Tunnels, we found out that one of the dudes was an actual legit preacher. So right there in the tunnel as the sun went low, I got down on my knee and asked Cadence to marry me. She thought I was just yanking her chain at first, but finally I convinced her that my love went beyond this world and that even though she was just a kid, only eighteen, she was way older than that, considering all the stuff she's been through. Life made her like twenty or older—really, man. So with the sun shining on her face, giving it this cool glow, she said she would marry me. Right then and there with a handful of people we hardly knew and with Moon—that's the dude doing the ceremony—we got married." Kevin's smile broadened as he told the story, and he got a wistful look in his eye.

Tony noticed a game of volleyball starting on the front lawn, while a few people played horseshoes. He turned back and looked at Kevin. "You know, don't you, that legally you're not married?

You need a license and all that. Some guy can't just marry you because he's a preacher."

"Moon said we could take care of all that later. 'Course now I can't find him, and who knows what he did with Cadence."

"So what now?" Tony asked.

Kevin nodded toward the house. "Norma said I could keep using her car, and she's already—"

"No, no, no! That isn't going to happen. Just because you can take advantage of some old woman doesn't give you the right to do it."

"But maybe, if you could prove you were sincere, like I don't know—turn yourself into the police . . ." Kelli began.

Kevin stood up, gesturing toward Norma as his voice grew louder. "No, I can't do that, not yet. I'd never find Cadence. And besides, Norma needs me to help her find someone, too. I told her that while I'm looking for Cadence I can, you know, look for her missing person as well. I'm going to need wheels to do that."

"Who is Norma looking for?" Tony wondered aloud.

"She's missing a stepchild. It's weird, but I keep thinking maybe Grouse Creek is where Cadence was headed. 'Course she's way too young to be Norma's stepchild, but she was trying to find someone too. Maybe there's a cosmic connection. Man, if I could find Moon and the dudes we were with and go from there, but I don't have any idea where to find them. Plus what if the guy that hurt me hurt Cadence too?"

Kelli grasped Tony's arm. "We better get over to the program, since you're going to play. You ready?"

"Oh, yeah. Norma's gonna read a couple of poems, and I think some of their grandkids are singing, but I need to get going." Tony glanced up at the sun, high in the sky.

"Considering Cadence's situation, eight months along, I would start by checking the nearest hospitals," Kelli advised.

"Yeah, that makes sense. I hadn't even thought about that—I mean, she wasn't due for another month."

"Babies can come early," Kelli said. "Was she being checked regularly?"

"Well, a friend of ours checked Cadence over good and asked her some questions and stuff and then told her she thought the baby would come in August. That was in L.A., but since we sorta left there she hasn't been seeing anyone."

Kelli's eyebrows rose. "Was the friend a doctor?"

"She had some medical experience."

"Where's the nearest hospital?" Tony asked Kelli.

"Well, from the Sun Tunnels, Tremonton. Or maybe Wendover."

"Tremonton—it's in Utah right? She'd stay in Utah, I'm pretty sure," Kevin said.

"Yeah." Kelli nodded. "It's about two hours away, going east. We should call and see if there is anyone by the name of Cadence."

"She'd be long gone by now if she had the baby right away, plus she ain't goin' to use her real name, so I think I better check personally," Kevin said.

"Maybe . . ." Tony said.

Kevin stood up and stretched. "Let's get going. We can stop at the church until you're finished with your part, then get to the hospital by three or four this afternoon."

"Whoa, what's this 'we' thing? Kelli and I aren't going anywhere."

Kevin looked at his shoes. "Whatever, I just thought you'd be in on this, man. What was all that Quixote stuff if you weren't planning on helping? Well, I guess I can go to the church first, and we can decide later." He motioned to Norma's car. "Do you want a ride?"

"No, we'll walk."

Kevin shrugged his shoulders and walked to the Subaru.

"So what do you think?" Kelli asked when Kevin was out of earshot.

"I don't know. I never knew my father. That was hard for a kid. It made me feel so . . . I don't know how to explain, but so left out." Tony stopped, remembering Kelli had lost both of her parents to a car accident. "I'm sorry. I know what you went through was harder. I forget sometimes."

"But at least I knew my dad. Don't apologize. I can't imagine not knowing your father. That must've been so hard."

Tony shrugged. Sometime he'd have to tell Kelli the whole story about his father.

Kelli began to run towards the church. "Beat you there."

Tony couldn't run with his guitar slung over his shoulder, since he didn't want to risk damaging the instrument. When he walked up to the doors to the church, Kelli stood there trying to catch her breath. They walked inside and saw Bishop Jed Watkins slumped on the sofa in the foyer, his head slung back and snoring. He jerked awake when the front door closed.

"Hey, there. You're just the two I need to speak to. Since you're going to be here all summer, I'd like to put you to some good use. Our new schoolteacher moved into Logan a while to take some courses, and that's left me up the creek. He's been my counselor and I can hardly ask you to do that, but if I could get you to help out with some of my workload, mostly looking after the elderly. And, Kelli, we need a Primary teacher, too. I know the Relief Society is a little shorthanded as well."

"Well," Tony said, taking his hat off and setting it above the coat rack. "Whatever you want me to do, I'd be happy to,"

"And what about you?" the bishop asked Kelli.

"Sure, I love to teach."

"Great. Then you'll teach the five- and six-year-olds. Mainly, Tony, I just like all of the older folks in town to have an extra visit or two each month, you know, to make sure they're all right. My counselor did a lot of that and right now my biggest concern this month is the sisters, Norma especially, bein' her husband died recently. But it's also a good opportunity to visit with Mabel, who's a little less than active in church."

Tony nodded his head and the bishop continued, "Yeah, now you're lucky, though. Normally we have to go clear out to Montello to see Mabel, her bein' the only member there, but sounds like she'll be staying on with Sister Norma for a spell, so that ought to take a load off."

"Yeah, lucky," Tony said.

"'Course now, Mabel usually won't let you in the door anyway—I mean on official Church visits. That's why I thought it would be good to ask you to go there. Bein' new in town, she won't suspect you. Ya kinda got to sneak up on her, so to speak. Go there for some other reason, like to visit about politics, for instance. Now she likes talkin' politics. Just make sure you've read the newspaper from cover to cover before you go, and don't be sayin' anything good about the current state politicians. Just listen and sympathize and you'll get along dandy. And Tony, I'm mighty glad you're willin' to take this on." Bishop Jed put his hand out to shake Tony's.

"No problem." Tony turned to Kelli. "I'd like to practice my song once before the program starts."

Kelli walked with him into an empty classroom and watched him take out his guitar and strum a few chords. Then he ran through his song. At the end Kelli smiled, so he continued:

I once met a girl
Or should I say she once met me.

Her eyes were the color of a pine tree after
a rain.
Her smile, so beautiful it could stop a
freight train.
Her hair, thick, long, and red—I mean auburn.

Tony sang and Kelli tossed her head back and laughed.

But there was one thing men should learn.
She isn't what you think.
She'll drive a man to drink.
Better not fall for those flashing eyes.
You're better off staying far away.
'Cause there's one thing you don't know, you
don't know.
She can't play the piano worth a lick.
Her beauty, her personality, her goodness—
it's all a trick.

When he finished, Kelli clapped her hands. "You're such a tease."

Tony sighed quietly as he followed her outside. She never took him seriously when he hinted that he was falling for her.

Fourteen

AN AMERICAN FLAG STUCK STRAIGHT OUT OF THE three-year-old's ear. Worried that Colton, the youngest of Mabel's four great-grandchildren, would hurt himself, Norma leaned over and whispered, "Careful with that stick, dear."

He scrunched his face and stuck his tongue out at his great-aunt as his older sister gently pulled out the flag.

Norma shifted her focus to the people now streaming into the chapel, chattering and finding their seats for the annual Fourth of July patriotic program. Norma was third on the program. Known in town for her poetry, she shared her newest pieces each year. This year, because of her husband's death, she'd almost declined to participate, but she'd decided at the last minute that getting back to some sense of normalcy might help her in the grieving process. She sat in the front of the chapel in one of the aqua-blue choir seats next to Mabel's great-grandchildren. They were a boisterous bunch—four in all—varying in age from three to ten. Norma felt bad that none of her children or grandchildren were coming, but at least they'd all come out for the funeral.

The chapel pews soon filled and people even stood along the back wall. Norma recognized nearly everyone in the audience—a collection of Grouse Creekers and their relatives who made the annual trek to participate in the festivities. For many it was a pilgrimage to the land of their heritage; to others it was just another weekend visiting relatives they only saw once a year.

Jean Brooks, who ran the tiny country store, stood at the microphone and announced the program. As soon as Jean sat down, Mabel's great grandchildren marched down the center aisle singing "It's a Grand Old Flag" while enthusiastically waving their small American flags. Norma silently read through her poetry again, clearing her throat in hopes her voice wouldn't give out. She had picked up one of those nagging summer coughs. When she glanced up, the children were on their return trip, and their tiny voices were barely audible. The three youngest children quit as soon as they spotted Mabel sitting in the audience on the third row back and slid in next to her, leaving the oldest to finish the song by herself. She managed the feat without a pause before running off to join her siblings.

Next, Tony Stratton began a rendition of "America the Beautiful." Norma gasped, surprised that such a raucous-looking though handsome boy could have such a beautiful voice. He sounded just like an angel. She wiped away a tear. Then Tony performed an original composition called "Raccoons on the Back Porch." The country tune that mocked typical love songs left Norma laughing so hard she had to grab her papers before they jiggled off her lap.

While Tony sang the second verse, Norma noticed Kevin leaning against the back wall with his hat over his eyes. *Oh dear*, she thought. She tried to motion to him to take his hat off, but he wouldn't look up. *What is he thinking, wearing his hat in the church? Most likely bad upbringing.*

Finally, Kevin glanced up just as Tony began the third verse. Norma motioned with her hands and mouthed, "Take off your hat." Kevin looked confused and gazed around. Finally, he pointed to himself and mouthed, "Me?" Norma nodded, pointed to her head, and pantomimed taking a hat off. He smiled as if he understood and then strode right up the aisle.

When he reached the front, he took the hat off, handed it to Norma, and then whispered. "Meet me in the parking lot right after your poems."

Norma pushed the hat back toward him and whispered, "It's not mannerly to wear hats inside, especially not in a church."

Kevin glanced around and then pointed at Mabel, who wore her flag-adorned baseball hat.

"The rule doesn't apply to women," Norma whispered.

"Huh? Well, that's dumb, but then don't you want to wear it?"

By now Tony had finished and Jean Brooks announced Norma's name.

"Absolutely not," she whispered as she stood up. She watched as Kevin held the hat against his chest and slipped out the side door.

Norma's hands trembled as she smoothed the paper out on the podium. Usually she wasn't nervous speaking in public, especially among friends, but Kevin's behavior had unnerved her. Why would he think she would wear a cowboy hat anyway? It'd certainly mess up her hairdo, to say nothing of the fact that it just wasn't her style. She shuddered, then made her way to the podium and began her poem.

Memorable moments of giddy joy
And searing pain.
A sky painted with colors of an autumn tree
Follows dismal, dark rain.

The death of a loved one, husband or son.
Searching the black night for a glimmer,
Instead finding only misery.
Holding a baby in your arms
A reminder life continues on—
Hope follows pain,
A rainbow—rain,
A new breath follows death.

Norma looked up at the audience again. She had paused on the last few words, hoping to emphasize each, so that the audience would grasp the meaning. There was a general hush, broken only by a wail of a baby.

Norma tried to paint a smile on her face as she continued with two lighter poems. When she finished, she heard a few claps and then widespread applause. Instead of returning to her seat she slid out the door, hearing Jean Brooks encourage all the veterans of war to come to the front.

In the parking lot, Kevin already had her car started and positioned to take off at a moment's notice. She walked up to his window to see what he wanted.

"Are you sure it's okay for me to take your car again?"

Norma wasn't sure. And now that she saw the car in better light, she wasn't at all sure about the color and quality of paint. But then she caught a glimpse of the boy's eyes, still bruised. He did remind her of her grandson Zach. For a second her mind flashed back to when that grandson was born. As a preemie, he'd spent weeks in the neonatal unit at Primary Children's Medical Center in Salt Lake. And now he was married. *My goodness, time flies.* "It will be all right, Kevin. But be careful and keep in touch."

"Thanks. I just wanted to tell you goodbye and to thank you once again for everything—ya know, for trusting me." He put his hand out and Norma took it.

Her mind raced back to her own husband. It'd been just over a month and a half since she had held his rough hand, weathered from years of mending barbed wire fences, hauling hay, and branding calves. For an instant, as clear as day, she saw Wes, young and handsome, holding an infant child who wasn't theirs. His face held that fleeting smile she longed to see again, and she felt her eyes swim with tears.

"Yeah, when I hook back up with Katie, we'll—"

"What?" Norma interrupted. "Katie! Did you say Katie?"

"Katie. That's Cadence. 'Katie' is short for 'Cadence.'"

"Your girlfriend's name is Katie?"

"Yeah."

Norma's mind raced. Could it be a coincidence? She didn't think so. The mysterious girl who had called looking for Wes—the girl who clearly needed help—had said her name was Katie.

Without another thought, Norma got in the car with Kevin.

Fifteen

Sam,

You're right, as usual. Kevin is probably a jerk, but he totally related to the story of Don Quixote, which makes me like him a little. Tony still puts me on such a pedestal that I know there's no chance I won't disappoint him. He is, like Stacey said, too good to be true. Tell Stacey that Mom used to make ginger tea for the neighbor, Sister Beaswell. Mom said it was good for her morning sickness. Of course at the time, I had no idea what morning sickness was, and I kept telling Mom I had morning sickness so she wouldn't make me practice the piano. I had no idea why she knew I was faking. LOL. Tony is so nervous about his audition, but you wouldn't know it. I tell you the guy is a genius on the guitar. Your last email got spammed! I hope that isn't a sign. ☺

We found out Kevin is supposed to be on meds. I think he's ADHD, but Tony thinks he's bipolar. Either way, you never know what makes people the way they are. I emailed Stacey, but she hasn't responded. Tell her I'm mad at her. ☺ Texting doesn't work here—I know that's her thing, but tell her I need her!

Love ya, Kelli

P.S. I ripped my new jeans climbing over a barbed wire fence. BLEH!

TONY AND KELLI DIDN'T KNOW KEVIN HAD LEFT town until a good hour after the Fourth of July program ended. Tony had noticed Kevin talking to Norma during the program, but that was the last he'd seen of him. After searching through the crowd at the rodeo, Kelli and Tony decided to head back to Norma's house to see if Kevin was there. When they rounded the bend they saw Mabel standing by Norma's white-picket gate.

"Yoo-hoo!" Mabel called to them, waving a piece of paper. "Did you see Norma and Kevin leave?"

"No. Aren't they here?" Tony asked.

"Darn it all," Mabel said. "Adele Adams said she saw Norma talking to Kevin and then get in the car with him. No one has seen her since, and all I can find is this note by the telephone. It's a list. Now what would possess her to leave right in the middle of the festivities and abandon me with all of our guests?"

Tony felt his gut tighten at the idea of a sweet elderly woman riding in the car with Kevin. He'd thought Kevin would still try to talk him and Kelli into going with him. If only he'd known Kevin would approach Norma instead. "What does the note say?"

"Chicken food, hose, light bulbs. Chicken food? Why chicken feed, today of all days? In mid-summer, free-range chickens have all those insects. About the last thing she'd need to run into town for is chicken feed. Besides, there's a full sack on the back porch, I checked. I wonder . . ."

Mabel looked worried.

Tony took the note from her outstretched hand and looked at it. The note had clearly been written in a hurry, and he was surprised Mabel could read it. "When did she write the note?"

"I don't know. I don't remember seeing it earlier. I hate to say it, and I certainly hope that I'm wrong, but—" Mabel swallowed hard.

"You think she might have been forced to go with him?" Kelli asked.

"It says chicken food." Mabel sighed. "How could it mean anything else? I suspect Kevin was looking over her shoulder."

"So she pretended to be writing an ordinary shopping list," Kelli said, "knowing that Kevin wouldn't suspect anything, but that you would catch the clue. Chicken food—very smart. You are the only one who could know that."

"Oh, dear. I just realized something. Someone called looking for a young woman by the name of—something like Candace. The call came yesterday while Norma was out. I forgot to even tell her about it, since I thought it was a wrong number. And the caller didn't say who he was."

"Could they have said Cadence?" Kelli asked.

"Cadence, that's right."

"Cadence is Kevin's girlfriend."

"Heavenly days." Mabel's eyes widened.

"Can we go inside?" Tony asked.

"Oh, sure, sweetie." Mabel grabbed Tony's hand and walked with him into the house. Kelli held onto Tony's other arm. The living room was bursting with people, one man stretched out on the sofa, while a redheaded toddler stuck leaves in his hair.

"Come into the kitchen and sit down while we decide what to do next," Mabel said.

No one was in the kitchen. They sat down at the table and Mabel brought them ice-cold lemonade. Tony took a sip. "Did they say Cadence's last name?"

"They did," Mabel said. "Now if I could just remember. It had something to do pigs."

"Pigs?" Kelli frowned.

"I just know when the man said the name, I thought of little pigs. What could it have been? Let see Pigs, Thriggs, Diggs, Biggs—none of those. Hog, Nog, Cog—that couldn't have been it, since I would've thought of dogs instead of pigs."

"How about Sty or Mire?" Tony asked, trying to make a connection.

"No." Mabel furrowed her brows together and fiddled with her glass. Then she smiled broadly. "Ah, I've got it. Wolf."

"As in the big bad wolf?" Kelli asked.

"Yes. I mean no. Oh, never mind. I don't think that's right after all. But it did have something to do with a wolf or a pig." Suddenly, Mabel's face broke into a grin and she held her hand in the air. "Puff—no Huff. It's Huff. I'm sure of it."

It took Tony a minute to make the connection between pigs and the big bad wolf and huffing and puffing, but it made him smile. "Well, maybe we should start calling hospitals, starting with Tremonton, to see if a Cadence Huff came in to have a baby. I'm pretty sure that's where he's headed, and he could have Norma with him."

A knock sounded on the door and as Mabel hurried over to answer it, Tony grabbed the phone and dialed the Tremonton hospital. When a woman answered the phone, he said, "Yes, I'm calling to see if a young woman named Cadence Huff delivered a baby there sometime in the last two weeks."

"You and everyone else," the woman muttered. "And who's this?"

"Uh, Tony Stratton. I'm . . . who else has called?"

"I'm really not allowed to give out that information. Who are you again?"

"I'm just a friend of a friend who's looking for her." Tony had no idea how to answer the question. It was difficult to explain that being asked to look out for Norma made him interested in Kevin, who was interested in Cadence. "Births are public record, aren't they?"

"Sure. We list them in the paper."

"Then you could tell me if she delivered, right?"

"She did. But I can't tell you where she is now. That isn't public record. Not that I know, which I don't. Which is what I told the police—that I don't know." Tony wondered how things had gotten so complicated.

"Were you there when she delivered the baby, then?"

"If it's night or a holiday, I'm here. I get all the shifts everyone else wants off." Tony walked into the hall to see whom Mabel was talking to. A uniformed officer stood in the doorway. He was relieved, knowing Mabel would pass on their concerns that Norma may have gone unwillingly with Kevin.

"So you were there? When was it?" Tony looked at Kelli and winked at her. She smiled and took another sip of her lemonade, then got up to join Mabel in the hall.

"No, I wasn't here when she delivered, but I came on right after. Scrawny baby, only weighed five pounds two ounces,"

"So Cadence was released?" Tony asked. "And when again was this?"

"Guess I can tell you, since they print the police report in the paper too. No, she wasn't released, not properly. Slippery little thing just walked out. I mean Cadence walked out, with the baby. That would've been about a week ago. Caused quite a stir."

"A stir? With the police?"

"Like I already said, yes. But now we're getting into stuff I probably shouldn't tell you."

"I'm just trying to help her, ma'am. "

"I've already told you everything I know."

"Listen. A kid and woman were headed there to look for them." Tony glanced at the clock on the wall and figured Kevin and Norma could've arrived by now. "Are they there? A blond guy in his twenties and an older woman."

"No, we've had hardly anyone in today."

Tony sighed. He sure hadn't planned on getting involved in all this. "If they show up, please at least tell the woman to call home. She's small, just over five feet tall with brown hair, and she's seventy or eighty years old."

"What is she wearing?"

"I—I—uh, Kelli, what was Norma wearing?"

"Bright red polyester slacks and a matching striped blouse with a pocket on the right side, and pearl clip-on earrings with silver clasps."

"Here, you tell her." Tony said, handing Kelli the phone.

Tony noticed the police car leaving. Mabel stood in the kitchen humming as she wiped the counters. Most of the visitors had gone outside again.

"So what did he say?" Tony asked.

"He just wanted us to know that the young man who stole Norma's car is wanted in the case of a missing woman—Cadence Huff. So I did have the name right."

Mabel looked pleased with herself. "I showed him the note with the clue, but he didn't think it was anything, so I offered him some lemonade and told him I'm sorry he had to work on the Fourth. And he said, 'Someone does.' And I said. 'Yes, I guess, that's true. Someone does, and it brings me comfort to know that no matter what day of the week or time of the day, we're being guarded over by someone as fine a person as I'm sure you are.' He didn't even smile when I said that. You'd think he would, but he was more intent on finding out if we'd seen Cadence or Kevin. He said today was a good day to investigate with so many folks out here to talk to." Mabel plunged her hands into a sink full of dishes and soapy water.

"So did you tell him anything else?" Tony asked Mabel.

"I just didn't know what to say. I still can't believe Kevin would harm Norma, so there must be a good explanation." With a wet hand she fished the note out of her shirt pocket and held it out to read through the list once more. She shook her head and stuffed the slip of paper back in her pocket.

Tony figured the officer was on his radio right now issuing an alert for Kevin in Tremonton and the surrounding areas. Depending on whether Norma went willingly or not, she might be charged with aiding and abetting a fugitive. Tony's heart sank for her. When he'd sat down after playing his guitar in the program, Norma had leaned over with tears in her eyes and patted his hand. Now, he closed his eyes and silently prayed she would be safe.

Sixteen

"KEVIN! SLOW DOWN!"

Norma watched as the odometer went down a few notches and let out a sigh. "Okay, Kevin, I know you want to find her, but it won't help if we're dead."

Kevin laughed and slowed a few more miles per hour, and Norma released her death grip on the door handle.

As they neared the crossroads Kevin turned to Norma. "I heard your poetry—some of it, that is. It's dark and deep. You don't seem like a gloom-and-doom type person."

"Not all of it is dark. Didn't you hear my poem about the cat that fell down the well?"

"Yeah, I heard it. You don't think a cat drowning in a well is dark?"

"But it's supposed to be funny," Norma said. "See, the cat chased a mouse down the well. It was being greedy, but the mouse made it out and the cat drowned. It was a cautionary tale—a fable."

"Like I said, dark." Kevin adjusted the rearview mirror.

"Well, I guess. Maybe we ought to turn on the air-conditioning. It's awfully hot in here."

"Damages the ozone layer," Kevin replied. "And uses more gas."

"But I'm paying for the gas, and I think they've fixed that ozone problem."

"Open your window."

"Obviously, you don't drive these kinds of roads much. There's a lot of dust. If I open the window you won't be able to breathe with all the dust." Kevin didn't respond but stared straight ahead. By the time they reached the end of the washboard road, Norma felt beads of sweat run down her face. She flipped the air-conditioner on. Kevin flipped it off.

"We aren't on the dusty road anymore. Which way?"

"Left to Tremonton, but look at my gas gauge. We need to go into Montello to get gas or we'll never make it." Norma turned the button back to COOL. "Look, dear, this is my car, so in my car we do what I want."

Maybe if she was as young as Kevin the heat wouldn't bother her, but at her age it seemed like her blood pressure rose with the heat.

"Guess that's true." He shrugged.

Before long Norma could see the large sign that read Welcome to Nevada—the Silver State. She tuned the radio dial to a soft-rock station.

"Hey," Kevin said, starting to reach for the dial. "Oh, yeah—your car." He pulled his hand back as if he'd been burned.

"No, go ahead and choose what you want," Norma said, deciding there was hope for the boy's manners after all. "Oh, look! That's Pilot's Peak coming into view." She pointed to the tallest peak in the Pilot Mountains. Sagebrush and junipers covered the base, but dark pines painted the top.

"Yeah?" Kevin peered out the left side of the car. "Tell me about it."

"As you can see it's the highest mountain in the area. I wonder if even Charles Lindbergh himself used it to mark his flight."

"Charles who?"

Obviously not a history buff. "Lindbergh." This was just another reminder to Norma that schools weren't teaching what they used to. She remembered studying Charles Lindbergh in the sixth grade.

"That right?" Kevin asked. "So was Lindbergh after the silver?"

"What silver?"

"The sign said the silver state. I thought maybe he was after it."

"No, he was a pilot. Made history as the first person to fly nonstop across the Atlantic Ocean"

"Oh." Kevin sounded uninterested.

"That was in 1927," Norma said. "The town is coming up soon." She rummaged through her purse until she found her credit card.

Montello, Nevada, came into view. Strewn across the barren landscape were a few scattered trailer homes, junk cars, and rusted farm equipment planted for decades wherever it happened to break down. The town boasted a population of 103, a frog's hair larger than Grouse Creek. On one side of Main Street, railroad tracks paralleled the road. On the other side, a few businesses and homes made up the town.

Norma and Kevin filled the car with gas at the Cowboy Grill and then went inside to pay and get something to drink. The place was deserted. Apparently, most of Montello had journeyed into the larger cities for the holiday weekend. Norma and Kevin took seats at the counter and waited for someone to help them. There was a pool table, a few slot machines, and a jukebox. Dozens of one-dollar bills with customers' signatures on them papered the wall behind the counter. Expensive wallpaper, Norma thought, recalling that customers wishing the owner well would sign their names on the bills. She noticed Mabel's name scrawled in red ink on at least two of them. Finally, the bartender appeared from the kitchen area. He was around sixty with short, gray hair poking out beneath his straw Stetson. He wore blue jeans and a T-shirt. "Hot day to be out. What can I do you for?"

"How far to Tremonton?" Kevin asked.

"Ginger ale," Norma said at the same time. "What would you like?"

The man said. "It's about hundred and twenty."

Kevin looked confused. "A cold beer."

"He'll have a root beer." Norma gave Kevin a disapproving scowl.

Kevin moaned but said nothing. A man sat down at the end of the counter and removed his wide-brimmed hat, revealing long, gray hair. He ran his fingers through his beard. His jeans were tucked into his knee-high, lace-up leather boots. His khaki shirt was worn through at the elbows. Norma felt his eyes on her, but didn't look his way. "Say, ain't you Mabel's sister?" he finally asked.

Norma stared at the man and finally recognized him as LaVell, a man Wes had introduced her to a couple of times. Wes had known LaVell well when they were younger. Norma nodded and smiled, then took a sip of the ginger ale the server had put down in front of her.

"Norma, right?" LaVell said.

"That's right." Norma nodded.

"Say, sorry I never made it to Wes's funeral. Tried to make it over, but everyone and their mother wanted me to chase a cow for 'em that day. Good man, your husband. Never turned a soul away that was down on his luck, that's for sure."

The mention of Wes tugged at Norma's heart. She tried to force a smile, but knew she hadn't managed it very well. Without asking him what he wanted, the bartender brought LaVell a cup of coffee.

"Say, LaVell, you knew my husband pretty well, didn't you?" Norma asked suddenly.

"We was buddies before the war and then fought in the same unit." LaVell opened a packet of sugar and stirred it into his cup.

"That's what I thought." How should she word this? She didn't want to make him wary. "I'm having trouble locating the child he had, the one before he married me."

He looked into his cup and stirred. "Not too many folks knew about her. 'Course I did because we was tight, but I can't help you. I don't know what became of her."

Wes's first child was a girl! Norma's hand shook and her heart jumped. She glanced at the dollar bills on the wall and watched the names blur as her eyes filled with tears.

"We've got to get to Tremonton," Kevin said, gulping his root beer. He burped loudly. "Trying to find my, uh, wife."

"What's she doin' there?" LaVell asked after taking a sip of his coffee.

"Lost track of her out at those Sun Tunnels. Now we're just following a hunch and trying to find her."

LaVell shook his head. "Nowhere to hide out at those pipes. If she got lost out there, then she was aimin' to get lost."

"Something happened to her," Kevin said, gulping his drink.

Kevin scanned the dollar bills on the wall as if he'd just noticed them. "We're already wasting too much time. We'll never make it by 4:00 now." He turned to LaVell. "Dude, do you have a cell phone I can use?"

"Got one, but it don't get reception here."

"What do you have it for then?" Norma couldn't help but ask.

"Confounded salesman talked me into it when I was in the mall in Elko. Thought it would be just the thing, so folks can track me down when they're needin' me. You know, for business purposes. Now if I'm up there on Pilot it comes in fine, but on this side and down in the valleys, not a thing. Purt near useless as a sled in summer. And if I was to string a line up to my place I imagine it would cost a pretty penny."

LaVell took another sip of coffee. "Now if you're wantin' to, young man, while I'm visitin' with Norma—you can get on Brandy, my Palomino, and ride 'im up Pilot until you get a signal. Wouldn't mind at all. Got lots of minutes." LaVell fished in his pocket and pulled out a tiny silver phone, then slid it across the counter.

Kevin grabbed it and flipped it open. "Okay. That might work. I've got a Subaru four-wheel drive. Where do I go?" Kevin swigged the last of his root beer and wiped his face with the back of his hand.

"That green car out there? It's too low to the ground. You'll bottom out."

"Nah. That's what these cars are made for," Kevin said. "That's why me and Norma got it. It's perfect for the kinds of roads we have out here."

That's pretty nervy, Norma thought. *He acts like he owns the car.*

"I'd be careful, but if you step out front, I'll show you where to go."

"Go ahead, I'll get this," Norma said, handing her credit card to the manager as he stepped up to the cash register. Then she noticed a dollar bill stapled to the wall with the word "Moon" scrawled on it in blue marker. At the picnic, Kevin had told a romantic story where a preacher named Moon had performed a marriage ceremony for Kevin and Cadence.

"Kevin!" Norma shouted as she scrambled out the door to find him. LaVell pointed across the train tracks. "Kevin! Moon has been here."

Excitement lit up his face. "Just a minute," he said to LaVell before following Norma back into the cafe.

The bartender disappeared into the back but then stepped out again. "What can I do you for?" he asked like it was the first time he'd seen them that day.

"Uh, the man that signed that bill behind you there, Moon. Do you remember him?" Kevin asked.

"Yeah, I do." The bartender adjusted his cap. "An odd bird, that Moon feller. He and a bunch just like him—long hair, rings, needles, nails, and things poking out all over their bodies, like they was human pincushions. They was here right during the solstice. We always get those kind in here that time of year. So what was that, two weeks back? Haven't seen them since."

Kevin pulled the cell phone out of his pocket. "Did they have a pregnant woman with them, about five feet five inches high with short blond hair?"

"There was more people with him than beans in a barrel," the manager said, fiddling with his suspenders. "But now that you ask, I do think one of them was pregnant."

Kevin looked at Norma. "I'm going to call the hospital and then I'll come back and get you in about fifteen minutes."

"You go ahead. I'll be here when you get back."

Norma watched Kevin drive across the railroad tracks, scowling when he didn't slow down at all.

"Kinda young to be married, but seems like a nice enough kid." LaVell nodded toward the door.

"He might be. I don't know him all that well," Norma said without thinking.

"Huh?"

"Well, I just met him. We're both looking for someone. He's looking for his wife. And I need to let Wes's child know about his death, but I don't even know her name. Maybe you can help, since you and Wes were friends back then. He, uh, lost track of her." Norma realized she had hardly touched her ginger ale, so she took a few sips. It tasted good and helped settle her nervous stomach.

She closed her eyes and tried to formulate in her mind an image of another branch of family who should know about Wes. Or should they? If he'd wanted them to stay in touch, wouldn't he have stayed in touch? And did she *really* want to meet these people? She vacillated a few more times, then gave in to the same determination that had brought her this far. She had to do this.

She opened her purse and pulled out a pen and notepad. "Can you think of anything that would help me find Wes's—" She didn't know what to call her. How should she acknowledge her husband's first love, the first woman he'd made love to? Or was that woman even the first? The thought was so unsavory that Norma almost forgot the question she needed to ask. "His girlfriend, the mother of his child." She forced the words out, but LaVell didn't seem to notice the long pause or the change in her tone.

LaVell ran his hand through his beard again. "Well, me and Wes was high school buddies at the time. It's possible I have a picture or two up at the house of her. It's just a hop, skip, and a jump to my palace."

"I don't know." Norma glanced at the door.

"We can be back here before you can say, 'Jack Daniels.'"

LaVell left instructions with the owner to send Kevin up to his place if he got back before they did. LaVell helped Norma climb into his truck, a 1955 Ford that may have been green or blue at one time but now looked like solid rust. Norma was about to roll the window up so the dust wouldn't blow in on her when she noticed there wasn't a window.

The entire town of Montello was about two blocks square. They passed by Mabel's house, one of three homes on Main Street built in the early days of the railroad. Another house, if you could call it that, seemed to be a trailer house with an addition made of railroad ties. The owner clearly had a sense of humor, as a sign nailed to the house read Montello's Finest Hilton—Vacancy.

Soon, LaVell pulled up next to a camper across from the city park at the edge of the tiny town. A tall chain-link fence surrounded the dirt yard, with rubber tires, car parts, and dog feces scattered everywhere. A Rottweiler bounded from under the camper and jumped at the fence, barking fiercely.

"That dog'll have you for supper if I don't chain 'im," LaVell said with a chuckle. "Just a minute."

Norma looked across the graveled road to the city park with its swing set, teeter-totter, monkey bars, slide, and half dozen picnic tables. There wasn't a single tree, a patch of grass, or landscaping of any kind to cool things down. With no children playing there, weeds were the only sign of life.

Norma glanced back at the trailer house to see LaVell trudging toward her. His snarling dog ran to the end of its chain and jerked in mid-air, then ran back and did it again. Norma nervously stepped out of the truck with her hand on LaVell's arm for support.

LaVell's dwelling place was nothing more than a camper sitting on top of an even more dilapidated truck than the one they'd ridden in. Several horses were corralled near the camper. The dog continued to bark, and as Norma headed up the path, a mangy cat slithered between her legs.

"Truck don't work. Parked it up here the night I rented out my other place, and haven't got it goin' again. I managed to throw stuff together and haul it up here. It's a might bit cramped. Suits me well enough, but I'm sure you're used to lots nicer."

Norma ducked her head and still felt the top of her head brush the doorframe as she stepped into the dingy camper.

"Make yourself at home there while I get the things," LaVell said.

Although the space was compact, it was tidy in contrast with the cluttered yard. Norma sat down at a built-in kitchen booth and pulled open the blinds. LaVell fumbled through a cabinet above the bed at the other end. "Just came across all this when I moved my things up here. Wanted to sort through 'em then, but time gets away."

He set a worn shoebox down on the table and opened the lid. "Not all this will interest you." He flipped through the stack of photos and newspaper clippings. "Here's something—had 'em put that plastic coating on it—trying to keep it from disappearin' altogether."

Norma picked up the yellowed newspaper clipping and scanned the photos, recognizing young Wes and LaVell dressed in U.S. Army uniforms. The story told of the soldiers' bravery in liberating a concentration camp. Norma knew the story but didn't know it had been featured in the newspaper.

"Here's somethin', too." LaVell handed Norma a photo of two beaming couples who stood with their arms linked. "Think that was before you—while Wes was courtin' your sister."

Norma held the photo closer to get a better look.

"You can have that one," LaVell went on. "I've still got one similar to it. But in this one" —he set another photo down— "we're lookin' like we just won the lottery. That was just days before we shipped on out."

Norma sighed at the reminder that her husband had courted her sister.

LaVell continued to shuffle through the photos. "There's gotta be one here of you and Wes on your wedding day. You know I wasn't there, but my sister took a couple snapshots for me. Oh, here we go."

Norma picked up the black-and-white photo. She had worn her nicest dress instead of a wedding dress, not feeling as if they could afford the "whole kit and caboodle," as Wes had always called anything fancy.

"Can you tell me more about the child?" she asked softly, feeling her heart thump. "My understanding is that the baby spoiled LaRue and Wes's wedding plans."

"I don't know a doggone thing you're talkin' about." LaVell picked up a stack of photos and squinted. "Gotta get my readin' glasses to see these better."

"The baby never spoiled any plans?" A bead of sweat trickled down Norma's hairline. The late afternoon sun poured through the window, turning the living quarters into a roasting oven. Norma fished through her handbag and found a handkerchief to wipe her face, then picked up a stiff photo and fanned her sticky skin.

"It's sweltering in here, isn't it?" LaVell jumped up and turned on a fan. Papers scattered in the breeze, but Norma gathered them again and held onto the photos.

"Norma, I have to say I'm mighty confused." He scratched his bearded chin and pulled the blind down. "I don't know why Wes would tell you the child came between him and LaRue. That's not at all what he told me. Wes tried awful hard to keep track of the baby, too, but the mother didn't want to marry Wes and worked against him. And far as I know, he only saw the baby once or twice after the war. Wes knew the mother had a hard row to hoe, so he didn't blame her none, but I know it broke Wes's heart. That's why it always made me happy as a lizard in the sun to see you two and the family he had with you. Doubt he ever forgot that first one, but still he had a fine family, and he was always a proud of that—proud of you, proud of the kids.

"Remember when Marianne graduated cum laude? Thought he'd bust a gut when he told me. Then the first grandchild—I helped Wes buy a pair of cowboy boots, hand-tooled, for the little tyke. Kinda tugged at my heartstrings. Wanted that sorta thing for myself." LaVell started putting the photos back in the box.

Norma tried to sort through the new information, but something didn't fit. Tears formed in her eyes and she dabbed at them with her handkerchief. Wes must have seen the child after she married him, and the thought nearly tore Norma's heart out.

"The thing is," Norma began, "Wes didn't tell me anything about the child, and it hurts me now to find out that he didn't think enough of me to share his most painful part of his life. How did he not trust me enough?" This man seemed like he would never judge her, so she found it easy to confide in him.

LaVell put his hand over Norma's and patted it as if comforting a child. "You think that child was the most painful part of his life? If you're thinkin' that then you've got it all wrong." LaVell held the newspaper clipping in front of her. "Those are just bunch of words on that page, honorin' us, but they don't begin to tell the horror we seen with our own eyes. Piles of dead folks discarded like yesterday's trash." LaVell turned his face and his voice broke before he went on. "Seein' what Hitler done over there . . . there's no way to describe it. It sure made us grow up in a hurry. Until then I was just some hotshot kid, you know, like young-uns today who don't think about no one but themselves. When you seen what we seen, it changes you deep. We seen the ovens built to burn folks. We seen the trenches full of those lucky enough to escape life. And those left, those we got medals for liberatin', they was just a hairbreadth away from death. When you seen all that, you never look at life the same way again. Things happen to ease that memory, but the nightmare is always there, waitin' to be sprung up before your eyes again. Wes come to grips with the horror. He married you. Wes was lucky. You helped ease that burden. But me—after seein' what humans could do to other humans—"

Instead of feeling sad, Norma felt anger—anger at herself for not recognizing the burden Wes carried, and anger at Wes for not letting her help him.

The photo of LaRue and Wes lay on the yellow Formica tabletop. LaVell picked it up and pointed at LaRue. "Yeah, you two sure were the spittin' image."

"That's right. I looked just like LaRue. When she wouldn't have him, he settled for me." Norma thought she'd put that part of the equation behind her, but hearing LaVell verbalize the similarity reopened the wound.

"So that's what's botherin' you. Did LaRue tell you that? 'Cause I'm sure as shootin' Wes didn't." The old man's brows knitted together.

"Not in those words, but she said she broke things off with Wes after she found out about the child."

"Hogwash."

"What's that?" Norma wondered if she'd heard LaVell correctly.

"Hogwash. It wasn't LaRue that wouldn't have Wes. It was Wes that wouldn't have LaRue."

"What do you mean?" Norma dabbed at her face.

"LaRue knew about the child—that part's right. But she still wanted Wes after that. She even offered to marry him before he shipped out, like so many couples done. But Wes wouldn't have that—he said he wouldn't leave no widow behind. If things worked out like he hoped they would, he'd come back, you know, and marry her right proper."

"I don't understand. What happened?"

"I'm pretty darn sure things just weren't the same after he come home. It's a lucky son of a gun who can just pick up the pieces of his life and continue on after the war like nothin's different. I guess Wes needed to start over. What's past is past, you know."

"But he didn't start over. He tried to pick up where he left off by finding someone who looked just like LaRue—the spitting image, you said yourself."

LaVell shook his head. "Sure, you mighta looked like LaRue, but he wasn't lookin' to replace her, that I'm sure of. After the war, I can recall how sorry he looked after he saw LaRue again. He'd gotten all spiffed up, like we used to do back then."

As LaVell rifled through the stacks of photos, Norma noticed the ragged edges of his fingernails that looked like he'd trimmed them with a pocket knife.

"Anyway," LaVell went on, "he was all downtrodden when he come home. Said LaRue wasn't the girl for him after all. He'd felt mighty bad about breakin' the news to her, but he said it wouldn't be fair to marry someone he couldn't love."

Maybe LaRue had her own version of the truth, Norma thought. Sometimes you were sure you were right about something, but it turned, and a new truth presented itself, making the old truth an illusion. Norma had a feeling this information would turn on her again and again before she discovered what was right. Still, her heart swelled with the knowledge that Wes hadn't wanted to marry LaRue. "LaVell, tell me more about the young woman—the one Wes had the baby with. You thought you might have a photo."

LaVell dumped the remaining photos onto the table. "Now, I didn't know her that well. We was just so young. But I'm pretty sure she was from Garland too, or one of those little places that came into Bear River High."

"Do you remember her name?" Norma scrambled through her handbag and found her pen and notebook. She wrote down "Garland" and waited for the name. When she looked up at LaVell, she could tell he was desperately trying to pull the name from his buried memories.

"It'll come to me, but I can't seem to remember her name right now." He scrambled through the photos again, finally handing Norma a snapshot of a young man. He was so young, fresh-faced, and vibrant that she looked twice before recognizing Wes. He held an infant in the crook of his arm like a football.

"That's the baby there. Wes and I roomed a while during college, and he left some of his things with me. Figured he planned to retrieve them, but he never did. This was among his things. Most of his stuff I quit haulin' around with me, but the photos, 'course I hung on to them. Thought maybe there'd be one of the mother, but can't see one in here."

Norma flipped the photo over and read the barely legible scrawl on the back. Catherine May. Norma jotted the name down on her paper, just finishing as she heard a car honking out front. She parted the blinds and saw her Subaru, then saw Kevin jump out and run to the camper.

"Come on, Norma! We've gotta get going!" Kevin shouted as he banged on the flimsy door.

Norma stood up and looked at LaVell. "Can I take this with me?"

"Sure. Take 'em all. What use are they to me?" After quickly sorting through the photos left on the table, LaVell handed her all those that included Wes. Norma placed the snapshots in her handbag.

"When's your sister Mabel comin' home?" LaVell asked. "Things just ain't the same around here without her."

"Oh, I'm sure she'll be here by next week or so. She was sticking around Grouse Creek more or less to keep me company and so I could use her car. I didn't know you were friends."

"Mabel's everyone's friend."

"True."

Kevin banged on the door again, then stepped inside and handed LaVell the cell phone.

"She had the baby a week ago in Tremonton. Let's go."

LaVell touched the brim of his tattered hat and looked at Norma. "Glad to get reacquainted with you again."

Norma nodded. "Stay in touch. And don't forget to call if you remember anything."

"Sure as shootin'."

As Norma got into the car, she remembered she should've called Mabel to tell her she'd gone for the day. But everyone was so busy that she doubted they'd even missed her yet. She'd call from Tremonton. LaVell said the cell phone didn't work at his place anyway.

Fifty miles later as they passed through the little town of Park Valley, Norma still clutched the photo of Wes holding his first baby girl in his arms. She could not stop looking at it. Kevin stared straight ahead and hadn't seemed to notice her intense study of the picture. "Lost babies," she finally said. "Wes's baby is over sixty, and yours is only two weeks old. Funny, isn't it?"

"Huh?"

Norma held up the picture and Kevin gave it a quick glance. "This is my husband's first child, the one I'm looking for. She just might have something to do with Cadence." Norma stared at the photo and felt her anger begin to dissipate. *Babies have a way of making a person forget the pain,* she thought.

"Yeah, okay," Kevin said. "We'll find our babies together—find Cadence and . . ."

"Catherine, Catherine May," Norma said.

"We'll find 'em both."

Seventeen

Stacey,

It's about time! I guess you've been too busy throwing up to stop at the computer and write a note. ☺ I loved the 4th celebration, especially Norma's chicken. She puts this tangy sauce on it that is to die for. Now Norma has left town without telling anyone where she was headed. Weird. My grandpa used to always tell us the truth is stranger than fiction, and in this crazy town he was right for sure. I'm glad the ginger tea is helping. I've also heard vitamin B helps. But what do I know? I can't believe I'm giving you advice on the subject of pregnancy. Tony is so cute! And while I can tell Sam almost everything, there are a few things I just want your advice on. The other night Tony gave me a hug and for a brief second, I wished we were more than friends.

Maybe if the circumstances of our meeting weren't so strange . . . But every time I look at him, I know *he thinks I'm such an idiot. Who could like a girl who almost became the 5th wife of a false prophet? I need someone who doesn't know my past, don't I? Got anyone in mind?*

Kelli

LARUE SAT ON A LOUNGE CHAIR BENEATH AN OLD sycamore tree with Patty and Mabel. "Let me see that note," LaRue asked, turning to her daughter and her sister.

"I'm stymied as to why she'd be buying chicken feed for them when they can eat all the bugs they want." Mabel shook her head. "I'm hoping she just wanted to go along for the ride with Kevin."

"I'm just sure that even Norma wouldn't leave on her own with him. After all, it would be unseemly for her to be riding around with that rapscallion." LaRue dug into her hand basket, pulled out a magnifying glass, and scrutinized the note. "What about these other words on the list? Light bulbs—that could be so we'd see the light, not stay in the dark, so to speak. And hose, what about a hose? I saw a case just like this on Matlock. If only I could remember . . ."

"Fiddlesticks," Mabel said. "I thought that too for a second, but then I remembered Kevin's face when he told us about his wife. A boy that much in love would not resort to kidnapping."

Tony wasn't so sure. Love can make a person desperate. He turned to see Kelli toss a ball to a little boy. He watched her pat the boy on the head as she leaned down to talk to him. Tony watched her face break into a smile as she spoke to the child. She was a beauty, inside and out.

Still, Tony couldn't think of a logical reason for Kevin to kidnap Norma. "Mabel, I think Kelli and I will head into Tremonton just in case LaRue's right. And since the police are looking for Kevin, even if LaRue's wrong, Norma could still be in a jam." Suddenly, Tony had a thought. *Who better to hold for ransom than a sweet, elderly woman with a family and a whole town who cared about her*?

"Wait just a minute, then. I'm going with you. LaRue do you want to come too?" Mabel asked.

"Where?"

"To Tremonton to find our baby sister."

"Now you know I never go to Tremonton," LaRue said, fanning herself with the mysterious list.

"Oh, yes, dear, I'd forgotten. You still haven't gotten over the possibility that you might die in Tremonton." Mabel turned on her heels and headed toward the house.

"I've got to die one of these days, and the odds of that are getting higher every day." LaRue shook her head and clucked her tongue. "So now, more than ever, I avoid going to Tremonton."

Within minutes, Mabel hurried out of the house with an overnight bag. Tony grabbed it and tossed it into the pickup. "So why is it LaRue doesn't want to die in Tremonton?" He held the truck door open for Kelli and then helped Mabel climb in.

After Tony jumped into the driver's side, Mabel answered the question. "Oh, because when she was sixteen or so she was sweet on Selmar Peterson."

"And so what does that have to do with anything?" Kelli asked.

"Because he's the mortician there."

"And?"

"Now, would you want someone you were sweet on at one time, and even courted briefly, to prepare your body for burying?

I wouldn't mind, but LaRue has a good point. Anyway, ever since 1971 LaRue has avoided Tremonton as if it was the plague. It's hard to spend thirty some odd years of your life going out of your way to avoid a place, but she's managed it." Mabel chuckled as Tony drove past the Grouse Creek sign.

"If all three of us went to Logan," Mabel went on, "we had to drive the country roads out to Elwood, then down to Brigham, and up through Sardine Canyon. It's a burden beyond imagining to avoid Tremonton, but few people have the gumption to argue with LaRue. I've tried telling her it wouldn't matter one iota if she died in Elwood, because she'd be sent to Selmar anyway. And even in Grouse Creek our bodies are sent on to Tremonton. Selmar is very good at what he does. Why, dear Denton Wireson looked like he could've sprung right up and shook your hand and thanked you for coming out. I stood there a while at his casket half expecting him to."

Kelli laughed at the image as Mabel continued, "But LaRue says, 'No, siree.' She doesn't care if Selmar can bring back the dead. She's going on to Burley. She's got notes all around her house with just those instructions—even in her handbag, just in case. Doesn't want anyone to send her on for Selmar to be looking at what he not ought to be looking at. LaRue says, 'I kept my body from Selmar when I was sixteen and I'll keep it from him now, thank you very much.'"

They were halfway to the crossroads when Tony noticed the needle on his fuel gauge dropping close to the empty mark. It hadn't occurred to him to fill up with gas before he left Grouse Creek. They wouldn't make it to Snowville. He wondered if there was a farmer's place in Park Valley where they could beg some gas. In Montana, rural farms often had unlocked gas tanks, free pickings to anyone without a conscience. He figured it was the same in Utah. "I'll be needing gas by the time we hit Park Valley. Do you know anyone there, Mabel, that we can beg, borrow, or steal a couple of gallons from?"

"Surely do, hon. My baby brother Deloy. Keeps chocolate under the bed if you've got a sweet tooth. He'll have gas." Mabel giggled as if catching the double meaning of her words. "And if you're needing anything else, he'll have that too, if you've got time to let him sort through a lifetime's collection of odds and ends."

"A packrat, huh?" Kelli hadn't stopped smiling since Mabel revealed LaRue's secret.

Mabel gestured with her hands. "That's putting it mildly. He's saved every one of his hunting licenses in his sock drawer. They're sorted by year. Even has his first tooth that fell out when he was eight."

It would already be late afternoon by the time they made it to Tremonton, and the detour would slow them down even more. When they reached Park Valley, Deloy's house was just off the main road near the schoolhouse. Deloy stood leaning on the fence watching a young colt frolicking around its mother.

Mabel rolled down the window of the pickup. "Can we buy some gasoline off of you?"

"Hey there, sis! Sorry I didn't make it out to your shindig today. What's going on? Just saw Norma a while back, racing through here like a house on fire. She pretty near run me down. Now here you are. What's so goll-darned important?"

"So she kept going?" Kelli asked.

"I stepped outta the post office after getting my mail and was about to cross the street when she just about mowed me over. Didn't realize it was her at first. While I was cussing at 'em, the car slowed down just a tad and Norma hung her head out the passenger window, waved her arms, and hollered something. 'Course I thought she'd stop, if for no other reason than to see if I was okay, but she just kept right on a goin'."

Tony and Kelli shared a look, and Tony knew she too worried Norma might have been yelling for help.

Deloy walked up to his front door and beckoned the group inside. "So, anyway, come on outta the heat and I'll get you a bite to eat. Did I ever tell you I joined the chocolate-of-the-month club? Dropped the package from Switzerland when Norma tried to run me down, but it didn't hurt it none too bad. Broke some pieces, is all. Those Germans make some mighty good candy." Deloy's face was a leathery tan and his stomach hung over his belt. He wore new jeans, polished boots, and a crisp, short-sleeved shirt.

"You mean the Swiss make good chocolate," Mabel said.

"Same thing," Deloy replied. "Anyway, take a load off and come on inside."

"We really don't have time to stay," Tony said. "We were just hoping to buy some gas from you."

"I'd be happy to sell you some."

"Awesome," Kelli said.

"That is, if I had some. Thing is on holiday weekends, with the price of gas so high, I get robbed blind. People on their way to Grouse Creek, Wendover, or Elko get this far and realize they don't have enough gas to make it to the next town, and it doesn't take them long to figure out that these big gas metal tanks so many of us have on our ranches ain't just fancy yard decor. So by the time I got up today to fill up my own truck, the tank was bone dry. A couple of years back I sat up all night guarding the tank with a shotgun, but I kept nodding off, so folks got their gas anyways and I lost sleep in the process. Now I just take my chances, but I sleep like a newborn lamb."

"Now what?" Tony said.

"Like I said, come on in and take a load off and I'll call around, see if I can't round you up some fuel. But I have to say I'm scratching my head as to what got into Norma." Deloy opened the blue wooden door, its paint worn by the years until the wood grain showed through.

So Norma hadn't gone along with Kevin of her own volition, Tony decided. Until now, he'd considered it quite possible that the chicken feed message was nothing more than diligence on Norma's part, but why would she allow Kevin to nearly run her own brother over and not stop? Why wouldn't she tell anyone where she was going?

Tony, Kelli, and Mabel followed Deloy into the house. Deloy's wife had passed away several years earlier, and what had probably once been orderly clutter was now disorganized junk. Boxes, magazines, clothes, dishes, and just about every imaginable thing lay in piles all over the front room.

"Chocolate is on the table. I'll see what else I can round up." Deloy fished in his refrigerator and clunked a six pack of soda in the middle of the table."

"Thanks," Tony said, removing a can from the plastic rings and handing it to Mabel. He pulled two more out and placed one in front of Kelli. "Allow me to buy you a drink."

"Don't mind if I do," Kelli said. She opened the can, took a sip, and set it down. Then she whispered to Tony, "We need to call the police and get out of here. I'm worried about Norma."

"Me too," Tony whispered back. "I'll call them before we leave."

Mabel seemed frozen to her chair. Tony watched her face but couldn't detect her thoughts. Finally, she cleared her throat. "Tony, dear, I can't think of a reason why Norma would nearly run down our brother on the street, so I can only conclude one thing. Something must be wrong. Maybe Norma was having a heart attack. Norma doesn't let on how old she's getting."

"I hope not," Tony said. "But for some reason, they drove through here not too long ago—much later than we expected them to. They might not even be to Snowville yet. I'm sure the police are already looking for them. It would surprise me if they haven't been found yet. In fact, Norma's probably getting help right now if she needs it."

Kelli took a bar of chocolate from the table, unwrapped it, and ate a small piece. Then she placed a piece in front of Tony, saying, "Allow me."

"Thanks." Tony grabbed the chocolate and stood up. When Deloy hung up the phone, Tony said to him, "Before you call anyone else, I need to make a quick phone call, please."

Deloy motioned to the phone and stepped away from it. "I thought if anyone would have gasoline, it would be Porters. You know their place, don't you, Mabel? It's so remote that most folks don't see their tank. He seldom gets his gas stolen, and as luck would have it, with the high cost of gasoline, he won't sell you any, seeing how he got this at last month's rate. I told him you'd be more than glad to make up the difference, but then he can be an ornery cuss when he wants to be and he said no, he'd just as soon save money as make a profit. Anyways, that was a dead end, so next thing—"

Tony went into the hallway and called the police to report the possible abduction. Then he stepped back into the kitchen and heard Deloy speaking.

"—a half gallon in a can for her lawn mower, and then Clem said he's got a gallon or more. Between those two, you could make it to Snowville, and you can fill up there."

"Then that will have to do," Mabel said. "Tony, Deloy found us some gasoline."

"Great. We'd better be on our way. Mabel, why don't you stay on with your brother? We'll call you as soon as we find Norma and make sure she gets the help she needs. No use all of us going."

Mabel acted like she hadn't heard Tony and strode purposely through the front door. Only after she'd given Tony directions to the two homes for gas and they were back on the highway did she say, "Did you expect me to leave off looking for my baby sister? A youngster, especially a man, can't possibly be expected to know what to do if anything happens. No offense, sweetie. Norma needs her older sister to find her and take care of her."

Tony sighed. At least there was one good thing about having the elderly woman along. With Mabel in the front seat of the small pickup with them, Kelli had to sit close to Tony and straddle the gearshift with her legs, so he had to touch her knee every time he shifted gears. So while he prayed this would all resolve quickly and happily, he couldn't hide his smile as they drove toward Snowville.

Eighteen

NORMA NODDED OFF. WHEN SHE OPENED HER EYES they were already in Park Valley. She knew she should stop at her brother's house to call her sisters—just to make sure they weren't worried—but she hated to ask Kevin to stop. Getting away from Deloy in a timely matter was almost impossible, and Kevin was in a hurry.

As luck would have it, Norma saw Deloy leaving the post office. She lowered the passenger-side window, leaned her head out, and shouted, "Tell everyone I'm fine."

Good. She leaned back in her seat, feeling satisfied that everything was fine. Deloy would call their sisters and tell them he had seen her, and they wouldn't worry about her one bit.

After another hour, they neared their destination in Tremonton. Norma spotted three police cars parked in front of the hospital and knew Kevin was driving into a trap.

"Uh-oh," Norma said.

Kevin stopped the car, stared at the police cars, and slowly turned the Subaru around.

"Before you do anything crazy, drop me off," Norma said, a feeling of dread in her stomach. She saw the look in Kevin's eyes and realized he was panicking.

No sooner had Kevin turned the car around than the sound of sirens pierced the still summer air. All three police cars were following them. Kevin pushed the gas pedal to the floor and Norma grabbed hold of the handle above the door, her whole body tensing with the advancing speed of the car.

"Pull over and let me out!" Norma shouted. "You'll get both of us killed! Pull into that church parking lot."

Kevin whizzed past the small Catholic church. A few people stood on the lawn after attending Saturday mass. A woman clutched her baby and a young man crossed himself. Norma could see Kevin had no intention of letting her out of the car.

"Listen to me. You've got to stay alive to find Cadence and the baby. And I need to find Cadence too."

A police car pulled up alongside the Subaru and an officer motioned to them to pull over. Then the officer backed off slightly.

"Pull over this instant!" Norma shouted at the same time the police broadcasted the same message. *Don't let me die—not now—not this way*, Norma prayed as Kevin increased his speed.

"Think of Cadence!" Norma shouted again. People say that in moments of great distress, when the possibility of death is imminent, one's life flashes before her eyes. But Norma's life didn't flash before her. The only thing she thought about was that she might die before finding her husband's lost child.

Kevin missed the turn at the intersection and headed straight into the Box Elder County Fairgrounds. The three police cars tailed the Subaru. Norma glanced at the speedometer as the needle still crept up. The car swerved toward an open arena and she could see people on horseback inside. Heads turned toward the sudden commotion.

Norma could think of only one thing to stop the recklessness that could be the end for both of them. She fished through her purse and found her bottle of pepper spray. "Stop now or I'll spray you!"

Kevin ignored her a moment too long, so Norma sprayed him in the face. He yelped and threw his hands to his face.

Norma grabbed the wheel and tried to steer away from the arena. They zoomed through a chain-link fence onto the manicured greens of the Tremonton Golf Course. Seconds after the car came to a rest on the seventh hole, it was surrounded by police cars with flashing lights and blaring sirens. Kevin moaned softly and cursed as he slumped against the steering wheel.

Mabel's useless gun had slid out from under the seat in all the commotion. Norma worried that the officers would think Kevin might use it on them, so she picked the gun up off the floor and slipped it into her purse, hoping no one had seen it. She knew enough to know that even the most minor offense was compounded severely if a person used a gun, even if, she imagined, the gun didn't work.

Kevin's shoulders shook as he let out a tiny sob. Norma felt sorry for him. She knew he might not deserve her sympathy, but still he was young, impulsive, and desperate—all things she could understand.

"Now, now, dear, I hate to say I told you so, but your stupidity could've killed the both of us. You'll thank me someday for doing what had to be done."

Large, calloused hands reached into the car and gently tugged Norma out of her seat. Another officer searched Kevin and tossed him into the back seat of a vehicle marked Tremonton Police—to Protect and Serve.

In a daze, Norma realized hands were patting her body. Her purse, the leather one Marianne bought her in Mexico, was wrenched from her grasp. She glanced at Kevin but couldn't see his face.

"Please don't damage my purse!"

"Ma'am?"

"My daughter gave it to me."

The next few seconds were a blur. Norma's arms were pulled behind her in an uncomfortable position, and cold metal clamped her wrists together. Then she was pushed, though gently, into the back seat of a police car. Her heart raced, but finally, she managed to ask, "What on earth is going on?"

"Ma'am, you have the right to remain silent . . ."

Through her brain fog, Norma heard several police officers discussing the gun and trying to figure out who had abducted whom. They couldn't believe such an old woman would be friends with a criminal like Kevin.

After piecing things together in the back of the police car, Norma realized the officers had jumped to the ridiculous assumption that she was a criminal too, perhaps because they found the gun in her purse. What if they somehow came to the preposterous conclusion that *she* had abducted Kevin? She wondered how they could possibly suspect her to be a criminal. After all, she was wearing a vermillion pantsuit she had ordered from Sears. Someone asked if she had an attorney, and she blurted the name of Milton Jackson in Brigham City, who was overseeing her husband's estate. She doubted he was a criminal lawyer, but since she wasn't a criminal she figured that wouldn't be a problem.

When the police cruiser stopped moving a few minutes later, Norma was led into the basement of the police station and put in a small room filled with clothing.

"I didn't do anything! The gun is my sister's—it's useless," she tried to explain to no one in particular as she was led into the small room. The officer left her alone and she pushed aside a box overflowing with mesh jerseys with vinyl numbers printed on them. She sat down on a bench and felt her arthritis acting up. She tugged one of the jerseys out of the box. It was dark blue with magenta numbers—probably a soccer uniform. By all appearances she had been placed into a storage closet, only it locked like a cell.

As Norma sat alone in the cell, waiting for someone—anyone—to come get her, she thought about all the moments of the day that had brought her to this point. If only she had listened to the warning that went off in her head when Kevin zoomed out of the church parking lot. From that moment on, she had never felt quite safe.

Her instincts had told her to stay in Montello with LaVell. The photograph of her husband holding the baby had caused her to set her misgivings aside and forge ahead without precaution.

Eventually, the door was unlocked and a couple of youngsters trudged in. At first they looked startled to see Norma, but then they relaxed. The biggest boy pushed the black hair out of his eyes, stuck out his hand, and said, "Hey, I'm a Blue Devil. We both are." He motioned to the skinnier blond boy with freckles spattered across the bridge of his nose. They couldn't have been older than thirteen.

"And what did you do?" Norma asked, shocked that the police were locking up children these days. Then she reminded herself that they seemed to have no problem locking up elderly women. Norma hadn't done anything illegal since she jaywalked as a young mother while pushing a stroller across the street in Ogden, back in the 1960s. She'd had just cause too, having realized that

Woolworth's was closing in five minutes and that she still had several items to buy before heading back to Grouse Creek.

Her mind jolted back to the present when the smaller of the two lads spoke. "Tore a hole in my knee when I tried to out a Cougar on third. I missed. Next time, though, I'll be ready. I'll get that sucker if it kills me."

"Oh, no!" Norma gasped. She believed the time to train a dog not to bite was when it was a puppy. The same thing went for children. "It's better just to calm down and let those kinds of things slide."

"Ah, sliding hardly ever works. You come up short and they get you anyway," the bigger boy said.

"No, you should never react in a rage. If Kevin had remained calm then perhaps I could've steered us out of danger instead of ending up on the seventh hole. Try this." Norma pressed on her abdomen. "Take a deep breath, hold it for three seconds, and then slowly release. Repeat until you feel your heart slow down and the top of your head start to tingle. Then you know you're doing it right. It might sound crazy, but it works."

The boys just stared at her and backed up until they were against the door. The tallest one pounded on the door and hollered, "Let us out."

"Oh, they won't let you out. Not until you've answered all their questions. I imagine they'll want to know exactly what you ended up doing to that cougar. I'm sure you're way too young for a permit, and even if you're not, aren't they on the endangered list? I know they were once, although one ate several of Deloy's chickens. He's my brother in Park Valley. They never did catch up with the furry thief. Next thing you know, two little ones ended up dead." Norma knew she was talking a blue streak, something she tended to do when she was nervous. She also knew the young boys thought she was crazy—she could see it written all over their panic-stricken faces. She took a deep breath and spoke more slowly so she would appear more rational.

"Babies?" one boy said with a squeak before pounding on the door again. Norma thought perhaps she should join them, since they seemed so sure they'd get out. She stood and banged on the door also.

"Sure, they were babies—Bertha's babies." Bertha was a big Hereford cow with twins that had survived their frigid February birth, just to fall victim to a cougar kill. Mountain lion kills were more rare than they used to be, but occasionally some of the outlying ranches suffered an attack.

Within seconds of their pounding a uniformed woman opened the door and the boys burst out through it.

"Did you find what you were looking for?" she asked.

"Nah, we'll come back another time," the blond boy answered. Then the two rushed out of the room and down the hall.

"I think I managed to talk some sense into them. They won't be chasing down any more cougars."

"Well, still, that was a mighty big hole he tore in his uniform. I should've warned them about you being in here, and not to worry when they heard the door lock behind them." The woman chuckled. "Must've scared them some. We turned our cell into a storage closet since we seldom use it. Any dangerous criminals go on down to Brigham, but it being a holiday weekend, they're full up."

Norma was confused. "So what exactly did those two young boys do to land them in jail?"

"Didn't do a thing. They just came in looking for a new uniform. The coach'll be upset that we didn't help them get one, but they skedaddled out of here quick as lightning, didn't they?"

"They surely did." Norma started to giggle.

"We're ready to book you, ma'am. Just follow me."

The billy club swayed with the swaggering of the woman's ample hips. Her dark hair wound on top of her head in a swirl. "We've checked our computers. This being a first offense, and considering your age, I doubt they'll hold you overnight, but then I've been surprised before. Okay, we'll start with your thumb."

The woman helped Norma press each finger in ink and then onto card stock.

"I think they sent the young man who was with you on down to the county jail. They'll squeeze him in somewhere. We just don't have anything here to hold dangerous criminals and—"

"I don't think he's truly dangerous." As Norma spoke it she knew it might not be true, but she still held onto an inkling of hope that it was. Nonetheless, Kevin had nearly gotten her killed. He was desperate, and desperate people could be dangerous.

After going through the booking process, Norma was allowed to go free on her own recognizance. Her court date was set and her belongings returned. The Subaru had perfectly even scratch marks all along the hood and top from speeding through the chain-link fence, as though someone had taken a wide-tooth metal comb to it. Now the original red of the car peeked through the green paint. It looked quite Christmasy, Norma decided.

She drove to her friend Ruth's house, knowing she would let her use her phone and stay with her while she searched for Cadence. Norma was fairly sure that Katie was actually Cadence and that Cadence was Wes's granddaughter, so finding Cadence was crucial.

Even though the temperature was close to ninety degrees, Norma trembled as she waited for Ruth to answer the door. When she opened it, Norma fell into her arms.

Nineteen

Sam,

I'm at the Tremonton Hospital. We're looking for Norma and Kevin. You know our cousin Josh. Grandpa always said he could get away with murder because he could charm his way out of anything. It finally dawned at me who Kevin reminds me of—Josh. As Dad said, I wouldn't trust him as far as I could throw him. Well, we're off now. I just wanted to let you know in case you tried to call me. And NO! I am not falling in love. I thought you were setting me up with that guy in your ward—the cute one. I don't trust YOUR opinion, but Stacey said he's cute, so now I'm ready. Well, not yet, but soon.

Love, your favorite sister ☺

TONY KNEW HE COULD COVER MORE GROUND without an eighty-two-year-old woman in tow. But he had to admit Mabel seemed spry for her age, and he did enjoy her company. It was late evening when they pulled into the hospital parking lot, and Tony noted that there were no Subarus in the lot.

"Maybe I'll just hop on in and see if I can find anything out." Tony expected Kelli and Mabel to wait for him in the truck, but by the time he reached the hospital entrance, both women were at his heels. But no one at the hospital had seen Norma.

When they returned to the truck, Tony opened the door for the two women and helped them step up into it. "Might need to invest in a crane if I keep getting into this thing," Mabel joked. "Let's drive over to Rocket Road. Norma's friend Ruth lives out there and she might know something about Norma. If she wasn't feeling well, maybe Kevin dropped her off."

"Shouldn't we call her first?" Kelli pulled her cell phone out of her purse.

Mabel opened her plastic grocery sack. "Here, have a cookie, and don't waste your time with the phone. Don't know her number anyway. Just turn south at the corner, then keep going until we get to Rocket Road. Ruth will be happy to get some of my cookies."

Tony reached for a cookie and wondered why Mabel had taken so long to get them out. Come to think of it, all they'd eaten since the picnic lunch was chocolate, soda, and now cookies. But as the cookie practically melted in his mouth, he knew the wait had been worth it.

When they pulled into Ruth's driveway, the truck headlights revealed a welcome sight: a green Subaru. "Sweet mercy, Norma is right here! Providence led us to her," Mabel exclaimed.

Norma's car had deep scratches, but Tony didn't pause to inspect it, not wanting anyone else to be alarmed.

Inside the house, Tony saw Norma sitting on the sofa, looking perfectly fine. Mabel ran to her and tugged her to her feet for an embrace. Norma's eyes were moist and she dabbed at them with her handkerchief. "Oh, Norma dear, we thought something terrible had happened to you—heart attack, maybe. Some even thought you may have been kidnapped."

"Good heavens! Didn't Deloy tell you I saw him in Park Valley? I thought he'd call you. And then when I did get a chance to call, no one answered."

"We've been looking for you, dear."

Norma shuddered. "But I have to say I am lucky to be alive. You can't imagine the day I've had. Sit down here and I'll tell you all about it." The two sisters embraced again.

Ruth wore flowered lounge pajamas, white anklet socks, and gold slippers. Her coiffed white hair looked as if she'd just come from the hair salon.

"I do apologize for my appearance," Ruth said. "If I'd known I was going to have so much company today, I would've stayed dressed. Most nights it's just Wendell and me. And Wendell hardly seems to notice whether I fix up or not, although he does seem startled at times when I first get up in the morning and my hair is such a fright. Doesn't even recognize me at times."

Ruth hugged Mabel, then put her hands out to Tony and Kelli. Her tiny hands had bulbous knots on the joints from advanced arthritis. "Wendell," she yelled. "Come out here and meet our guests!"

A small white dog bounded around the corner. He barked, bounced, and skidded across the floor, his toenails clicking on the hardwood surface.

Kelli and Tony smiled as the little guy jumped at Tony's legs.

"He's so protective of me, and jealous at the same time. He

hates for me to have any men over. Don't take it personally, but he only attacks males."

"How cute!" Kelli bent over and patted the little dog. "My grandma had a dog a lot like this one, only her dog's named Johnny Cash. When I was growing up I always thought the singer was named after my grandma's dog, and not the other way around."

"I brought you some cookies."

"Thank you. Oh, where are my manners? Please sit down. After I got over the initial shock of what happened to Norma, we've been catching up. She brought some photos for me to look at from ages ago."

When Ruth retreated into the kitchen with the cookies, Wendell let go of Tony's pants and followed at her heels. Kelli followed Ruth as well, and Tony guessed she wanted to see what she could do to help.

He gratefully took a seat next to Norma, who held an old photo of a man holding a baby. Tony glanced around the room. Glass mirrors surrounded the white brick fireplace, giving the illusion that the room was twice its actual size. The hardwood floor featured several braided rugs.

"So, anyway, it turns out that Kevin nearly killed me when he fled from the police. And he ran my car through a fence."

"It's poor upbringing, is what it is," Ruth said when she returned to the living room with a plate of cookies. "But then you never know. My friend Dora's oldest grandson got arrested for cooking up his own hallucinogenic drugs right in her own kitchen. I swear she thought he was making candy to sell to the neighbor children. She had actually complimented him on his work ethic. Not until the police surrounded the house and dragged him out on the front lawn in front of everyone on Rocket Road did she suspect he was up to anything criminal. And Dora's a member of the Daughters of Utah Pioneers and sings in the church choir!"

"But Kevin has an honest face," Mabel protested, munching on a cookie as Kelli sat down in a nearby recliner.

"That isn't necessarily an indication of anything," Tony said.

"Well, I just need to find Cadence before Kevin gets out of jail." Norma paused from studying the photo in her hand.

"Why the sudden urge to find Cadence? And why did you take off in the first place? And why did you leave a note saying chicken food on it? And where is Kevin?"

"Hold on a minute—one question at a time. Kevin is down at the county jail. He tried to outrun the police. Today was certainly a day of contrasts. Just when I thought everything was going wrong, I learned that Kevin's Cadence—and this is the most astounding part—may well be Wes's granddaughter. And she is the one who made the desperate phone call to me two weeks ago. Cadence is Katie. I don't know why I didn't think of it earlier. So now I'm trying to find her. When I found out, I just jumped into the car with Kevin without thinking." Norma held the photo out again. "I wonder if Wes . . . do you believe it's possible that my husband orchestrated all of this?"

"Certainly not. If Wes had planned this, then I don't think he would've had you arrested and thrown in a jail cell piled with soccer uniforms," Ruth said as she tickled Wendell's belly.

"I don't know, dear. I'd heard Wes was quite a tease before the war. And you know what scripture says, that not one hair will be lost in the resurrection. I'd like to think that means instead of getting hair as thick as shaggy dogs, all the good parts of our personality will be restored. I, for one, am hoping to be able to touch my toes again." Mabel bent over and touched her calves. "Perhaps we could just take a few minutes and run on down to Brigham and check to see if Kevin's all right."

"It's practically nine o'clock and Tony's wife has fallen

asleep. You can all stay here for the night. I have church at nine in the morning." Ruth smoothed her hair. "If you want you can attend with me before going down to Brigham."

Tony glanced at Kelli, who was indeed asleep in the recliner. "She isn't my wife," he said quietly. *Although I wish she were.* Tony felt like stretching out on the sofa and going to sleep himself. "Listen, folks, I think we'll head out of here. You're okay now, aren't you, Norma?"

"Of course, dear," Mabel answered for her sister. "We can finish things up now on our own. I'm here now to help Norma. And Norma, if you still need chicken feed we'll have to stay until Monday when the feed store opens again."

Norma still held the snapshot in front of her. "Chicken feed? Why on earth would I need chicken feed this time of year with all the bugs? It's healthier for the chickens, adds good protein to the yolks for us, and keeps the insect population down. Besides, I have a full bag on the back porch."

"That's exactly what LaRue said. But there it was right on your cryptic note, 'chicken food.' That's why some folks jumped to the conclusion that Kevin had kidnapped you."

Norma stood up and slipped the photo back in her purse. "I don't know what one's got to do with the other."

"Maybe I can explain," Tony said, flipping his ball cap around. "We thought maybe Kevin forced you to go with him and that he watched you write the note, so you wrote 'chicken food' to give us a clue. And then when you raced through Park Valley nearly running down your brother, we were pretty sure something bad had happened."

"Even I was beginning to wonder, dear." Mabel frowned. "So what did you mean?"

Norma tapped her hands together, trying to think. "Oh, I remember now. I need chicken for next week's church supper, so

I wrote 'chicken.' You know that orange chicken recipe?"

"Certainly. It's my favorite," Mabel said. "I especially like it with green peppers, although they sometimes give me indigestion."

"And then I tried to think what else I needed, then thought better of it and realized I needed just about everything, so I just jotted down 'food.' But I wrote that grocery list last week."

Tony chuckled as he realized they had shown an ordinary grocery list to the police as a clue in Norma's suspected kidnapping. And even though their meandering conversations drove him crazy, he liked how these older women tended to think the best of others even in the worst situations. Norma didn't seem to be as put out by Kevin as she should have been, and Mabel still insisted that he was a dear boy. Tony shook his head in wonderment.

"Oh, Norma." Mabel laughed. "We were so worried."

"Well, it gives me something interesting to write about for this week's newspaper article. But I have to say, I had just about lost all respect for Kevin. When he ran through the fence at the golf course that was the last straw. Of course, he may not have done that if I hadn't sprayed him with pepper spray."

"Well, I have to admit it sounds as if he may have deserved it," Mabel said.

"And I spent the day in the jail, thanks to that silly gun of yours."

"But, Norma dear, that gun doesn't work. It hasn't worked since 1973."

Norma huffed. "Mabel, the police don't know it doesn't work."

"But didn't you tell them?"

"I did, but they arrested me anyway, and I was even wearing my vermillion pantsuit."

"Can I look at that photograph one more time?" Ruth interjected, ignoring the ongoing conversation.

"Which one?"

"The one with Wes holding the baby."

Norma removed the photo from her purse and handed it to Ruth, who disappeared into the kitchen and came out holding a magnifying glass up to the photo. "Lookie here. I know where this picture was taken! See this—" Ruth held the photo under the lamp light so everyone could see. "This lamppost Wes is standing by was custom made with fixtures to look like apples. The owner of the house was an eccentric man named Appleby. He had an apple mailbox, an apple-shaped bathroom window, and a wooden bench on his front porch with apple spindles. When old man Appleby passed on, the new owners let it all decay and eventually replaced the lamppost with one from True Value."

"And you know where this place is?"

"Not only do I know where it is, I'll take you there after church. But for now, let's all get some sleep."

Tony was glad that Norma was safe, Kevin was in jail, and no one needed his help anymore. Tony stood up, grabbed a few more cookies, and gently woke Kelli. In two hours, he would be back in Grouse Creek, crawling into bed.

Twenty

Another Eventful Week

by Grouse Creek Correspondent Norma Weaver

Everyone will be as pleased as punch to know that Norma Weaver got her car back, though she isn't thrilled with the front-end damage the car received after a chase with the police where Norma was an unwitting and unwilling participant. This correspondent can verify to the fact that the police department has no qualms about handcuffing and jailing perfectly innocent and harmless law-abiding citizens. Yes, dear readers, Norma Weaver was arrested! Her crime, you ask? May you be as horrified as this correspondent was to find out that merely trying to do right can land you in jail these days. But fear not, she was released before succumbing to her stifling and deplorable conditions. Her sister LaRue would most definitely have called the situation "unseemly." On a more pleasant note, Norma was overjoyed to be reunited with her good friend Ruth. (They both attended Bear River High, meeting in the debate club that took first place at the regional meet in 1947.) As always, Ruth looked the picture of health, and her furry companion, Wendell, is just as spunky and amiable as ever.

Grouse Creek's Fourth of July celebration was well attended, with folks joining in from as far away as Colorado. Although Norma missed the rodeo, she was informed by LaRue that the only mishap occurred when eleven-year-old Cody Esplin from the Bar T Ranch was bucked off his Palomino. The judges offered a re-ride, which Cody declined, saying his arm hurt too much. This correspondent is sorry to report that the tyke's arm is indeed broken. He

> is now sporting a fluorescent green cast that has already been signed by every child at Grouse Creek School, plus Mavis the custodian. Cody's dad said, "It'll be tough to get by without him during haying season, but we'll manage." The school put on a satisfying dinner, serving Dutch-oven beef, corn, and salad. At times the line wound all the way to the street, which made it a mighty hot wait indeed. Norma and her sisters made fried chicken for their clan, and they enjoyed a friendly visit from some out-of-towners. Herman Anders says he appreciated whoever "borrowed" his truck, Ol' Blue, putting it back in its proper place next to the house, but says, "Next time you're needing my truck, it'd be kind if you'd put some gas in it." Finally, Jean Brooks will be out of town to visit her sister, so the co-op will be closed until further notice.

NORMA WAS NOT USED TO RUTH'S COMPUTER; nonetheless, she was able to print out a copy in only an hour. She smiled as it came crisply out of the printer. She figured that while she was in town, she might as well drop off her weekly column over at *The Tremonton Leader*. She glanced up at the old clock as it chimed the half hour.

"Goodness gracious, it's almost time to go!" Norma hurried to finish getting ready for church.

⊰⊹⊱

After church, Ruth, Mabel, and Norma stared at the once-stately home from the photo. Green paint peeled away from the wooden front porch, revealing the original white, and weeds edged the crumbling stone foundation. A tire swing filled with leaves and dirty water hung from a gnarled apple tree, and Norma decided it must be the perfect breeding ground for mosquitoes.

She walked up to the door and knocked, careful not to stand where the porch had rotted through. There was no response. Then she thought she heard a radio, so she knocked again and waited. Mabel disappeared around the back, while Ruth stood next to the car fiddling with a small green apple that had fallen onto the hood.

"Guess no one's home." Norma sighed.

She had just started back to the car when Mabel appeared from the back with a young man. His hair was long and stringy, and he wore baggy pants and a white undershirt that revealed a dragon tattoo on his shoulder. Norma was sure he hadn't been to church, and clearly he was the type of person who drank beer in the middle of the day. Then Norma chided herself for her judgmental thoughts, knowing that was something LaRue would not only have thought, but would've shared with everyone around her. LaRue never had an unexpressed thought. *Oh, my goodness—it's snowballing now!* Norma thought as she realized her own unkind thoughts about LaRue were judgmental as well.

Norma smiled as she greeted the young man. She showed him the photo and learned he had only been renting the house for a year. He didn't know the landlord personally, and he knew nothing about the history of the home. Norma wished him luck and scurried back to the car, only to discover that Mabel had disappeared again. She started her car, gave the horn a quick honk, and turned the radio to a "Sounds of Sunday" music program.

Ruth got in the car and began humming to an instrumental version of the "Battle Hymn of the Republic." The music matched Ruth's attire: red slacks paired with a festive red, white, and blue blouse that complemented her dangling flag earrings.

"Shame that boy didn't know anything. Where's Mabel gone off to?" Ruth asked, dropping the small green apple into the gutter.

"Who knows," Norma said. "Goodness, it's already hot, and it's not even noon."

"There she is. Who on earth is she walking with? Your sister Mabel still hasn't lost her talent for picking up strange men, I see."

Irritated at the mention of the rumors, Norma snapped, "He certainly doesn't look strange to me. The gentleman is wearing a suit coat even on this hot day. Why he looks like he's just been to church!"

Mabel could've walked a bit faster, but she matched her pace to the hunched man, who held onto her arm to balance himself. He seemed so feeble that an unexpected swift breeze could have toppled him. His thin, gray hair was parted in the middle and combed close to his head.

"Look who's coming to dinner! You don't mind do you, Ruthie dear?" Mabel poked her head in the car window.

"Well, I hadn't thought—" Ruth began.

"Marvel has lived on this street his entire life," Mabel said.

Marvel, what kind of name is Marvel? Then Norma realized what Mabel was hinting at. Marvel could know what happened to Wes's baby! Norma unsnapped her pocketbook and fished the photo out, but Marvel was already sitting in the back seat of her damaged car, with Mabel scooting in next to him.

"Guess I could warm up a frozen lasagna from Schwan's. Schwan's comes every other week now. Have you ever tried their bagel dogs? They give Wendell indigestion, but they're really tasty." Ruth craned her neck to peer at Marvel.

When Schwan's frozen foods decided to include Grouse Creek on their home-delivery route, the entire town thought they'd died and gone straight to heaven. It was the next best thing to living close to a supermarket. Norma chuckled, remembering the first time she'd heard the Schwan's truck would be coming. LaRue had called her early one morning and asked Norma if she'd heard the news—Schwan's, only it sounded like she'd said "swans"—were coming to Grouse Creek. Norma imagined a big flock of the giant white birds migrating through and wondered how someone had been able to pinpoint their route so precisely, and what on earth she was supposed to have her checkbook ready for.

Now, Norma remembered Ruth needed an answer on the lasagna. "That'd be great."

Norma tried to hand the photo to Marvel, but Mabel pushed it back to her.

"Let's have a nice sit-down dinner before we go bothering Marvel about anything. Okay, Norma dear?"

"Goodness, I'm not bothering him."

"Still, it's so much easier to think clearly on a full stomach," Mabel explained. "Marvel has forty-nine grandchildren. Can you imagine that? That's more than twice as many as any of us has."

"Going for an even fifty," Marvel said in a raspy voice.

"The problem is," Mabel said, "his youngest son is currently divorced, and the rest of his children seem to be done with childbearing."

"Going for an even fifty," Marvel repeated.

"Oh, dear." Norma wasn't sure this man would be any help at all, but Mabel must think he would be or she wouldn't have asked him to dinner. Norma repressed a sigh as she drove back to Ruth's house, noting how peaceful everything was on Sunday.

When they arrived at Ruth's, she pulled a box out of the freezer and plopped it into the microwave. "Norma, would you mind opening a can of green beans while I fix the lasagna?" Ruth pointed to a lower cupboard and proceeded to watch the lasagna turn in the microwave.

Norma found a small saucepan and dumped the beans into it, then turned the stove to medium heat. Wendell barked furiously at Marvel, and Norma worried he would scare the gentleman away before she got a chance to find out if he knew anything.

"Maybe you could set the table while the beans warm up," Ruth suggested, not budging from her post in front of the microwave.

When Norma began searching for silverware, Ruth said, "I just keep all the dishes in the dishwasher now. No point putting things away twice."

"But what about the dirty ones?" Norma asked.

"They aren't dirty if they're in the dishwasher."

Norma frowned. "What do you mean?"

"What do *you* mean?" Ruth countered.

A thoroughly confused Norma opened the dishwasher. Sure enough, the dishes looked clean, and she remembered hearing the noise of the dishwasher running following their breakfast of frozen waffles.

By the time Norma set the table, the microwave timer had dinged and the beans had boiled over. She moved the pan to a cool stove coil, then opened the dishwasher again in search of a bowl to put the beans in.

"Dinner's ready," Ruth chimed in a singsong voice as she

carried the lasagna over to the table with oven mitts on her hands and set it down on the table. Then she bowed her head and said, "Dearest Lord, let this stifling July heat give us strength to endure the freezing cold winter ahead. And today let us be truly grateful for good friends, frozen food, and a working microwave. Amen."

Without sitting down, Ruth held her hand out to stop anyone who dared help himself or herself to the lasagna, then dished out a large spoonful and plopped it into Wendell's dog bowl. "Come on, Wendell darling. Dinner's ready."

Wendell bounced into the kitchen, his tail wagging enthusiastically. Norma found comfort that at least Wendell wouldn't be joining them at the table. In the past, she'd never thought of Ruth as one of those dog-obsessed people, but now she wondered if pet obsession came naturally in the aging process. Before she passed, Deloy's wife had allowed their pet poodle to sleep between them on their king-sized bed.

Ruth did seem a bit off since the last time Norma had visited. She quickly tallied Ruth's age in her head, then remembered they were only months apart. How discouraging. An old saying came to mind: "All the world 'tis strange except for me and thee, and sometimes I wonder about thee."

Realizing Ruth wasn't planning to serve anyone but Wendell, Norma served Marvel, took a serving of lasagna herself, and then stood up to serve Ruth and Mabel, since the cardboard baking dish was too awkward to pass. Feeling her heartburn start up within just a few bites, Norma tried to scrape off the acidic tomato sauce, then filled her plate with green beans. "Doesn't the lasagna give Wendell indigestion also?"

"No, just the spicy bagel dogs. He chomps them down as fast as an Indy 500 racer, then upchucks just as quickly," Ruth said as she took a bite of lasagna.

"How old is Wendell?" Norma asked.

Ruth smiled. "We celebrated his eighth birthday on June seventh."

Norma finished her dinner and then anxiously waited for Marvel to finish. "How did you get your name, Marvel? It's an interesting name."

"These beans from the garden?" Marvel asked. "I used to keep the biggest garden on Factory Street. That was back when Emma Jean was alive. She'd pick the beans and fill all the jars in the pantry with them. Those that she didn't have a jar for, she'd give away to the neighbors. But it got so folks just didn't want them anymore. People stopped putting God's goods away for the winter. Everything is instant now. Instant everything."

Norma laughed a little uneasily, not sure if Marvel was trying to make a joke or not. The old man rambled and didn't seem lucid enough to answer any questions.

"I agree. Pretty soon they'll be having instant funerals." Mabel put down her fork. "Folks'll be able to stop by and leave messages on one of those automated machines like they got at the gas stations now. The sign'll flash, 'Do you wish to leave a message of condolence? Yes or no.'"

Now Norma giggled and continued the imaginary scenario. "'Are you glad this sorry, no-good bum is gone? Yes or no. In lieu of flowers, insert credit card into slot.'"

Marvel looked confused. "Mabel, have I told you, you remind me of my Emma Jean, who's passed, bless her heart?"

"No, no, you haven't," Mabel replied, scooping up Marvel another serving of beans.

Marvel tipped his head to her as she continued.

"Now how did you get such a marvelous name Marvel?" Mabel emphasized the word "marvelous" as if she were advertising a cleaning product.

"Born premature. Said I was such a scrawny little thing, delivered by the neighbor woman, Mrs. Lillywhite. She thought I was stillborn, but when she held me up by my feet, I sputtered a few breaths and Mrs. Lillywhite announced, 'Do marvels never cease?' Then my mother said, 'If the boy lives, we'll name him Marvel, but if he dies during the night we'll name him Cease.'"

Wendell barked and begged for more. As Ruth dished him the last few bites of lasagna, Norma noticed Marvel's face fall.

"What a wonderful story," Norma said.

Mabel laughed. "Your mother had a sense of humor, didn't she?"

"Not that I recall," Marvel said.

Norma's faith in Marvel's with-it-ness was somewhat restored, so she pulled out the photo and set it in front of him. "Do you know whose baby this is?"

Marvel fished his reading glasses out of his pocket. He put them on and held the photo up for a good look. "That's the Appleby's home, all right, but whose baby is this?"

"That's what I was hoping you'd tell us." Norma forced a smile.

"Don't ask me about today, but I can sure tell you anything you want to know about the past," Marvel said.

Ruth began picking up the dishes and placing them in the dishwasher.

"Oh, Ruth, the dishes in the dishwasher are already clean," Norma said.

Ruth looked at her a bit crossly. "'Course they are, Norma."

Norma realized Ruth must put the dirty ones right on top of the clean ones. She turned her attention back to Marvel.

"See, I might've been off to the war during this time. But Mr. and Mrs. Appleby were too old to have an infant this young. Jacob was near my age—he was killed in the war. Then there was Mark, a bit older than Jacob. Then Nathan was a tad older, and they had one or two older than that. So the baby couldn't be theirs. Then they had one pretty girl, Caddie, after all those boys—a tail-ender. Blond hair, blue eyes, dimples, and a smile you'd do anything to see. But she was a funny little thing. Her parents were too old by then to know what to do with a girl, so she sort of raised herself."

"What about the girl?" Realizing the baby could be Caddie's, Norma felt her heart quicken with excitement. "Did she ever have a baby?"

"I imagine she did, eventually. I recall getting a letter while I was serving overseas that said Caddie left home and poor Mr. and Mrs. Appleby just couldn't bring themselves to go after her, though she couldn't have been more than sixteen or seventeen when she disappeared. I don't like to admit it, but since Emma Jean's no longer with us, I guess I can tell you. See, I took a fancy to Caddie ever since grammar school."

Ruth started the dishwasher. "Marvel, isn't it possible that while you were serving overseas, Caddie had herself a baby?"

"She wasn't married, so I don't know how she would have."

Mabel laughed. "Oh, Marvel, you're such a tease. You know a marriage license isn't required to produce a child."

"No, but it entitles one now, doesn't it?" Marvel said.

The sound of the dishwasher made it hard to hear. Norma stood and slid her chair back under the dining table. "Why don't we go in the living room for a minute before we take Marvel back home?"

Soon everyone followed and sat down in the living room, whereupon Wendell started barking at Marvel again.

"Oh, Wendell, you've already met Mr.—" Ruth paused. "Oh, dear, I've forgotten your last name."

"Just call me Marvel." The old man stuck his hand out to Ruth, who took it and pumped his arm up and down as she scolded Wendell for barking.

Irritated, Norma pointed at the photo in Marvel's hand. "Is there any chance you know the man in the photo?"

"Oh, sure. That's Wesley. I didn't care for him much. He was a two-timing, no-good-for-nothing—"

Mabel cleared her throat as if it were filled with cotton. "Marvel, Wesley is Norma's husband."

"Who's Norma?"

"I am." Suddenly, Norma felt quite ill. "Why on earth didn't you tell us you knew Wes?"

Marvel went a little pale. "You asked about the baby. I figured you already knew the man in the photo or you wouldn't have had it in the first place. Sorry about what I said. Come to think of it, he might've been a fine man by the time this photo was taken." Marvel held the photo up in the light. "I always did admire the way Wesley dressed in high school. I used to sit on my front porch and watch him walk up in his fine apparel to woo Caddie. I figured Caddie would take one look at me in my dungarees and think I didn't hold a candle to Wesley. But one day, my folks wrote me that Wes had shipped out after I did, so I got my hopes up that maybe after the war Caddie would want me. Uniforms equalize everyone and dignify just about anyone. After the war I thought I'd wear that uniform and it'd be me strolling up that walk to the Appleby's home, holding a bouquet of roses and asking for Caddie's hand in marriage. But I didn't count on her running away from home. The day I got home from the war, I walked into the corner drugstore, still dreaming about Caddie with her golden hair, when Emma Jean bounced out from the soda fountain and said, 'Well, well, do marvels ever cease? Marvel's back from the war.' She smiled and I forgot Caddie had ever existed."

"Was Caddie her real name or just a nickname?" Norma wondered aloud.

"Now let me think. I guess that's all anyone called her. Except for her mother." Marvel rubbed his chin. "What did her mother call her? I remember pushing Caddie in the swing in the apple tree behind the house. She wore her hair in curly pigtails on the sides of her head, and they bounced as she swung. Her yellow frock billowed out, too. And Mrs. Appleby stood at the back door and shouted her full name."

Again Norma's heart quickened. All she needed was a name, and she could find Wes's child!

Marvel looked up at the ceiling and sang, "'Catherine May Appleby, come into this house this instant.'" Then his voice sounded masculine again. "That was our signal. As soon as her mother hollered we'd take off running. She must've been in the fourth grade, and I was twelve. We'd run down the street and hide behind the factory and talk. She'd let me grab her hand when we ran. I used to live for those moments."

"Catherine May," Norma mumbled to herself. It was the mother's name not the baby's. "Thank you, Marvel. You're truly a marvel to behold. You've given us the name of the mother."

Twenty-One

Hey, Stacey,

I hope to get over to Burley one of these days—that is, if you feel good enough for lunch. I agree, that place next to the bank where I used to work would be fun to try. It's weird when you have to get away from life in Peyton Place AKA Grouse Creek. Since you grew up in the city, you probably thought things would be safer way out in the boonies. But could anything be further from the truth? Crazy! Herman and Maggie said to tell you hello and to come visit.

Soon, Kelli

P.S. You didn't tell Sam what I said about Tony, did you? Cuz I'm back to normal now.☺

TONY WAS GETTING FRUSTRATED.

Before sacrament meeting began, he had watched Kelli stand momentarily at the back door of the chapel, look around, and then sit down by Jean Brooks. Hadn't she seen him?

After sacrament meeting, he tried to talk to her in the hallway, but Kelli hurried into the Primary room with her arms full of teaching materials.

When church ended, Tony stood by the Primary room door, waiting for Kelli to come out. Then Bishop Watkins saw him and waved him into his office.

Tony followed him, and just before the bishop shut the door, Tony saw Kelli walk out of the Primary room, chatting with another woman. He sighed and turned toward the bishop.

The bishop's ruddy complexion contrasted with his stark-white forehead, weathered from years of wearing a cowboy hat. "Hey, there, take a seat. I've got a few things to talk to you about."

Tony sat down across from the bishop.

"How are things going with the older folks in town? Have you had a chance to meet Norma yet?"

"Fine," Tony said. "I, uh, really haven't had an official visit yet. I've spent a lot of time with Mabel and Norma, though. Sort of accidentally, but still—" Tony glanced at the door, hoping Kelli would talk long enough for him to meet up with her.

"Oh, of course. I didn't mean to imply that you should've visited with them already. I'd just like to get to know you a little better since you're going to be here a spell. See I've got this niece coming out to spend a few weeks—she'll be helping me out with our busy season. I thought since you're single, it'd be nice to line the two of you up. So, my wife and I would like to invite you over for dinner tomorrow. You can meet my niece and we can play some games, that kind of thing."

It was a setup! "I don't know," Tony stammered. He couldn't think of anything he'd rather do less. "I'm pretty busy at the Box C. We'll be fencing tomorrow up on the north pasture. I can't see— "

The bishop smiled and leaned back in his chair. "Real pretty gal. You two have a lot in common. She's a musician, can play the piano like nobody's business, and sings, too. Thought you could bring your guitar along and we could have a little jamboree. I play the guitar a little too, not like you, but I thought I could get it out and see if you can't teach me a thing or two. My daddy played pretty good, taught me. Who taught you to play so dang good?"

Not my daddy, that's for sure, Tony thought. "My mother taught me some, but mostly I picked it up myself. My mom said music is in my blood." He ran his hand through his normally unruly hair, combed for church. He hated being put on the spot.

"We'll be expectin' you around seven, then. I already checked with your boss, since he's in the bishopric. He said it'd be no problem—that you don't have much work right now."

Tony felt his face grow hot. He hadn't meant to lie, but he really didn't want to spend time with any girl except Kelli. "Bishop, I appreciate you thinking of me, but I'm sort of seeing someone."

"I'm certainly not askin' you to marry the girl, just show her some fun. I thought you might be with Kelli Carson, but she said you two were just friends. And if you can spend time with Kelli, meeting one more gal couldn't hurt." The bishop winked. "Remember, you've got to kiss a lot of frogs before you find your prince, or in this case, princess."

Tony squirmed in the chair and felt a new heaviness in the pit of his stomach. "Well, okay then. I'll see you tomorrow." After shaking the bishop's hand, he hurried out the door.

Tony stepped into the hall. It was true; he and Kelli were

just friends. So why did he keep hanging onto the hope that they could be more? She had made it clear to him, and now she was apparently making it clear to everyone else. They were just friends. She had no interest in him romantically. He'll go meet the bishop's niece and who knows, maybe she'd be the one. After all, she was a musician. All Kelli could do with music was listen to her iPod, she'd said so herself.

Still, when Tony glanced down the hallways in the church building and didn't see Kelli, he was disappointed. When he got home, Tony picked up his guitar, tossed a pillow on the floor so he could lean against the wall, and started to play. He played melancholy songs he made up as he went—songs about lost love, fatherless children, and lonely nights in a remote town.

He plucked the strings and closed his eyes, trying to imagine what his audition would be like. Would he actually meet his hero, Buck Branson, or would Mr. Branson send someone else to listen to him? If he made it in the band, would it be because he had talent or because of who he was—who his mother was?

"Hey."

A voice startled him out of his daydream. He looked up to see Kelli standing in the doorway of the bunkhouse.

"Hey," he said.

"I missed you today at church."

"I missed you, too."

"I waited around for you." Kelly smiled at him.

"Yeah? Well, the bishop wanted to talk to me about something."

"Oh, so are you going?" Kelli sat on the edge of the bed. "Keep playing. I love to hear you."

"Nah, I don't feel like it anymore." Tony sat up straighter, realizing she must know about the family home evening at the bishop's house.

"Don't feel like going or don't feel like playing?"

"I don't feel like either, but I kind of have to go to the bishop's. I told him I would."

"That's good. I think you should. His niece sounds perfect for you. From what he said, she's really smart and graduated in biology. Besides, she can play the piano really well. Who knows—it could be really great."

"Yeah, but I doubt it."

"Why not? You're the-glass-is-half-full kind of guy, so why not her? You deserve to find someone. I can see you two in years to come, playing together, maybe even touring together—all your little kids singing in a family band."

Tony plucked at his guitar strings. "'Cause I don't see it. I envision myself with someone else." He looked up and tried to hold her gaze, but she avoided his eyes.

"You're just being silly. You haven't even met her yet, so you don't know. Anyway, I came to tell you that something weird happened." Kelli stood and paced across the small room.

"What?"

"I don't know. Maybe I'm just being paranoid, but when I got home from church, I walked into my cabin and could tell someone had been in it."

Tony bolted upright and set his guitar back in its case. "Herman?"

"I asked him and he said it wasn't him and that Maggie had been at church, so it wasn't her either. I'd left it unlocked, so . . . I'm sure it's probably nothing. Sometimes I have a hard time knowing what is a big deal and what isn't anymore."

"You have every right to worry after what you went through last year in Montana. Kelli, you've been chased by men with guns—that would keep anyone scared. Let's go check it out."

Tony ran his fingers through his hair, then grabbed a baseball cap off a hook and put it on backwards. He still wore his white shirt and tie, but he had put jeans on. "We need to find out if Kevin is still in jail. My guess is he's out already and has made his way back to Grouse Creek. For some reason he seems kind of fond of the country lifestyle."

A few minutes later they were at Kelli's cabin. She went up to her dresser. "This drawer was open, and my purse had been rifled through. I left it hanging next to the bed. I didn't have any money in it, and no credit cards, either. I'm sure if it was Kevin, he's picking through someone else's belongings right now."

Tony looked around the room. "Did you call the police?"

"No. I guess I'm a little hesitant to talk to them. I'm afraid, they'll say, 'Why should we believe someone with a rap sheet as long as yours?'"

"They would never say that! The police should've given you a medal for doing their work for them. If it hadn't been for you, that cult would still be committing terrible crimes."

Kelli smiled. "Well, when you put it like that, I guess escaping from them was pretty brave."

"You keep focusing on the wrong thing. You got involved at a low point in your life, but it took a lot more guts than most of us have to stand up to them. It's incredible, really. Because of you, Kelli Carson, an entire criminal organization was brought down. It wasn't just a few women who were being victimized. It was children, too. Besides, their illegal business dealings came out in the trial." Tony grinned and winked. "I'm honored to hang out with such a hero."

"Now you're just being ridiculous, but okay, whatever. Let's call the police before Kevin can get any farther. The Anderses had a phone installed for me this week. After what happened when Kevin was here the first time, they didn't want to take any chances." Kelli pointed to the wall near the kitchenette.

Tony reported the crime to the Box Elder Sheriff's Department, but he was unable to find out if Kevin was still incarcerated. He doubted the sheriff or his deputies would be out to investigate any time soon. Attempted burglary wasn't as urgent if you lived two hours away from the nearest sheriff's department.

"I'll just keep the door locked from now on. If it is Kevin, I'm not afraid of him, and if it isn't, chances are they won't be back anytime soon."

Tony hesitated at the door. He hated to leave Kelli if there was a chance someone—anyone—might do something bad to her again. He watched her slip her church dress onto a hanger. He thought about how pretty she'd looked in the lime green dress. She opened her small closet and put it in. Tony noticed her shoes lined up neatly on the floor.

"Hey, call me tomorrow and tell me about your date." Kelli flashed him a smile.

"Why?"

"Because I want to know all about her."

Tony shook his head and took a breath. "Kelli, I really, really . . . care about you." He'd wanted to say "love," but he didn't want to shock her when she obviously didn't feel the same way about him. *Still, she should know that she is torturing me when she talks like this.*

Kelli began putting the scattered items on her bed into her purse.

"Did you hear what I said?" Tony felt a lump in his throat.

"Yes." She flipped her hair over her shoulder and then looked him straight in the eyes. "You need to find someone who deserves you."

Was that the problem, that she didn't think she deserved him? "But *you* make me happy," he said.

"Call me tomorrow, k?"

"All right, fine. See ya." Tony walked out to his truck and stretched out on the seat. Until Kevin turned up, he didn't dare leave Kelli by herself at night.

He slept restlessly, hearing Kelli say over and over, "Find someone who deserves you."

Twenty-Two

NORMA WOKE UP EARLY MONDAY MORNING AND tried to clear her head. She seldom slept well away from home, but the night before had been especially bad, as images of Wes, Catherine May, and then LaRue kept creeping into her thoughts.

Mabel had already slipped out of the double bed they'd shared, and soon Norma emerged from the guest room. The morning sun streamed through the sheer yellow curtains that hung in Ruth's kitchen.

Mabel hummed as she sat at the table, stirring her tea. "Good morning," she said brightly. "Sit down here and join me in a cup of peppermint tea. It's just the right thing for a nervous stomach."

Norma scrutinized the cups in the dishwasher, chose one that looked clean, and sat down across from her sister, glad Ruth wasn't up yet. "Sorry, dear, that my tossing kept you awake. I couldn't clear my mind of the cobwebs that have plagued me lately."

"Oh, no matter," Mabel said. "Important thing is to convince you that you were the one who warmed Wes's heart—not

Catherine May, and certainly not LaRue." Mabel reached out and touched Norma's hand.

"It's all that, but it's more, too. I haven't had a chance to tell you about LaVell. You know him."

"LaVell in Montello? Surely do, dear. He was a dear friend of your Wesley's." Mabel retrieved a tea bag from her purse and handed it to Norma.

Norma placed the tea bag in her cup and got up to get some hot water out of the kettle. "Well, he said he's pretty sure Wes stopped seeing LaRue, not because she wouldn't have him, but because he wouldn't have her."

"Well, I'll be. LaRue certainly said otherwise." Mabel chuckled. "She was a prideful girl, wasn't she? Remember that time she walked all the way home from the Simpsons' house in Etna just because she'd spilled a little punch on her dress and didn't want anyone to see it? Then she told Mama that Dale Simpson had spilled it on her, just because she couldn't bear to make a mistake. Even though that pink punch stain was in the fold of her party dress and practically matched the color, to my knowledge she never wore the dress again."

"Still can't bear to make a mistake. But I don't know . . ."

"What don't you know? You know now that Wes loved you and not LaRue. Isn't that enough? Are you sure you still want to find Catherine, Cadence, and the baby? Won't that just open more wounds?"

Norma took a sip of warm tea. It felt good even though the day promised to be hot. "It might, but I feel compelled to find her. You know the morning Wes died, just before he walked out the door to do chores, he stepped back inside, smiled, and gave me a kiss. He said he had something to tell me—something he wanted to do. Or maybe he said it was something he *needed* to do. Anyway, I said, 'Sounds serious.' And he said something like,

'Depends on how you look at it.'"

As she gazed out the window and watched a ruby-throated hummingbird hover near Ruth's feeder, Norma tried to remember. Now the difference between the words "need" and "want" seemed important, but she couldn't recall which Wes had said. She felt Mabel's fingers squeeze around hers.

"When Bishop Jed came pounding on my door, I nearly jumped right out of my skin. I'd been trying to imagine what Wes had to tell me after all these years. As you know, Wes was a man of few words.

"When I found out Wes was dead, I assumed he must've not felt well that morning and that's what he wanted to talk to me about. But what if it wasn't that at all? What if he'd planned to tell me about all of this—this child, the romance, all of it?"

Norma knew if anyone could understand her feelings, Mabel could. "I just wish I knew for sure what it was he had planned to tell me. I'm not ready to forgive him for not telling me, but knowing would help."

"So do you feel if you find the missing girl, you'll find out what Wes wanted or needed to do?"

A deep pain gripped Norma's chest and she felt tears well up in her eyes. Mabel pulled a clean handkerchief from her skirt pocket and scooted it across the table. Norma dabbed at her eyes.

"That's exactly right. And now I've been given this chance to get to know Wes better through his grandchild. You know the saying, 'Where God closes a door, He opens a window'? I think Cadence may be that window."

"There's something I've been wanting to say." Mabel took another sip of tea. "You think maybe Wes was going to tell you about all this on the day he died. If you're right, there had to have been something that happened recently to prompt him to suddenly want to talk. You had the impression that Katie, who we think is Cadence, had talked to Wes before and probably recently, right?"

Norma mulled this over in her mind and tried to conjure the young woman's voice. She did sound desperate, but why? Why the sudden need to talk to Wes after all these years? "Yes, that's right. So what now?"

"One thing's sure. I don't believe in coincidences. All your life you've been kept from the truth about Wesley, then right before you find out, you get this phone call from a distressed girl. He talked to her recently—I'd bet money on it. And you are being led right to her, if you're sure you want to pursue that. I just hope you aren't putting too much hope in this. She might not be the answer you're looking for."

In Norma's mind, she heard the tiny sob in Katie's voice when she'd told her Wes was dead. Norma wanted to find Katie, and in order to do that, even though it would be difficult for her to face, she needed to find Wes's first love. What kind of a person was she? What did she look like? And would they be able to find her?

⁂

Things seemed to be going Norma's way. By late Monday afternoon, Ruth's son Carl, who worked at Thiokol Rocket Company but dabbled in private investigative work as a hobby, had located a Catherine Appleby Brown, who had passed away a decade earlier. He found the obituary in the archives of the *Salt Lake Tribune.* The obituary listed five children as survivors. The first child, Sarah, lived in Las Vegas, Nevada. Norma read through the rest of the obituary, searching for any other clues. Nothing told Norma anything about her husband's first love.

While the obituary said Catherine May had twenty-three grandchildren, none of their names were listed. The photo was of an ordinary elderly woman. Norma took one more look at the woman, searching her face for clues, and then handed the photocopied obituary back to Carl with a trembling hand. They were close now. "Is there any way we can find out if Sarah still lives in Vegas, and maybe get her phone number?"

Carl, a fiftyish, baby-faced man with a receding hairline, grinned and said, "Actually, she does. I found her online and have already talked to her."

Norma cocked her head. "Well, what did you find out?"

"She said she knew the man who raised her wasn't her birth father, that she remembers talking to her real dad on the phone when she was just a little girl, but she doesn't recall much about him."

Norma heard a gasp escape from her mouth. "Can I call her?"

"Yeah, she wants to talk to you."

Within minutes, Carl had dialed a number and handed Norma the phone. Sarah sounded young, but Norma reminded herself that the woman had to be in her mid to late sixties. "I'd like to ask you some questions," Norma said hesitantly. .

"Did he leave me any money in his will?" Sarah wondered.

This unsettled Norma, but she replied honestly, "I don't know. I'm not even sure he had a will. There's a small life insurance policy, I imagine . . ."

"How much?" This woman sounded so cold. Could she really be the person Norma was searching for? Could this Sarah provide her with the answers and the peace she desperately needed?

Mabel smiled encouragingly.

"When I cash in the policy, I'll send you a portion. But we had five children together, so it won't be much."

"Well, from what Mom always said, Hummer was rich and had a big cattle ranch in Utah—"

"Hummer? Why did you call Wesley that?" It stung that this woman knew the nickname Norma had only recently learned.

"I'm certainly not going to call him Dad. Besides, that's what Mom called him."

"Did your mother ever see Wes, have contact with him?" Norma breathed hard, not sure she wanted to know. She reached out her hand and felt Mabel's reassuring squeeze.

"I don't know. Only thing I know is Daddy treated me different. When I was about five years old, I noticed that Daddy played with my younger sister all the time, ignoring me. I remember asking Mom why Daddy loved Beth so much more than me. I thought maybe it was because my little sister was prettier than me, but we both looked a lot alike, with blond curly hair and blue eyes like Mom's. That's when Mom told me that my real father was a rich rancher and that when I was old enough it'd all be mine."

Norma's mind went back to Wes's sudden heart attack. He'd put on his chore jacket, slipped on his tall rubber boots, and stepped out into the unusually crisp May morning. It had been one of those days when the clouds hugged the earth, filling Norma with oppression and dread even before Wes's death. She'd hollered to him to be sure to keep his ears covered so he wouldn't catch his death. *Ironic*, she thought, shutting out the voice on the phone. Now she heard Wes's voice in her head again, "There's something I *need* to do, and I want to talk to you about it. I've got something to show you." He *had* said "need." It had been Bishop Jed Watkins who had found Wes. Jed fed his cows in the field adjacent to theirs. He said he'd noticed Wes's truck idling in the field and had climbed over the fence to say hello.

Sarah droned on and Norma's mind jolted to the present. Sarah hadn't even asked how Wes, her father, had died. "I'm sorry that your mother misled you about Wes. He wasn't rich. No one is rich around here. Most years we just scrape by. Occasionally when cattle prices are up, we buy a newer truck for the farm and go out to dinner to celebrate. If there is a life insurance policy, I'll see that you get a portion of it, if my attorney thinks it's fair."

"Oh, it's fair. More than fair. I spent my whole life with an ornery stepfather and mother telling me that everything would even out for me someday."

"It wouldn't be for much." Norma took a deep breath. "Tell me about Katie."

"Don't know a Katie."

"You don't have a granddaughter or a daughter named Cadence or Katie?"

"How do you know Cadence? Did she show up there? No one has seen her for sometime now, a good year or longer. Last I heard was when the police called and said she and her baby had disappeared from the hospital. It was obvious from the start she had more of her grandfather's genes in her than anything." Sarah sighed. "When I got pregnant with her, I though I'd already gone through menopause, you know."

Norma tried to squelch the anger rising in her chest. She felt as defensive as if Sarah were disparaging her own flesh and blood, and the woman had the nerve to hint that Wes had been inferior in some way. Just to make sure they were talking about the same person, Norma asked, "Does Cadence go by the name Katie sometimes?"

"Well, once when she was twelve years old, she asked me to call her Katie. Said Cadence was a name for strippers." Sarah laughed. "But I hear she prefers Cadence now."

"Cadence is beautiful name—a name for a poet," Norma said. "Did Cadence know about Wes?" Her voice quivered.

Sarah ignored the question. "My mother told me Cadence got her dark eyes and dark hair from Wes. Cadence always wanted to know why she didn't look like anyone else in the family. I always told her she was the lucky one because she didn't have our awful blond hair. Once when . . ."

Norma thought about Wes's dark eyes. It had been those eyes that had first intrigued her. She had thought his eyes held the answers to life's biggest questions. Now a young woman existed with those eyes, and, even stranger, she was Kevin Frazier's girlfriend. Norma and Kevin were indeed searching for the same person. Could this be why she had felt compelled to help him?

Sarah continued, "Yeah, she was definitely Hummer's, my mother said. According to her, Cadence even had his odd quirks, like humming while she colored, a passion for horses, and her crazy love for stray pets. She dragged home strays even though I'd ground her for a week every time she did. I never understood the girl, always begging for a horse, as if we had room for one in the suburbs with lava rocks for a yard. She was a fish out of water. I figured when she ran away I'd never see her again. It's easier without her—I'm way too old to have a twenty-two-year-old child anyway—but I still miss her sometimes. Tell her to give me a call if you see her, will you?"

"Okay," Norma said. After saying good-bye and promising to look for the life insurance policy, she hung up the phone. She held her head in her hands. "Let's go home," she finally said to Mabel. "I need to find out what Wes had planned to show me that morning he died."

Twenty-Three

NORMA WALKED BACK INTO HER HOUSE, KNOWING right where to look. The day before Wes's funeral, she had rushed around tidying up loose pieces of paper, then crammed them all in the lowest drawer in the pantry. Now she carefully opened the drawer and pulled the pile of papers out, setting them on the kitchen table. They were mostly bills and receipts from the veterinary clinic, the feed store, and the farm-supply store. She'd always taken care of the household bills, but Wes took care of the ranch. Some of the bills were overdue. Norma stacked the late bills in a pile and set them aside, then fished through the rest of the stack.

Under the bills was a blank white envelope. Norma's heart almost stopped as she reached inside and found a long, handwritten letter. Holding her breath, she began to read.

Dear Mr. Wesley Weaver,

My mom is your daughter, so that makes you my grandpa. All of my life I've known I was different. Everyone in my family has blond hair and blue eyes, and I have coal black eyes and dark hair. Mom joked that a Native American family came to Vegas and lost their money gambling at the casino where she worked, so they used me to pay their debt. When I got older I realized I wasn't Native American—that it had been a joke all along. Once, my grandma, Catherine May Brown (Appleby when you knew her), said, 'She is exactly like her grandfather—walks like him, looks like him, and even has the same wild look in her eyes.' Well, I knew my grandpa and knew I was nothing like him, so when I asked Mom she told me about you, my real grandpa. From that moment on I knew someday I had to find this man I was so much like. When I was seventeen I left home, and, unfortunately, I got into some trouble. Now I'm pregnant and the baby is due in the next month or two—I'm not exactly sure. Now it's really important that I find you. I want to come live with you. I belong where I can work with horses and animals. My baby and I belong with you. I don't know where I'll be, so I'll contact you after I have the baby, so you can come and get us. I look forward to meeting you and know we'll be happy there with you.

Your loving granddaughter, Katie

Norma held the letter to her chest and began to cry. This was what Wes had needed to talk to her about the day he died. He had wanted to show her the letter! And he'd probably planned to ask her if his granddaughter and baby could come live with them.

Norma knew she would've hesitated. After all, they had their own grandchildren. They had their lives, their ranch, and their friends, and they were well liked in their community. Norma couldn't just welcome a total stranger into the family, and, even worse, one who had by her own admission been in trouble. Norma couldn't be expected to just drop everything and bring a baby into the family. A baby changes everything.

Was Kevin the father of Katie's baby? If so, why had he said he wasn't? Was he afraid to take responsibility for the child?

With that thought Norma started to sob even louder. Wes hadn't taken responsibility for his child, either. And he'd over sixty years to tell her—his wife—that he'd fathered a child before meeting her. Why did he wait so long? Had he considered it his responsibility to take in his pregnant granddaughter? If he had and they'd taken her in, much of the work would have fallen to Norma. Would she have resented Wes for that, especially if he hadn't been around long?

Norma set the letter down, struggled to pull herself up out of the chair, and called Mabel in from the front porch. Norma handed Mabel the letter before calling Bishop Watkins on the telephone.

"Jed?" she said when he answered the call. Norma had a hard time calling him "Bishop." After all, she remembered when Jeddy had soaped all the windows in town and hadn't even spared the church, the co-op, or the post office. It was hard to forget a thing like that. But still, if the Lord had enough consideration for Jed to call him as bishop, then she should respect the man. "I mean Bishop, I was wondering if you could come over and visit. It's been a while since Wes passed on, and something has come up."

Jed agreed to come over and Norma hung up the phone. Then she looked at Mabel, who held the letter in one hand and dabbed at the corners of her eyes with the other. "We don't need to do a thing," Mabel said. "She'll come to us. I'm sure of it."

"I don't know. By now, she's obviously found somewhere else to go. She's had the baby. We know that because she ran away from the hospital without paying her bill. She's still desperate. I told her Wes was dead—her only hope, bless that little girl's heart. Why would she come here?"

"She'll come," Mabel said again.

When the doorbell rang, Mabel handed the letter back to Norma and disappeared into another room, leaving Norma to welcome Jed. "Come on in, Bishop,"

"You can call me Jed, Norma, just like always."

"Bishop, I've asked you here for some official advice. I need the help of God, it seems. You know I'm not one to ask lightly the advice of the Church. If I weren't urgently in need here, I'd sort this out for myself. So in that light, I've decided to call you 'Bishop.'"

"Well, then, that's mighty nice of you."

Norma could tell Jed had dressed up for the occasion: black jeans, his nicest boots, a cowboy hat, and a belt with a large, silver buckle.

He took his hat off and sat down in a living room chair. Norma held the letter in her hand and handed it to him. He nodded as he read and then handed it back to her.

"Sister Norma," he said with a compassionate smile, "this isn't news to me. Brother Wesley visited with me shortly before he passed on, and he told me this whole story, even about this letter."

Norma gasped. Another betrayal! Wes had shared this information with someone outside of the family before telling her. "Why did he do that? I'm his wife and this is the first I've heard of it."

Jed cleared his throat and stared at his calloused hands, which held his hat. "Forgive me, for not knowin' how to tell you this. I'm fit to be tied, Sister Norma. See, your husband talked to me because he felt right bad about what he'd done in his younger days. We all done things we ain't so proud of, and, well, Brother Wes, he wanted to get this weight off his chest. Now what he shared was confidential and I never planned on tellin' you, nor anyone for that matter. But things've changed now that you found the letter. I'm not one to betray the trust your good husband put in me by sharin' the secrets of his soul, but now it seems he would have wanted me to tell you at least part of it. I don't know if I should give a call over to Burley and talk to the stake president to see what the correct procedure is, or if I should check with headquarters in Salt Lake."

"Darn it all, Jed Watkins!" Mabel shouted from the kitchen. "Have you been out in the sun so long your brains have been baked? Just come right out and say it! You don't need to call over to Burley or Salt Lake to know what the right thing to do is, now do you?"

Jed's eyebrows went up. "Your sister's here?"

"Yes, she's still here."

He turned toward the room. "Well, um, I guess not, Sister, er, I mean Mabel."

Mabel disliked the Mormon custom of being called "Sister," and before Norma could warn the bishop, Mabel shouted. "I'm not your sister, Jed!"

"I'm sorry, Mabel," he called, then dropped his voice to a whisper. "Ya mind if we go somewhere else a little more private?"

"We could step out onto the porch."

Soon, Norma sat in the rocking swing and Jed leaned against the railing.

"As I was a sayin', your good husband told me just days before he passed that he had some things to confess. He said he'd never seen the point in comin' forward since it wasn't a secret from God. But I said, 'Nothin' is secret from God, but that isn't the point of confession. The point of confession is to humble yourself enough to admit to a wrong.' He said he also didn't see no point of it after so many years. What's done is done. Mistakes had been made, lessons learned, and him coming forward like a whipped dog don't undo a thing."

Jed chuckled and shook his head. "Wesley throwed in a string of cuss words there that I seen fit to leave out. Anyways, he went on to say that he'd told your sister LaRue before he shipped off to the war that he'd fathered a child, and so he just assumed you knew. He admired that you hadn't held that fact against him and had never even brought it up."

Norma gazed off into the distance. "I didn't know."

"Yeah. It seems he figured that out some years ago and didn't see the need of upsettin' you at that point in your lives. But then, see, the letter come from this youngster. Wesley figured maybe his wrong could be made right by helpin' her out or at least seein' to it that she got the help she needed. In order to do that, though, see, Wesley had some explainin' to do. He was afraid that you might not understand."

Norma bit her lip to keep from crying. "What I don't understand is why he didn't just tell me. What kind of uncaring person does he think I am? We all did things when we were young that we're ashamed of. I know that, Bishop. I know that, Wes." Norma glanced heavenward.

Jed gently took Norma's hand, tears glistening in his own eyes. "He was afraid you wouldn't understand why he never told you in the first place. He knew you'd understand that he made a mistake and that you'd forgive him for that. But he'd sorta accidentally and then purposely kept a secret from you, one he shoulda shared long ago. See, that's the thing he was mighty afraid you'd not forgive him for."

"So why didn't he tell me before he passed?" Norma could hardly get the words out.

"I counseled him to share the letter with you, and I hoped he'd been able to do that before he died. See, I'd been wantin' to ask you if he'd done that, but didn't see how I could without betrayin' the trust he put in me."

Norma stood up, walked to the edge of the porch, and looked down at the bishop. "If Wes wanted this girl to come live with us, baby and all, then that's what I want too. Did he tell you what he wanted?" She held her breath and waited for the answer.

"Yes. He was wantin' her to come. He was purty sure you'd agree once he got up the gumption to talk to you about it. I told him I thought it'd be wise for the two of you to decide together and seek the Lord's will in prayer."

Suddenly, Norma was angry with God for taking Wes when He did, and she couldn't stop herself from crying again. "Oh, why did Wes have to die?"

"I wish I could answer ya that."

Jed retrieved his hat from the living room a few minutes later and was about to leave when Mabel showed up holding a piece of the lemon meringue pie she'd baked the day before.

"Can't be thinking of leaving so soon, can you, Jed?" Mabel asked with a wink.

"Not unless you're just holdin' onto that piece of pie for yourself."

Mabel set the pie on the table and motioned for Jed to sit down. She whistled a tune as she poured a tall glass of cold milk and placed it in front of him.

"You wouldn't be a tryin' to buy your way into heaven, now would you, Mabel?"

"Why would I be needing to do that now, Jed Watkins? You said as much yourself at least a dozen times that my pie is heavenly. If that's truly the case then I'll have no trouble passing through the pearly gates. I'm sure I'll get there before you do. In fact, if you'd like, I'll try to hold the gates open for you."

It was true. Besides her delicious cookies, Mabel did make the best pie in all of Grouse Creek, and Montello to boot. LaRue and Norma always tried to match it, but couldn't quite get it right.

Exhausted, Norma sat down across from the bishop and rested her head in her hands. She closed her eyes and thought about what to do. When she opened them again, she saw a piece of pie in front of her. Norma took a bite and momentarily forgot her problems.

Twenty-Four

Sam,

Remember the pedestal I told you Tony had me on? Well, the ***bishop*** *knocked me off! He set Tony up with his niece. Too funny! Actually I'm excited. I knew Tony would eventually realize that he couldn't possibly be attracted to someone like me. And besides I am so NOT attracted to him. He's too much like you. ☺ He kind of acted embarrassed to tell me about her. What does that mean? I think she's perfect for him.*

Love ya, Kelli

WHEN TONY KNOCKED ON BISHOP WATKINS' DOOR, the bishop opened the door and ushered him into the kitchen. The bishop hadn't lied. His niece Jamie was pretty. She had big brown eyes, shoulder-length brown hair, and a cute smile.

Ann Watkins had cooked a beef pot roast with all the trimmings. At first, Tony felt a bit awkward, probably because Jed and Ann's children stared at him as he ate. In addition, Jed peppered Tony with questions that were obviously for the benefit of his niece, since Jed already knew the answers to most of them: "Where did you live before coming here? What was your major in school? How did you get into music? What are your plans for the future? What is your family like?"

Tony had trouble answering the last two questions. He wasn't sure what his plans for the future were, since what he wanted to do seemed less and less likely. "I'll be looking for a job in the agribusiness field."

Jed nodded as if he understood, and Tony didn't elaborate. Then he moved on to answer the next question. "You could say my mother got me into music. A long time ago before he was anybody, she sang with Buck Branson. She got me a guitar when I was twelve and taught me a few things."

"She sounds like quite a woman."

"Yeah," Tony said, "she is." *The trouble is*, Tony thought, *she could have been a lot more if she hadn't gotten pregnant just as her music career was starting*. He knew he'd interrupted his mother's life—she never let him forget it.

"My mom raised me. I don't have any brothers or sisters. We lived in Bozeman, Montana, where my mom ran a hair salon. She must be good because lots of clients won't go anywhere else."

Ann stopped eating, her fork pausing in mid-air. "Just you and your mother?"

Jamie stared at him. "I can't imagine that. In my family there are eight children, and I'm the oldest."

"Yeah." Tony smiled. "That's something I can't imagine."

After dinner, Jed led everyone into the living room for family home evening. It lasted less than a half an hour; Ann explained that it was impossible to hold the children longer than that. To Tony it seemed the whole thing was planned so that the children would be out of the way as soon as possible, since they were sent off to watch a movie upstairs as soon as the lesson was finished.

"How lucky that you brought your guitar," the bishop said. "We were hoping to hear you. Maybe Jamie could play something on the piano, too."

Tony chuckled to himself. The bishop had insisted he bring his guitar even when Tony'd told him he felt awkward about doing so. "What would you like to hear?"

"Can you play just about anything?" Ann asked, sitting on the edge of the sofa as if she would need to stand up in a minute.

"Pretty much, if I know the tune."

"What a gift," Ann exclaimed. "Well, there's a song I've wanted to hear for a long time. My mother used to sing it to me. It's about a brook—do you know it?"

Tony smiled. "Uh, I need a little more to go on. Can you sing the tune?"

Ann put her hand in the air like she was leading music and began to hum. "Hmm, hmm, hmm and then the brook ran down the mountain. Hmm, hmm, hmm, and doo de day. Lots of children came out to play. Don't go near that brook, their mothers say . . . "

Although Tony had never heard the song he was able to follow Ann and pluck out the tune.

"You do know it." Ann clapped her hands. "So what are the words? I can only remember some."

"I don't know it, but the tune is similar to other folk songs. Lot of melodies are so close, and it's no big deal to figure out what chord comes next."

Jamie sat down at the piano. "Let's try it again and I'll see if I can figure out the notes."

Ann supplied the words she could remember, and whenever she didn't know the words, she hummed. Tony listened and played and then joined in with his own version, filling in the blanks. Jamie could plink out the tune on the piano, and Tony was impressed with what a fine musician she was.

After a couple of songs, Jed stood up and stretched. "I've got to check the stock, so if you will excuse me."

Ann slipped into the kitchen, saying she needed to finish the dishes.

"I can help, Ann." Jamie stopped playing.

"Oh, no, I wouldn't hear of it. I'd much rather listen to you two play music than have your help in the kitchen."

"You sure?"

"Absolutely.

Jamie started playing a song and Tony picked his guitar. Then he started playing a song and she played along.

After they'd played about a dozen songs together, Jamie stopped and stretched her hands. "My fingers are getting tired."

"Yeah, I'd better go."

"I'd really like to just sit back and listen to you for a minute. Would you mind playing me something you wrote?"

"Here's something kind of fun." He sang an upbeat catchy tune.

She has long red hair and sad green eyes.
But falling for her will make you cry.
Look but don't touch, though you want her so much.
Life will never be the same and it's a terrible shame,
A terrible shame to be just friends.
Just friends for now and for forever.

That's all we'll be—just friends.
She isn't worth the pain.
She isn't worth the strain.
She'll break you.
She'll take from you.
She'll make you bleed.
Forget your need, just friends.
Now and for forever, just friends.
It's not the end.
Your heart will mend—just friends, just friends.
It's not the end, your heart will mend.

He ended the song with a fast picking melody, then looked at Jamie to gauge her reaction.

"You wrote that? That's so cool. You could totally record that, really. It sounds, sort of, I don't know, Bob Dylan meets Kenny Chesney." She put her hand on Tony's knee and he impulsively slid away from her.

"Uh, sorry." She moved her hand. "I didn't mean anything."

"No, it's cool. Sorry."

What was wrong with him? Kelli didn't want to be anything but friends, and already this great girl, with loads of talent and personality, acted interested in him. It was time he let go of Kelli.

"Hey, want to do something tomorrow night?" he asked Jamie. "Maybe head into Burley and catch a movie and dinner?"

"I'd love to."

Twenty-Five

EARLY TUESDAY MORNING, NORMA HAD JUST GOTTEN into the bathtub when she heard a frantic knocking on the front door.

Flustered, she reached for her robe and nearly slipped on the wet floor. Who would come over at seven in the morning? Before she opened the bathroom door, she heard LaRue's voice in the hall.

"Norma, are you in there?"

"Yes," she said in a panic, fearing the worst. "Be right out."

When she entered the hallway, LaRue stood there, holding a shoebox and wearing her lavender robe wrapped tightly around her flowered cotton pajamas. Norma knew something worse than terrible had happened to bring LaRue out in such a state. For one thing, LaRue never stepped onto her front porch without being fully dressed, and for another thing, she was wearing black rubber chore boots that must've belonged to her husband, Vernon—something LaRue normally wouldn't be caught dead in. Her normally tidy hair fell in loose strands around her face, and she looked as if she'd aged ten years overnight, her wrinkles deeper and her skin red and blotchy. Norma feared her sister's allergies had gotten out of hand, but then she realized LaRue had been crying.

"What's happened?" Norma's mind raced to all the horrible possibilities. Mabel, no—she was still asleep. Patty. DeLoy. Who? She hugged LaRue and felt the shoebox between them. "LaRue, honey, what is it? How'd you get here?"

"I walked."

"You walked?" Now Norma knew for sure something awful had happened. She pulled away from LaRue and looked at the mud on the boots. "I would've come and gotten you. What's happened?"

"I've had a terrible night, but nothing is wrong except that I'm just so sorry," Tears filled LaRue's eyes. "This is for you." She pushed the box toward Norma.

Norma put her hands on the box and they moved into the kitchen with both of them still holding onto it.

LaRue sighed as she finally let go of the box. They sat down across from each other and Norma lifted the lid. The box was stuffed with letters. "These should be yours. I wasn't completely truthful." LaRue choked on the last word and took a breath. "Patty and I had a long talk after the celebration. Until you came over the other day, I figured it was better to just leave things be. After all, we'd gotten along okay after I moved to Grouse Creek. I just stayed out of Wes's way and he stayed out of mine, but now that Wesley has passed—bless him—and after your questions, I know you need to see these."

Norma rifled through the letters. Each was addressed to LaRue, and each was from Wes. "But they're addressed to you. I don't want them." Norma slid the box toward LaRue.

"Patty asked me if there were any letters. I told her no, that I'd thrown them out, but then I got to thinking that maybe I hadn't. So I've been up all night, first searching, then poring over these once I found them. I'd planned to just read them before tossing them in the burn barrel, but as I read I came to understand some things. Some were written before the war. You know that Wes lived in Garland and we often saw each other on weekends at the dances. When he shipped out I wasn't sure I'd ever see him again. It was that way for so many of the boys. I wanted to marry him before he left, but he wanted to wait until after the war. So we promised to marry or at least get betrothed. I thought that if we were betrothed, even secretly, then nothing would take him away from me—nothing. But something did take him away."

Norma stared into LaRue's face, surprised at the sadness she saw there. Norma patted her sister's hand and started to cry. "I didn't know you loved him."

"Oh, dear, oh, dear. I prayed for the strength to tell you all this. Hummer broke my heart in a thousand pieces, and I blamed you for that. I've blamed you all these years. But now I know I was wrong. It wasn't you who took him away from me. It was the war. When he came back, I breathed an enormous sigh of relief and felt the deepest wish of my heart had been granted. He had lived. That's all I got on my knees each night and prayed for—that he would make it through the war. But I think I must've prayed for the wrong thing. I should've prayed that he'd come home the same person that I'd sent off. But he was never the same."

Norma squeezed LaRue's hand gently and urged her to go on.

"Oh, I still wanted him," she said. "But he didn't want me anymore. I was so mortified that someone would jilt me. I can see now that it was pride, plain and foolish pride, that kept me from whispering the truth to anyone. When he told me at the Idle Isle in Brigham that he didn't think we were well suited, I told him he wasn't good enough for me anyway and walked out before I'd had a chance to eat my cherry pie. And you know how much I love cherry pie! I just left it sitting there with only one bite taken out of it. I was halfway down the street when I remembered the pie." LaRue blew her nose, honking into her handkerchief.

"I made a quick decision that just because my heart was broken there was no need to let a perfectly good piece of cherry pie go to waste. So I walked right back into that café, held my head high, sat back down across from Wes, ate the pie without a word, wiped my mouth with the cloth napkin, and then left. Of course I had no way of getting home. I didn't even have a nickel for a phone call, so I just kept right on walking down Main Street. I planned on walking all the way home if I had to."

"Oh, LaRue dear! That must've been dreadful." Norma could see her sister marching down the sidewalk as if nothing had happened. "What did Wes do?"

"He drove right next to me in his Ford Club Coupe with a string of cars behind him, blaring their horns trying to get them to go faster, but he ignored them completely. Just drove five miles per hour as if he were the grand marshal in a town parade. And that's how I met Vernon."

"It was?" Norma remembered they had met in Brigham, but she had been under the impression it had been at a Church event.

"Yes, Wesley slowed his automobile to a stop just ahead of me and shouted for me to get in the car and he'd take me home. It was the least he could do, I remember him saying. I just kept right on walking as if I hadn't heard him. Then I ran into Vernon, literally. He was headed into the barbershop to get a haircut so he would look presentable as best man at a wedding in less than an hour's time. So as I was saying, I nearly knocked him down since I had turned my head to talk to Wesley. I had just said, 'Please leave me alone. I never ever wish to set my eyes on you again.' And then, *bam!*" LaRue clapped her hands together for emphasis. "I walked smack into Vernon. Wesley left his car running and jumped out to see if I needed help. You see, I'd fallen onto the sidewalk. Vernon helped me up in the most gentlemanly way, and I turned to Wesley and informed him that I had a previous engagement with this kind young man, and for all I cared he could go jump into the Great Salt Lake. Well, Vernon looked like he'd just won the lottery. 'That's right, Buster Brown,' he said. 'You can just hop right back into that hot-rod of yours—the girl is with me.' So I grabbed onto Vernon's arm and we strolled into the barbershop. After the haircut I attended the wedding with him, and right as he handed the groom the ring, he turned his head and in front of God and everyone, he winked at me. I knew before the day was over he'd ask me to marry him and he did."

"He did?" Norma couldn't believe how much of her sister's life she had missed. Was she just so wrapped up in herself that no one bothered telling her things? "So how did he ask you?"

LaRue blew her nose again. "Allergies," she muttered. "Anyway, as fate would have it, I caught the bouquet. It practically landed in my lap. As I recall, a group of girls had gathered around the bride, and believe me I wanted to, but since I didn't even know her I didn't feel it was in good taste. You know how mindful I always am of propriety."

Norma did know, so she nodded.

"So I had just sat down at a table to drink some pink punch when out of the corner of my eye I saw the bouquet sail by, so I reached up and grabbed it before it hit Vernon in the face. As I held the bouquet and laughed, Vernon looked into my eyes and said, 'Guess you wouldn't marry me, would you?' And all I could say was, 'Of course I will, silly. It's Providence that has brought us together. How can I go against Providence?' So from that instant he introduced me to all of his friends as his fiancée, but to introduce me as his fiancée he had to find out my name."

"Then you did love Vernon!" Norma stood up and stretched. She felt so stiff after missing her warm bath.

"Most certainly I did, but that doesn't mean I still didn't want Wesley to suffer. I was deeply hurt and wanted to make him hurt as badly as I did."

"But why? Other than almost not getting to eat your pie and that fall on Main Street, it doesn't sound like you had to suffer much at all."

"Even still, no one likes to be rejected, honey. So I made up my mind to be the one who rejected him, and I convinced myself I was saved from a fate worse than death by the grace of God."

"You mean Vernon, don't you? You were saved by Vernon. Let's not exaggerate, sister."

For a second Norma thought she'd pushed LaRue too far, but after a flash of anger in her eyes, LaRue went on.

"But the truth is, even though I should have told you that Wes and I courted, I vowed to myself to keep it secret. And as for the baby, I'd always assumed you knew, and it was only when you started asking questions that I realized you didn't. I didn't know what to say."

LaRue looked down at her hands and rubbed them together. She looked sad, sorry, and miserable.

Norma felt a lump in her throat the size of a boulder. She swallowed and then cleared her throat. "Why didn't I know you two had dated? How did you keep that a secret?"

"When we started dating, I was working and attending school in Tremonton. You were just a youngster here in Grouse Creek. Folks knew I was dating a man everyone called Hummer and that he went off to war. After we broke up, I married Vernon and went to California. When you got married, I realized Wesley didn't go by Hummer anymore, so no one made the connection between the two. Besides, most folks believed my soldier was killed in the war and I just let them believe it. It was easier than telling them the truth."

Of course, Norma thought. LaRue enjoyed being a martyr, and losing her love in the war would add to that.

"And I suspect you had blinders on," LaRue continued. "You were in love and I'd made up too many stories to try and set them right. But it doesn't matter much now, does it? So I want you to have these. Here, read this one first. It answers your questions."

LaRue fished through the pile and pulled one out. Her wrinkled hands trembled as she slid it across the table toward Norma. "It's the second-to-last one he ever wrote to me. Read the rest on another day. The ones about the war—make sure you read those when you're sure you have the stamina for it. Even without the censored parts, you'll read about a nightmare that will haunt you forever. See, I never read those war letters all the way through until now. I glanced through them, but I didn't want to know about the human suffering. I didn't want to internalize the war. So I didn't read them, and I'd write cheery letters back, telling Wesley to keep his chin up and to fight hard, and I'd quote other meaningless platitudes that I thought would help him fight like a man. Now after reading what he went through, I'm ashamed. And this letter says it all."

"Just a minute." Norma retrieved her reading glasses from the top drawer by the fridge. When she sat back down, she smoothed the yellowed paper on the table. *Nice handwriting*, she thought.

LaRue,

I'm sorry that things won't work out for us after all. When I met you at the Idle Isle last

Wednesday, I had every intention of asking you to marry me. When I first saw you sitting in the booth—your beautiful, hopeful face, your lovely smile—my heart swelled. But when I tried to tell you about the war, you said, "How dare you tell such things to a lady," and that I was to put it all behind me, to put one foot in front of the other, to forget that it ever happened. Of course you're right, and if I could put it behind me I would, but I can't do that. What happened to me has changed me forever. I will from this day on be a person who lived with death day in and day out—ate with him, slept with him, woke up in the morning with him, ran along the trenches with him, and made him a part of my soul. You made it clear through your words and actions that the person I've become isn't the person you could be happy with. I was especially disturbed to find out you hadn't even read my letters. I needed support and you couldn't give it to me. I don't blame you for this—it's just not what I want.

I met men like you want out there—men who saw the same atrocities that I saw and managed to tell jokes among their pals, who even managed to scrounge souvenirs to take home so they could relive their glory moments. Believe me, I wish I could've done that, but instead of telling jokes about the endless piles of emaciated corpses and the stench of dead that filled the air for miles, I would vomit. And even more shameful, I would cry myself to sleep at night and pray for my own death so that I wouldn't have to take another minute of it—of the helplessness I felt when we'd reach a camp that was occupied only with the dead because we, who would have been their liberators, had arrived too late.

LaRue, you are a lovely girl who deserves the kind of a person who can make you happy. I'm sorry that it can't be me. I hope you understand. I'll forever wish the best things in life for you.

Wesley

"My poor Wes!" Norma's hand flew to her mouth involuntarily as if to stop the sobs that would follow. Just then she heard another voice.

"Oh, Norma dear. See? These letters are your answer—the gift you've been praying for. A chance to better know the man you married." Norma looked up and saw Mabel standing in the doorway.

"How long have you been standing there?" Norma asked.

"Long enough."

"But is it too late?" Norma thought of Wesley's horror when he saw the carnage at the death camps.

LaRue stood up and smiled. "Well, the morning is half gone and I need to get home and get dressed. Here I've talked your ear off and I've got an appointment in twenty minutes to get my hair done. And look at me—I'll never be ready!"

"I could find something for you to wear," Norma offered, "and, of course, drive you. Aren't you going to that new young gal who lives in the trailer home close to the co-op?"

LaRue touched her hair and tried to tuck the loose ends into a bobby pin that dangled from one of her strands. "Yes, that's where. And no, my dear sisters, I don't need your help.

I'll just walk on down there. I'm through being a bother. At least for today."

"My goodness, dear, it's no trouble, and you certainly can't go like that. People will think you've gone mad."

"I don't care."

Norma was a bit frightened by LaRue's devil-may-care attitude, since it was so uncharacteristic of her. "Here." Norma pulled a lacy handkerchief from her robe pocket. "Take this. You're eyes are puffy and red. If the hairdresser thinks you've been crying, she'll send the Relief Society ladies to your aid."

LaRue smiled and Norma had a sudden urge to hug her. Her mind flashed back to a time when she'd skinned her knee on the playground at school. It was her oldest sister, LaRue, who had helped her into the school, where she lovingly washed the blood off and covered the wound with a bandage. Somehow this felt the same. Norma had been wounded and even though LaRue had been wounded also, she had set that aside and come to her aid.

LaRue didn't protest as Norma hugged her. Then with a dignified air, she walked out the door.

"Come on." Mabel pulled Norma toward the door. "We've got to stop her. If someone sees her, they're bound to call the police, or at least that young whippersnapper you call Bishop."

Dressed in a khaki skirt, her usual Nikes, and a man's western short-sleeved shirt, Mabel hurried out the door.

Norma threw her robe off, pulled on some pink slacks, and tucked her nightgown into the top. She grabbed a sweater from the coat rack to cover up the bulge her nightgown had created around her buttocks. "Wait!" she hollered to Mabel.

Mabel paused at the gate while LaRue hobbled ahead down the lane.

"LaRue, honey, wait for us!" Mabel shouted. Just before

they rounded the bend to the co-op, LaRue turned her head and flashed a triumphant smile. Norma couldn't help but wonder if this miraculous change in LaRue was more than just a fleeting one. Then Mabel grabbed Norma's arm. "I think she's going to be okay, but let's keep following behind just to make sure."

Jean Brooks, back from visiting her sister in Twin Falls, bolted out the front door of the tiny clapboard store. "What on earth has happened? Who should I call?" she called as she ran toward them.

LaRue held her hand in the air, motioning for Jean to stop. "Have you never seen an elderly woman on her way to get her hair done?"

Jean stood speechless, watching the little brigade of sisters march down Main Street. When they reached the trailer that served as both a home and a hair salon, Norma helped LaRue up the steps, and since there wasn't a handrail she didn't protest. With scarcely any room for spectators in the tiny trailer, Mabel and Norma waited on the front stoop.

A truck with hay bales in the back barreled around the corner and screeched to a stop in front of the trailer home. Jed Watkins hopped out and jogged over to them. "What in tarnation happened?"

"Nothing at all, sweetie. Why do you ask?" Mabel asked.

Jed took off his hat. "I'm relieved to hear that. See, I was in the middle of hayin' when Ann came running out to the field to tell me that something mighty bad musta happened to the sisters, 'cause the two of you were following behind LaRue, who seemed a bit off was how Jean Brooks had put it."

"When one is our age, one is entitled to certain things." Mabel didn't budge from the stoop. "Wouldn't you agree?"

"Certainly." Jed wiped his brow with a bandana.

"Well, then, if LaRue wishes to march down Main Street in

nothing but her birthday suit, then she's entitled, wouldn't you say?" Mabel lifted her chin.

A look of sheer horror passed across the bishop's face. "She didn't do that, did she?"

"No, my good boy, she didn't. But what we witnessed here today was no more shocking and nothing short of a miracle. Nothing short of a miracle." Mabel looked thoughtful. "And you say you thought something must be terribly wrong?"

"Well, yeah, that was the gist of things."

"That's where Jean got things wrong. Nothing could be more right." Mabel reached over and grabbed Norma's hand. "Right, sister?"

"That's right."

"Glad to hear it. Guess I'll get back to my hayin', then." Jed put his hat back on and touched the brim. "Take care now, ya hear?" He hopped back into the truck, turned it around, and drove off.

Norma watched, hoping the haphazardly placed hay bales wouldn't topple out of the back when he made the turn.

Ten minutes later, Mabel grabbed Norma's arm. "Honey," she whispered, "you need to go home right now. I'll wait here for LaRue."

"I want to wait too. This is more fun than putting pickles up."

Mabel laughed at the old joke. "I'm serious—I think you need to be home."

Norma felt chills crawl up her spine and knew her sister was right. Those letters needed to be read. She hugged Mabel, then rose and started to make her way home.

As she trudged by the co-op, Norma saw Herman putting gas in Ol' Blue. "Herman, will you please take me home? I'm in a hurry."

Herman pulled the gas nozzle out of his truck and nestled it back in place. "Be glad to." He helped Norma climb into the truck. Then with methodic slowness, he drove her home. Norma realized she could've walked just as fast, but she thanked Herman and walked into her house just in time to hear the phone ringing.

Twenty-Six

Stacey,

Like I said—you married him, now make him behave. Did Sam tell you he pretended to be some guy asking me out on a date? I fell for it, too, until he mentioned dancing in Montana. I knew no one knew about that except for Tony, and Tony is into Jamie now. Just when I was starting to like him, too. J/k! Good thing that thing I had for him was short-lived, cuz he seems to really like Jamie. I'm going over there now to see how his date went. And I get to hear him practice. If he marries Jamie, does that mean I don't get to hang out with him anymore? ☺

Hang in there, Kelli

TONY WALKED OUT OF THE BUNKHOUSE TUESDAY morning, pausing to admire the soft orange glow of the rising sun. He breathed the country air and smelled the sweet fragrance of alfalfa blossoms. He thought about his upcoming date with Jamie that night; he looked forward to it.

As he set off for work, he realized he needed to, as the old saying went, "wake up and smell the coffee." Or, as Mormons said it, to smell the Postum. He needed to move on with his life, and he couldn't think of a better time. He knew he might be jumping ahead a bit, but Jamie was a better match for him than Kelli anyway.

As Tony worked with the ranch's new gelding, he thought about the first time he had danced with Kelli at the Lazy Moose Café. She'd already danced a few dances with some of the town's old-timers, so she was a little breathless. She and Tony did the cowboy swing, the two step, and finally a slower dance where he could hold her tight and feel her breath on his neck and catch the light scent of lavender in her hair. By the time they'd finished the dance, he knew he liked her a lot. He enjoyed the way she laughed whenever he said something funny. He liked how easy she was to talk to, how easily he could share his dreams with her. But he'd felt some of those things with Jamie, too.

Tony slipped the halter on the horse's neck and fastened the cheek strap. He would work the horse from the ground for a few minutes before saddling him and riding him in the round pen. As he attached the lunge line to the halter, he heard a female voice behind him.

"Hey there, good looking."

Tony turned to see Kelli leaning on the lodgepole fence.

"Hey, yourself." He felt annoyed when his heart raced a bit at the sight of her. He led the horse to the edge of the round pen. "What's up?"

"You never called me after your date."

"Oh, well, I forgot."

"So?"

"So what?"

Kelli laughed. "I've been dying to know how it went."

Tony smiled. "It was fun. She's nice."

"That's it? She's nice and it was fun."

"What else do you want to know?"

"Everything, silly."

"I'll tell you about it sometime, but I've got to ride this horse." Tony had hoped for a little jealously from Kelli, but she certainly didn't show any. If anything, she had proved to him that getting to know Jamie better was a good idea.

"I came to tell you Norma wants to see you. I guess she got the word that you are the official bishop's helper for the seniors in town. And I got a call from the county sheriff. They're looking for Kevin." She let out a long sigh. "He wasn't released like we assumed. He escaped. We're supposed to call if we see any sign of him."

Realizing he was running out of time, Tony decided to skip the ground work and quickly saddled the gelding. Then he stepped into the stirrup and put all his weight there without climbing onto the back of the horse. The horse kicked and Tony stepped off and stroked the animal's neck, then tried again.

"I'm okay," Kelli answered, then changed the subject. "You know my brother Sam is a horse trainer, don't you?"

"That right? He didn't tell me."

"One of the best. He's booked solid for the next year. People bring him their horses from all over."

"I'd love to talk to him about it sometime."

"I'm heading over there tonight. Want to come along? Sam would love to talk shop. He doesn't get a chance much to talk to other guys, especially guys interested in the same things he is."

"Can't tonight. Maybe next time, though."

"Oh, what you got going?"

Tony felt his face flush, but he didn't know why. After all, Kelli had encouraged him to date. "Got a date with Jamie. We're, uh, heading to Burley to go to a movie and out to dinner."

He watched Kelli's expression as he spoke. He thought her smile faded a bit, but it could have been his imagination. He stepped into the left stirrup again and then climbed onto the horse's back. This time, the animal didn't buck.

"Oh, well. Why don't you stop by after, or come over early? I'll already be there. I'd like to meet Jamie. She wouldn't mind hearing about horses, would she?"

"Uh, I don't think so. I mean, I don't think that's a good idea. I hardly know her. I don't want to . . . you know. It would be a little awkward." Tony felt beads of sweat forming on his forehead.

"No, it wouldn't. Sam and Stacey are so cool, they'd make her feel right at home."

"It's not that."

Then Tony heard another car and looked up to see Jamie climb out of a red sports car. She strolled toward the fence. "I hope I'm not interrupting anything. Uncle Jed told me your boss wouldn't mind me coming over and watching you work. It's kind of boring around here."

"Hi, you must be Jamie." Kelli smiled and stuck out her hand.

Jamie looked at Kelli, then at Tony and back at Kelli. She smiled and took Kelli's hand. "Hi. And you must be 'just friends,' by the looks of that long red hair and those sad green eyes."

"Huh?"

Tony's eyes went wide, and he hurried to head off that line of conversation. "Jamie this is Kelli. Kelli—Jamie. Kelli is working in Grouse Creek for the summer." He tried to catch Jamie's eyes to warn her to keep her mouth shut, but to his horror she continued.

"The song—you know, long red hair, sad green eyes, not worth the pain, she'll break you and take from you, just friends now and forever, what a terrible shame—something like that." Jamie looked at Tony and raised an eyebrow. She knew exactly what she was doing.

"No, I haven't heard it," Kelli said nonchalantly. "But I'm so glad you're here. After your date tonight I want both of you to stop by my brother's place in Burley for ice cream, so these two horse fanatics can talk shop or round pen or whatever."

"You haven't heard the song?" Jamie asked. "It's really great. Tony, you should totally sing it for her."

Tony felt like he'd been slapped in the face. *Is she crazy or jealous or what?* The song was personal and yet he'd sung it out loud to someone he hardly knew, and now he regretted it. He climbed off the gelding, led him to the side, and began to unsaddle him. He didn't feel like riding anymore today. Besides, now he had an audience, and he wasn't used to having people watch him work. He tried to think of an excuse to get both girls to leave.

Kelli looked down at the ground and put her foot on the bottom pole of the fence. "I'd like to hear the song," she said softly, not meeting his eyes.

"Some other time. I'm working."

"I'd like to hear the song now."

Kelli looked up and held his gaze. He felt his pulse quicken. Tony tossed the saddle on top of the pole fence. He looked at Kelli again and saw tears in her eyes. "No, Kelli. Some other time."

"Is the song about me?"

He slid the halter off the gelding's neck. The horse snorted and wandered off.

"Is the song about me?" Kelli's voice rose and her eyes flashed with something between pain and anger.

Tony let out a long breath. "Of course it's about you."

"I thought we were friends, and yet you mock me to others and sing that I'm not worth the pain?"

"No, it's not like that," Jamie said quickly. "He wasn't mocking anything. Really. It's very sweet, but you too don't need me hanging around. I remembered something important I have to do, so I'll just go now."

Jamie walked off and Tony heard the car door slam shut and the car drive away. All the while Kelli stared at him without saying anything, her eyes brimming with tears.

"Sweet?" Kelli finally asked, obviously unconvinced. "If the song is sweet then I want to hear it."

"Look, I said some other time. I've got work to do."

Kelli sat down in the dirt. "I won't leave here until you sing it."

Tony looked up and saw his boss walking down from the barn. He didn't want the boss to see him slacking off from his duties. But the way Kelli looked at Tony now, he knew he had no choice, so he quickly repeated the words to the song, mumbling the harshest ones.

"Is that it?" Kelli made swirls in the dirt with her finger.

"Yeah, that's it."

"All of it?" Kelli asked, pulling herself up and brushing off her backside.

"Yeah. 'Course, it's a lot better with the guitar." Tony tried to smile to lighten the moment. "Now I really need to get back to work."

"So, that's how you feel?" Kelli asked.

"That's pretty much it. Yeah."

Tears ran down Kelli's face. "What is it I've taken from you?" Her voice quivered.

Tony glanced back; his boss was getting closer. "My heart—you've taken my heart, then said over and over that you don't want it."

"That's because I . . . I don't deserve it."

"But I'm in love with you. Don't you get it? I'm in *love* with you, Kelli. I want more than this. It isn't enough for me to be friends."

"Isn't it?"

"No, it isn't."

Kelli stood silent for several seconds. Then her expression hardened and she lifted her chin. "Good, because I can't be friends with you anymore either, not knowing that you'll make fun of me behind my back. I can't do it. I'm sorry. I had no idea it was so painful being my friend." She turned and headed for her car.

Tony leaped over the fence and ran after her.

Before he could reach her, he heard a shout from his boss, Jay. "You have an urgent telephone call, Tony, from the police department."

Tony slid to a stop, watching Kelli drive away.

Twenty-Seven

NORMA REACHED FOR THE PHONE AND KNOCKED IT off the hook. The phone slid across the kitchen table and dangled by the cord over the edge. Norma retrieved it, but her "hello" was answered by a dial tone.

"Fiddlesticks," she cussed. Then she set the phone down and put her head in her hands, willing the phone to ring again.

She sat for nearly five minutes without moving, certain if she got up to finally get dressed for the day she'd miss the phone again. If the call weren't important, Mabel wouldn't have had such a strong impression Norma should go home.

The phone rang again. "Hello? What is it?" she answered on the first ring.

"Hi, Norma. This is Tony Stratton. I heard you needed some help. I thought I'd come by during my lunch break. Will that be okay?"

"That will be great." *This must be the important call,* Norma thought, disappointed it wasn't something about Katie. "I'll have lunch ready for you."

"Cool."

"Tony, did you call a few minutes ago," Norma asked.

"No, why?"

Norma relayed the story about waiting for LaRue to get her hair done and Mabel's impression.

"Does Mabel get impressions often?"

"Often enough that I've learned over the years to listen to her." Norma thought back to the first time she'd noticed Mabel's "sixth sense." They were playing near Trout Creek, jumping back and forth across its narrow banks. Suddenly Mabel shouted, "Stop, don't jump!" Norma stopped, her feet teetering on the edge of the muddy bank. And then they heard the telltale rattle and saw the huge snake coiled right where Norma would have landed.

After hanging up the phone, Norma bathed and dressed, deciding to keep the bathroom door ajar just in case the phone rang again. She heard her front door open. "Mabel, I'll be right out," she hollered. When she stepped out of her bedroom all she heard was the hum of the refrigerator and the ticking of the mantle clock. She was certain she'd heard Mabel come in. Norma looked in the living room and Mabel's bedroom, but couldn't see her anywhere. *She must've gone outside again.*

Norma sat down at the kitchen table, picked up the telephone, and dialed Kelli Carson's number. Since Tony was coming over, it was an opportunity not to be missed. She hoped Kelli wasn't out counting birds.

"Hi, Kelli. Listen I was wondering if you wouldn't mind helping me out with something. I just need someone with good balance to change some light bulbs for me."

"Of course. I'll be right up." Kelli sounded like she'd been crying, but Norma decided maybe the girl had a sore throat.

"Not now. I'm, uh, not dressed yet. Could you come at noon? I'll have a bite to eat for you."

"Okay, I should be working, but I guess I can work after lunch."

"You've got to eat anyway. Goodness knows you're as thin as a pole."

"Okay, see you at noon."

The shoebox of letters still sat on top of the lace tablecloth Norma's mother had crocheted in the years preceding her death. Norma felt the edges and admired the delicate handiwork. Even before Norma's fingers had turned stiff with arthritis, she had never been able to crochet, not like her mother. LaRue had inherited her mother's keen eye and adept fingers for handiwork.

Norma thumbed through the letters again, noticing they were dated about a month apart. Her heart fluttered with excitement. This would be her new project. She would compile these letters into a brief history of Wes's war years. This memorabilia would help his children know him better. She could even include the medals she had found upstairs, the news clippings, and photos. Perhaps Cadence, if she ever found her, would appreciate the effort.

First, Norma organized the letters by date. Then she took a deep breath and began to read. Some letters were so censored that only the greeting and the signature were left; the rest of the letter was blacked out. After a while Norma found herself sobbing aloud at Wes's descriptions of the atrocities of the death camps. Finally, she pulled herself off the chair to find something to dry her tears.

A dish towel decorated with blue geese hung from a cabinet handle, so Norma snatched it and wiped her face. Then she pulled out the last letter and glanced at the postmark. It was dated over three years after the war, right after her engagement to Wes. She pulled the letter out of the envelope and felt her hands tremble as she spread it out on the table. It was written on lined white paper instead of yellow stationery.

Dear LaRue,

I'm sure you know that I've asked your sister Norma to marry me and she has accepted. As this may cause you some distress, I thought it best to clear things up. I assume you aren't terribly close to your sister, as she's never mentioned you. And I know that you still harbor deep resentment toward me. While I find this difficult to understand, especially since you are now married yourself, I don't want any of your bitter feelings to in any way affect my sweetheart, Norma. It's strange that fate threw Norma and me together the way that it did. When I first laid eyes on her, the resemblance to you was so startling that I practically ran the other way, because I'm ashamed to say I feared you'd disrupt my life yet again. Then I ran into her again and realized she wasn't you. It took me a while to get to know her for herself, since she looked so much like you, but finally her goodness won out and she just became Norma to me, nothing more. By the time I asked her to marry me, I'd almost forgotten that she is your younger sister.

Norma doesn't deserve to suffer because of any disagreements you and I had in the past. So my intention in writing this letter is to ask you to please not hold your anger toward me against your sister. I've always assumed that you told Norma what you thought about me, and the fact that she still allowed me to court her speaks highly of her character. I assume you'll be at the wedding, and

I hope you can set aside our differences and treat Norma with the utmost respect on this special day. I assume that you will do so, and I hope all is well with you and your husband.

Thank you, Wes

Norma twisted the damp dish towel in her hands into a knot, then untwisted it. Finally, she let herself feel the ache in her heart. She read the letter again and this time found herself smiling. *Wes loved me for me, not because of LaRue, but in spite of her.* She wondered how life would have been if LaRue had simply told the truth all those years ago. Norma missed Wes now more than ever, and she longed to talk to him. For a brief minute, she wished she could just die—die right there at the table with Wes's letters in front of her. Could a person just will death to come if she wanted it badly enough? She longed for a sudden heart attack to take her away in an instant. But then she thought about Cadence and the new baby. She thought about her own children, her grandchildren, and her great-grandchildren, her sister Mabel, and even LaRue. Norma still had so much to live for, and she let out a long sigh of relief at this realization.

Suddenly, she noticed the sun searing through the west-facing kitchen windows. She glanced at the clock on the kitchen range. *What is Mabel still doing outside?* It was too hot to do much of anything out there, and her sister would bake to death in this heat. Norma went to the front door and shouted, "Mabel!" The cattle in the nearby meadow answered with drawn-out bawls.

"Mabel!" she shouted again. She walked around to the back of the house and couldn't see Mabel in the yard. "Dirty elm trees," she muttered to herself as she started picking up twigs off the lawn. "I declare, they drop more limbs in the summer than they do leaves in the fall. They'll be the death of me yet."

Before long she'd picked up an armful of sticks. As she strode toward the burn barrel to dump them, she heard a humming sound. She emptied her load and turned to see Mabel and LaRue strolling arm-in-arm up the lane. More accurately, Mabel strolled and LaRue trudged. LaRue's newly permed hair radiated a silver hue as the sun rays highlighted it through the trees. She wore her pink polyester slacks and striped blouse, clothes she usually reserved for a trip into town—not Grouse Creek, but Burley or somewhere else. What had gotten into LaRue? Between her walk to Norma's that morning, her walk into town, and her walk back, she had probably walked three-quarters of a mile. That was at least twice as far as she'd walked in quite some time.

As they came through the gate, Norma could hear LaRue's rapid, shallow breathing.

"Help me inside," LaRue demanded, fanning her face with an AARP newsletter. "I think I'm going to die right here on the spot if I don't have water this instant."

Norma opened the door to the house and guided LaRue to a chair. "What would possess you to walk in this heat? You must be out of your ever-living mind! Mabel, why didn't you call me to come get you?"

"I did, several times in fact, but the phone was busy." Mabel filled a glass with water, set it in front of LaRue, and then got one for herself.

"But why didn't you just drive your car back to get LaRue when you came home the first time?" Norma asked, remembering that she'd heard Mabel in the house more than an hour earlier. "I can't imagine that you called several times, either, since I was only on the phone briefly."

It was nearly eleven o'clock, and Norma realized she'd have to hurry to get lunch ready. She'd gathered a few eggs that morning and had a sudden hankering for egg-salad sandwiches. "We're having company for lunch in an hour. Do egg-salad sandwiches sound good?"

"Weren't we going to fix your orange chicken?" Mabel peered into the refrigerator and pulled out the thawed chicken. "Oh, dear. I don't know how we can get this finished in time."

"Oh, that's right." Norma looked at the clock, then pulled some orange juice from the freezer and mixed up the marinade.

"Tony called, but no one else, and I've been at the table all morning. I think I missed the important call you told me to get right home for."

"No matter. I could've been wrong."

"Honestly, the way you run back and forth, Mabel, one would have a hard time believing you're eighty-two years old. You never did tell me why you came home about an hour ago."

Now Mabel rummaged through the fridge, no doubt searching for an onion and a green pepper. "Who's coming to lunch?"

"I invited Tony and Kelli." Norma grinned. "They'll make the cutest couple."

"Oh, sweetie, I don't know if that was a good idea. Tony is dating Jed's niece, Jamie." Mabel peeled the onion in the sink and began to chop it.

LaRue piped up with, "Yes, I saw Ann at the co-op today, and she said they are getting along famously. Ann was buying a can of Manwich—said it's Jed's favorite. A match made in heaven, she said. The perfect pair. Tony made another date with her for tonight."

Norma wiped her hands on a towel, hardly believing her ears. She'd seen the way Tony looked at Kelli. "Mabel, didn't you see it—the way Tony and Kelli are when they're together, the way they seem fit for each other?"

"I didn't see it. I could be wrong, I guess, but I'd bet money his head has been turned by Jed's niece."

Norma took a deep breath, afraid her sister was slipping, losing the gift, since she couldn't see something as plain as the nose on her face. "Well, I'll bet all the money I have in that number-ten can that his interest hasn't lessened."

Mabel chuckled. "That sounds like a fine bet."

"Since you're getting the chicken ready, I'll put the rice on." Norma washed her hands, opened the rice canister, and scooped out a cup. "What do I get if you're wrong, which you most certainly are?"

"My cookie recipe. Now, would you be a dear and turn the oven on to 375 degrees?"

Norma couldn't have heard correctly. "Did you say your cookie recipe?"

"I did."

Norma felt her heart race with excitement. She looked at the clock so she could remember the time. This day—this time—would go down in history.

LaRue fanned her face even faster with the AARP newsletter. "Mabel," she said sharply, "Norma seems to think you were here an hour ago. And you weren't, so why don't you answer her? An hour ago, Mabel sat in a chair reading the *Tribune,* sipping iced lemonade, and complaining about the doggone state legislature while I got my hair done. Didn't you now, Mabel?"

Norma's face went pale. "What do you mean?" She turned to Mabel. "I distinctly heard you come into the house. I even heard you go up the stairs."

Norma felt a little queasy. Whom had she heard? Instinctively, she grabbed a butcher knife out of the drawer and treaded up the stairs as quietly as possible. Mabel came right behind her. "What on earth are you doing with that silly knife?"

"Just being careful." They tiptoed down the hall and peered into the bathroom. Norma held the knife in front of her. When she pushed open the door to what had been her son's bedroom, she saw Kevin sprawled across the rumpled bedcovers. He lay asleep on his back, with the phone receiver on his chest beeping the off-the-hook signal.

"Oh, the dear boy," Mabel whispered. "Came all this way. He must be plumb tuckered out. When he wakes up he'll be extra hungry. Let's go finish lunch without waking him."

Norma glanced at her knife and felt foolish, but she decided to keep it close just in case. She didn't trust Kevin the way Mabel did. Mabel took the receiver, then gently hung it up. The two sisters backed out of the doorway. When they got downstairs, Norma didn't have the heart to do what she knew she had to do—call the police. Yet she couldn't knowingly break the law and keep a criminal—a fugitive from the law—in her home, so she decided to call the police later, after lunch. No reason to ruin a perfectly good meal. She slipped the butcher knife into the drawer.

LaRue had stopped fanning herself and had put together a salad of carrots, asparagus tips, and fresh spinach greens from Maggie Anders' garden. Norma felt a twinge of guilt. Herman and Maggie had been so kind to her lately, and she'd hardly done anything to return their hospitality. She vowed to bake them a pie as soon as the heat spell broke.

"Well, what did you find?" LaRue asked.

"Nothing." Norma decided LaRue didn't need to know Kevin was upstairs. "I guess I was imagining things after all."

Now she noticed the shoebox still sitting on the table. "LaRue," Norma said, "thank you for bringing the letters." She felt her eyes mist up and automatically wiped at them with her apron.

LaRue set the salad bowl on the table and looked at Norma with teary eyes.

"I read the last letter," Norma said. "The one where he tells you to be civil toward me at the wedding."

"Why, I cried all that morning, I'll never know, but I always blamed it on my delicate condition, since I'd already been married for some time. And even though I was perfectly happy with Vernon, I still felt jealous. My emotions were so topsy-turvy I could hardly think straight. I pulled myself together and got ready for the reception. I wore that blue taffeta party dress and was happy I could still fit into it and no one could even tell I was in a family way yet."

LaRue smiled happily before continuing. "People streamed into the church, and most everyone greeted me. I couldn't help but wonder if they knew Wes had jilted me. But of course they didn't. Delores Clayton, you remember her, she and her husband came out all the way from Garland. She knew Wes, so of course she knew all about his baby. She said to me, 'You must really be upset about this wedding. How could she marry such a man like him?' 'No,' I said, 'you mustn't think such things. After all, all is fair in love and war.' She laughed and went inside, and there Wesley stood. He pulled me aside away from the gathering. It was right under that tallest elm on the south side of the old chapel. 'You did forgive us, didn't you?' he asked."

LaRue took a breath as Norma and Mabel waited for her answer. She looked at their expectant faces and let out a quick laugh.

"'Of course, I did!' I said. 'Of course, I did!' I said it twice just to make sure he believed it, I guess. Then I promised myself I would never let it come between us. Wes smiled and said he'd forgiven me also, and he hoped we could be friends. He put his hand out and shook mine. And then he did something I'll never quite forget. He pulled me toward him and gave me a hug. 'Thank you,' he said. When he pulled away I could see the tears in his eyes. 'This is the happiest day of my life,' he said. Oh, and you were so beautiful, Norma. I've never in my life seen a lovelier bride, and never one so deserving of such a good husband. I hope—" LaRue paused, reaching up the sleeve of her blouse to pull out a lace hanky. "Oh, blast these tears. I can't afford to cry—not after my eye surgery. You know what tears do to my eyes. You'd think it all happened yesterday, the way I'm acting. Oh, my, I do hope you can forgive a poor, wretched soul."

"I can," Norma replied with a little sob, hoping LaRue could forgive her for all the nasty thoughts she'd had about her over the years. "Can you forgive me?"

"Whatever for?" she asked.

"Just you know—not always being the best sister in the world. One more thing, now that we can put this behind us, will you teach me to crochet?"

"Oh, dear." LaRue laughed. "If we could all die right this second, wouldn't that be something—to just die the instant all is forgiven and all is well? At least right after I teach you how to crochet."

"Mmm, smells good." Kevin stood in the kitchen doorway. "Hope you made enough for me."

Twenty-Eight

Sam,

I'm so mad! So Tony has been singing little songs about me—making fun of me. I feel every emotion you can think of: anger, hurt, sadness—well, yeah, I guess not every emotion. I'll tell you what I don't feel. Happy! I am not happy. I thought he cared about me. Who would think I could be so wrong about someone? I thought he was like you. But I was wrong, wrong, wrong. You would never hurt someone like that, if you loved him or her. Tony turned out to be nothing but a jerk after all. Oh, yeah, you asked about Kevin. He escaped from jail and is probably on his way to Mexico. Life sucks.

Love, Kelli

TONY WAS LATE FOR LUNCH. HE CHECKED HIS BOOTS for mud and scraped the hard soles against a metal rod at the side of the porch, installed just for that purpose. Norma answered the door, and Tony suspected by the big smile on her face that she was hiding something. He stuck his hand out to shake hers. "Hi, Norma. Good to see you looking so well."

"Come in, come in. Everyone else is already here."

"Everyone else?" Tony had thought Norma had wanted to talk to him alone. He followed Norma into the kitchen and saw Kelli first. She stood on a chair, screwing a light bulb into the ceiling fixture. The table was set for six.

Then Tony saw Kevin, leaning back on a kitchen chair, reading a magazine. *What is going on?* He hated this guy, yet apparently he was expected to sit down to dinner like everything was okay. Kevin leaned forward and let the chair fall into place. He glanced up from the page. "Hey, nice to see you, man."

Tony grunted a greeting and Norma pulled a chair out for him. He sat down, his eyes on Kelli. When she finished screwing in the bulb, she stepped down from the chair. "That'll do it for you, last one." Then she turned and saw Tony. Her eyes flashed and she said quietly, "I've got to go."

"What? Oh, no, dear! We've got lunch all ready for you. I'll be so disappointed if you don't stay, and I'm sure I'm not the only one." Norma gave Tony a sidelong glance.

"I'm sorry. I just remembered something I've got to do." Kelli glared at Tony.

"No, Kelli, it's okay. You stay. I'll go." Tony stood up to leave. He hated that he'd hurt her so badly, and he had no idea how he could make it better.

He strode out the door, the screen door slamming behind him. Then he heard Norma's voice. "Oh, dear, Oh, dear! This isn't what I expected. Tony?"

Tony turned on his heels and called to her. "It's okay, Norma. You didn't know." *How could she?* he thought, *I'm not even sure what happened.*

He got in his truck, but when he turned to look out the back window so he could back up, he noticed Norma had followed him. She approached the passenger's side of the truck, so Tony leaned over and opened the window.

"Can I get in?" she asked.

Tony held his hand out to help her climb in. "Guess you noticed Kelli's upset with me."

"What happened? Do you want to talk about it?"

"You're missing your nice lunch."

Norma waved her hand in the air. "Hogwash. They'll save both of us some. I'll fix you a plate and bring it out to you if you'd like."

"That's okay. I don't feel much like eating." He sighed. "Last night, I sang a song I wrote to Jamie—that's the bishop's niece. It was a song about Kelli. Then Kelli found out, and let's just say she didn't like the song."

Norma brows knit together. "Was there a reason for her not to like the song?"

Tony pushed his hand through his hair and then fiddled with steering wheel. "Yeah, I guess. I wrote the song to deal with how hurt I was that Kelli doesn't feel for me the way I feel for her. It's something I've learned to do over the years to deal with my problems. But Kelli, she's a little sensitive—overly sensitive, if you ask me. I know she's been through a lot in her life and I should've never sung that song. I just didn't think. And I guess I sort of wanted to impress Jamie."

Norma giggled. "Oh, if we could just take back all the things we do to impress someone, especially when that someone is of the opposite gender. Do you know that I once pretended that I could make a lemon meringue pie? I can make apple pie, pecan, and chocolate—anything but meringue. I couldn't get a meringue to set up if my life depended upon it. But see there was this fellow. He had dreamy eyes and biceps the size of Texas, and his favorite pie was lemon meringue. So I had Mabel make pies and I told him that I made them. Of course, Mabel eventually got tired of cooking them for me and so the jig was up. He dumped me and started courting Mabel."

Tony laughed. "That makes me feel better." He had a hard time imagining Norma being interested in a man's biceps.

"No, it doesn't." Norma looked him straight in the eye. "But I can think of something that might."

"What's that?"

"Write her a new song."

"I doubt she'll ever give me the chance, but . . . it's not a bad idea."

Just then, Tony saw Mabel standing at the truck window, holding two plates of food. Despite Tony's lack of interest in food, he rolled down the window and took the plates from her. Without a word, Mabel walked back up the sidewalk and went inside the house.

Tony took a bite of chicken, wondering how Kelli was doing. Norma picked at her food, but seemed to enjoy watching him eat.

"Tell me, sweetie," she said. "And take your time before you answer, because I've got a lot riding on this. Has the bishop's niece turned your head away from Kelli?"

Turned your head. While it was an expression Tony didn't hear often, he knew what it meant. *Had* Jamie turned his head? She was attractive, no doubt. In fact, she was, at least as far as he could tell in a few meetings, everything he'd ever wanted in a girl. She certainly could distract him from his anguish. "I don't know. Jamie is really great, but Kelli captured my heart a long time ago. Yet she's made it quite clear she isn't interested."

He took the last bite of his salad and handed Norma the plate. "Thanks for lunch. I better get back to work. I'll come by tomorrow. Save some jobs for me to do for you, will you?"

"Sure enough." Norma struggled to open the door.

Tony remembered his manners and jumped out and opened the door for her.

"Oh, I forgot. There is something I wanted to ask you to do." Norma balanced the two plates with one hand and leaned against the truck with the other.

"Okay, anything. Shoot."

"Find Cadence."

Find Cadence. Tony opened his mouth to protest, but Norma was already halfway up the walk. He watched her carry the empty plates into the house. He'd thought maybe she needed help with a job around the house, such as screwing in a light bulb, but of course she'd asked Kelli to do that. Why did people—first Kevin and now Norma—think he was good at finding people? And just how in the world was he supposed to find Cadence?

Twenty-Nine

"I'VE REACHED A DIFFICULT DECISION." MABEL PUT her plate in the sink. "I'm going back home to Montello soon."

Norma looked up with a frown.

"I've stayed so long here for you, dear," Mabel continued as she cleared the table. "After our jaunt to the Sun Tunnels, I felt like you needed me here. You're still grieving the loss of dear Wes, bless his soul, but now that Kevin's here and shortly you'll have Cadence and the baby, well, what do you need this old bag of bones taking up space for? I've sorely neglected things at home, and of course I certainly don't want to wear out my welcome, so when Cadence gets here, I'll be heading back. You won't have the room then anyway."

"I'll have plenty of room, and it would be an honor if you'd stay with me," LaRue said as she sucked the dressing off a carrot slice. LaRue's silver hair caught the afternoon light shining through the kitchen windows.

A look of shock passed over Mabel's face. "Oh, my," she said. "LaRue, sweetie, it's best not to take on too much at once.

Too many changes and you could find yourself, well, not yourself at all."

"Dudes—what's all this about Cadence?" Kevin interrupted. "When is she coming? She's called, hasn't she?" He jumped out of his chair, a look of wild anticipation in his eyes.

"No, Kevin, she hasn't called. Mabel just gets ahead of herself sometimes. One would think she'd know better than to get people's hopes up too early." *Oh, dear*, Norma thought. She'd just said something exactly the way LaRue would've said it. *Am I becoming LaRue, and is LaRue becoming, well, me?* "Mabel, please don't give the boy false hopes. The truth is that we haven't found her, nor may we ever find her."

"Oh, sweet Norma, don't dash the dear boy's dreams. What have we got but hope?"

Don't dash the dear boy's dreams. Norma wanted to remember that line; it sounded like a line of poetry. "I'm just trying to be the realistic one here, since the two of you may have simply lost your minds."

"Hey, whatever. It'll be cool." Kevin reached across the table and picked up a stray asparagus tip and ate it before settling back down. "Norma, mind if I borrow the car so I can go look for her?"

Norma couldn't believe he was serious. What had she gotten herself into? His manners were atrocious to say the least. She got a rag and washed the kitchen table before Kevin could find any more crumbs to eat. Then she went into the living room. "Wes," she heard herself say out loud. "I wish you would've just told me yourself."

"I didn't mean to upset you."

Norma turned to see Kevin in the entryway. "Just so you know, that's the best meal I've had since the last time I was here. That sticky chicken? Man, you ladies sure know how to cook."

"Thank you," Norma said curtly, not in the mood to talk to him. She pushed the front door open and stepped onto the porch, suddenly wondering what had happened to the steaks she had thawed out earlier in the week. When she'd come back from her trip into Tremonton, they were missing. *Just another mystery,* she thought with a wry chuckle.

Norma gazed across Herman's field and could just see the back of Meredith Watkins' home, where a little figure sat on the swings. Meredith's grandchildren must be visiting again, Norma thought. She sighed and sat down on one of the painted metal chairs Wes had brought home from one of his trips into town nearly forty years earlier. Norma had painted the chairs bright orange, and over the years they had faded to a pale peach color. She'd rocked all of their children on these chairs and listened to the sounds of the night—the howling of coyotes, hooting of owls, chirping of crickets, and bellowing of cattle. Life had felt so simple then. She'd known exactly what was expected each day: take care of the house, the kids, and Wes; do good to your neighbors; and if there was any extra time, read a few pages before falling to sleep each night. But now—just when she could see the sun fading in her own life, when life was supposed to be the simplest—it became the most complicated.

The phone rang.

"Just a minute," Norma heard Mabel say. Then she heard her steps shuffle across the tile floor, and then the creak of the screen door.

"Sweetie, it's her."

"It's her? Are you sure?" Norma pushed herself off the chair and hurried to the phone.

"Hello, Cadence?"

"How'd you know?" The voice was quiet and childlike.

"Mabel told me. Mabel's my sister."

"But how'd she know? All I said was hello."

"We were expecting you to call. I hope you've recovered from having the baby." Silence. "Cadence?"

"Yeah, I'm fine, but I need some money. Sorry to ask, but I don't know who else to ask."

Norma looked at the expectant faces in the kitchen. Mabel and Kelli stopped doing the dishes. LaRue stopped swaying in her chair, and Kevin looked like he wanted to wrestle the phone away from Norma. "Of course I want to help you. I've been praying you would call back."

"You have?"

"Wes would've wanted it."

Silence.

"There's someone here who really wants to talk to you. Remember Kevin?"

"Kevin Frazier? How did he—well, I sure don't want to talk to him. He's a—"

"He loves you intensely and has been looking high and low for you."

"Then why'd he dump me when I needed him most? The jerk left me out in the desert with Moon and a bunch of other creeps. I spent days in a cramped dive with a bunch of stoners. Then I went into labor and got one girl who had it halfway together to haul me into a hospital. I'm through with Kevin. I'll never speak to him again."

Someone wasn't telling the whole story here. "Oh, dear, I think there's been a misunderstanding."

"Look, all I want is to raise my baby the best I can, but I need some cash to do that. I've been staying in a sort of a shelter, but I can't stay here forever. I wanna get a job and set things up right for me and the baby."

"Well, now, of course you do." Norma thought Cadence

seemed flighty, maybe a little scared, but she wanted her to know she could trust her. "I'm not sure just giving you money is the best—"

Click. Norma jumped in disbelief and then muttered into the phone. "Well, I was just going to say I thought she ought to come stay with me, but she didn't give me a chance. Fiddlesticks."

Kevin grabbed the phone. "Cadence, Cadence, Cadence," he shouted into the receiver.

"Kevin, she thinks you abandoned her out there with those stoners—that's what she called them. Did you? Did you abandon her? Because if you left an expectant mother, then I find that unforgivable."

Kevin looked at Norma defiantly. He held onto the phone as if expecting Cadence's voice to return. Finally, he hung up the phone. "No way, man! But I don't know what happened. I don't remember. We got married—I told you that. Moon married us and I've never been more stoked, naturally, about anything in my whole life. Then we decided to celebrate. Cadence didn't drink nothing, 'cause of the baby and all, but the rest of us kind of got lit up. That's pretty much it, dudes, Scout's honor. That's the last thing I remember before I passed out. When I woke up, there I was lying in the hot sun with no clothes, a funny hat on my head, and a sack on me." Kevin shook his head. "Those dudes beat me up, took my clothes and my money, and left me out there to die, no less, but took the time to shade my body with an open umbrella stuck in the sand."

"No, dear, I was the one who put that umbrella up for you," Mabel said. "But we thought you were already dead."

"Huh?" Kevin stared at Norma.

"Had we known you weren't dead, we'd have left some water for you, wouldn't we have?" Norma asked LaRue, since she'd been the one with the water.

"But what would I have taken my medication with?" LaRue huffed.

Norma smiled, glad to know LaRue hadn't changed completely.

Kevin shook his head in confusion. "You mean you ladies found me out in the desert nearly dead, and you just left me there with an umbrella, a cloth sack, and a hat? I mean, that's harsh!"

Now Norma felt embarrassed. Of course they should've done more for him. But they weren't thinking right, and they did have strong reason to believe Kevin was dead.

"Oh, dear," Mabel said. "We didn't do right by you after all, did we? We would've done all those things and more, sweetie, had we just known you were still alive. As it was, the umbrella was just an afterthought—you know, so your body wouldn't bloat up in the hot sun. We couldn't bear for the vultures to pick at you before the authorities got there. So, see, we only did the best we could under the unusual circumstances. It's not every day we come across such things."

"That doesn't make much sense, but whatever. I guess you meant no harm."

"Humph." LaRue glared at Kevin. "No harm? By the way you're talking, one would think we hadn't saved your very life. One would think we hadn't come along, one would think we hadn't sacrificed our precious umbrella and Mabel's hat—although why on earth she wears those hats, I'll never know. And worst of all, that embroidered pillowcase you so callously referred to as a sack, was for my granddaughter's trousseau. One would think you hadn't put yourself in the unfortunate circumstances we found you in. One would think you hadn't stolen not one, but three vehicles. Why you needed more than one, I'll never know. You can blame yourself for that one, mister. No one put a gun to your head and told you to drink the devil's brew to the point of incapacitation. And why you felt the need to dance in nothing but your birthday suit is beyond me. You should thank your lucky stars you're still breathing. In my day young people knew when thanks were due." LaRue wagged her finger at Kevin.

"You're so right, m–ma'am. Thanks. Is that all?" Kevin looked like a whipped puppy.

"It'll do for now. But I have a mind to teach you a few manners myself. For instance, that habit you have of calling everyone 'dude.' Where do you get such disregard for your elders?"

"Du—I mean, ladies, I don't mean no disrespect."

"Sweetie, I know you mean no offense," Mabel said. "But out here where many a man makes a living as a cowboy, or rancher, if you prefer, 'dude' is a derogatory term. It's a term that casts doubts on a person's intentions. It's used to describe someone who just plays cowboy." Mabel put a hand on Kevin's shoulder as if to console him.

"Oh, a poser, you mean. Seriously, I had no idea 'dude' meant that, really man—ma'am. Now can we just call Cadence back?"

Norma took the phone and dialed *69. "That number is unavailable," came the reply.

"Let's call the police and see if they've found her," Mabel suggested.

"You can't call the police, dudes, I mean ladies. You know, I don't get why she didn't want to talk to me. I mean, Moon's the dude who would've hurt her. Not me, not never."

"We'll be needing to work on your grammar as well as your manners," LaRue said. "'Not never' is a double negative."

"Huh?" Kevin asked.

LaRue stood up and yawned. "I'm feeling mighty tired. Now that you've got everything squared away, I think I'll go home and take a nap."

"Would you like me to drive you home?" Mabel asked.

"No, no, the fresh air will do me some good." LaRue stepped outside.

Norma opened the drawer next to the telephone, pulled out the phone book, and found the number for the sheriff's department. "Actually Kevin, I think it would be for the best if you turned yourself in."

"Into what?"

"Kevin you've broken numerous laws and—" Norma began.

"Come on, man—I mean, Mrs., uh, Norma. We're friends now. You wouldn't turn me in."

Norma looked up at her Grouse Creek calendar, which featured a photo of two horses on a hillside. In the short time they'd known Kevin, their lives had been turned inside out.

Mabel put her arm around Kevin. "Sweetie, she's right. It's just a matter of time before the police come here looking for you. Your luck is wearing mighty thin, whether anyone turns you in or not. When you find yourself on the wrong side of the law, the best thing you can do is to step up and get yourself on the right side again. We'll be there standing right beside you, but it's best if you set yourself straight."

"You can't find Cadence without me."

"Kevin." Mabel paused with her eyes closed. When she opened them again, she said, "You need to call the police right now and tell them you're turning yourself in. You can't wait another minute."

"But—"

"Mabel's right, honey," Norma interjected. "She's always right. Well, almost always." Norma figured the jury was still out on whether or not Tony was interested in the bishop's niece. Even Tony seemed temporarily confused about that.

Norma dialed the number to the Box Elder County Sheriff's Department and handed the phone to Kevin.

Thirty

TONY WORKED WITH THE NEW BAY GELDING, wondering how long it would take the police to get out to Grouse Creek. Even with the best scenario, it'd be a couple of hours from now, and he didn't know if Kevin would still be around.

Today, Tony was trying to get the gelding used to noise and surprise. If they ever wanted to use the horse to work cattle, he would have to learn not to startle easily. Tony tied a plastic bag to the horse's tail, then led the horse around the corral.

Jay had told Tony he could name the gelding, and Tony had named him GC, after Grouse Creek, the town that had crept into his life like an addiction. Now that Tony lived in Grouse Creek, hardly a day went by without someone outside of work needing him, whether it was Herman calling to see if he was free to chase some stray cows or brand calves, or one of the kids needing help preparing the 4-H steers for the upcoming county fair. But now with Kevin, Jamie, Kelli, and the Hansey sisters, even his practicing for the Buck Branson audition had been regulated to a before-bed rush.

Tony sighed and focused again on the gelding. The horse's unruly, wild appearance would've scared off most folks. Even most cowboys wouldn't have bothered with a horse as uncivilized as GC. But Tony could see past that—he could see the horse's spirit. In much the same way, Tony had been right about Grouse Creek and its inhabitants. The remote town attracted a sturdy breed of people, and while Tony had wondered about some of them at first, he now felt honored to associate with them.

The gelding had been sorely neglected for the first few years of his life, so his training took a great deal of time and patience. Tony tried to remember what his instructor, a well-respected horse trainer, had taught him. "Always listen to the horse, and he'll tell you exactly what he wants." The trainer had added almost as an aside, "Not like a woman. With a woman you never know for sure if you've got it right, but with a horse it's easy." Tony now believed that to be an understatement. With women it was impossible, and with horses it wasn't all that easy either, but he was catching on. Eventually, Tony had learned to listen to GC and judge his reactions. When Tony shut everything else out and focused on the horse, GC responded to his signals. But today shutting everything out had been difficult, because Tony couldn't stop thinking about Kelli.

As the sun started to set, Tony drove home to clean up for his date with Jamie, then headed out to pick her up. But as he passed the church and the little town came into view, he saw several cars and trucks parked in front of LaRue's house. His gut tightened at the sight of the ambulance backing up to the door of the house. He parked his truck haphazardly behind a string of vehicles and bolted for the house. Inside, Tony saw EMTs placing LaRue on a stretcher. He noted the rise and fall of her chest. Thank goodness she was alive.

Tony watched as Mabel and Norma followed behind the stretcher and waited as the EMTs placed LaRue inside the ambulance and closed the doors. Tony reached Norma's car just as she started to back out of the driveway. She spotted him and rolled down the window. "Tony, it's LaRue—something's happened." Her voice broke. "Can you check on things for me at home just in case we don't make it back tonight?"

"Sure, but I'd be more than happy to drive you to the hospital."

"Oh, no, the bishop has also offered, but we'll manage. We don't want to burden anyone."

"Come on, let me do this for you, please." Tony opened the door and held his hand out for Norma.

She protested a few more times, but her words were swallowed by sobs. Tony helped her into the back and then got in the driver's seat. As he put the car into reverse, he remembered his date, so he rolled down the window and hollered for someone to call the bishop's house and tell them he couldn't make it tonight. He'd call Jamie later.

Tony drove the ladies down the gravel road until they caught up with the ambulance. "What happened to her?"

Norma sighed. "We don't know. I certainly hope it wasn't the chicken. But then I guess not, since none of the rest of us had a problem."

"You see, sweetie," Mabel said, "I called over to see how she was getting on after lunch, and after all the excitement, with a patrol car retrieving Kevin after he turned himself in. When she didn't answer the phone I worried something was wrong."

When they turned onto the paved highway, the ambulance picked up speed and the siren whined loudly in the desert. Tony kept up with the ambulance, fearful that if he didn't the sisters wouldn't see LaRue alive again.

"She only answers the phone at her own convenience. Remember, she doesn't think one should be programmed to respond to the sound of a bell—"

"Like Pavlov's rats, she said," Mabel finished. "But this time when she didn't answer, I felt it in my bones. It's like a form of arthritis. Your body, dear Norma, is like a barometer. You know when a storm is brewing, and I know when trouble is on the horizon. It's a gift either way."

Tony knew Pavlov's famous experiment was with dogs, not rats, but he didn't say anything.

"I don't see how my aches and pains can be considered a gift, but—"

"Certainly they are. Remember that time we all went with our children to show their steers at the county fair and you said, 'Be sure and take along your umbrella—a storm's coming'? The sky was as blue as a robin's egg. Remember that? So I grabbed my umbrella and so did Meredith Watkins because we knew you'd be right. We'd just gotten through the first round of judging, when *kaboom!* a lightning bolt crashed. Then rain came down so hard it sounded like bullets hitting the metal arena. Everyone ran for their cars holding programs over their heads." Mabel pantomimed the lightning bolt striking and rammed her hand into her palm.

"Well, sure, but how useful is that, really?" Norma asked. "We wouldn't have died or anything if we'd gotten our hair wet, but you've probably saved lives. Most likely if you hadn't gone and checked on LaRue she would've—"

"I'm sure she'll be okay," Tony said, but he wasn't really sure at all.

"No one's as good as the other. They're just different. If I'm sure of anything, I'm sure of that."

"What do you mean if you're sure of anything? Certainly you're sure of lots of things, aren't you? Your faith in God, for one." Norma fished through her purse to retrieve a handkerchief.

"If I was sure, how could it be defined as faith?" Mabel asked. "To be sure is knowledge, and I don't have knowledge."

"I don't know how you can say that."

"I can because it's true, that's how, dear," Mabel said. "Faith is fragile. Sometimes you almost know for certain and then something comes along to startle you back to reality, and all you know is that you don't know a darn thing."

"I know lots of things."

"And that's why I love you so much, dear. I'll just hold onto you and we'll fly into heaven together."

Norma reached up and tapped Tony on the shoulder. "What do you think, Tony? You seem like a person who would know. Does it work that way? Can one person get into heaven because of another?"

Tony craned his neck so Norma would hear him. "I hope so."

"That isn't what we're taught in church, though. We'll each be judged according to our own works, our own faith."

"It's always something isn't it," Tony teased. "Even Brigham Young said, 'If Brother Brigham should take a wrong track and be shut out of heaven, no person will be blamed except for Brother Brigham.' So if that's true, we can't rely on someone else to keep us on the right track either, I guess. On the other hand, I'm counting on lots of chances. You know we all mess up now and again."

"See, there you have it." Mabel said. "We'll all be together, the fools who think they are wise and the wise who know they are foolish."

Tony shook his head. "Hey, speaking of fools, what's happened with Kevin? You said he turned himself in?"

"Sure did. In the nick of time, too, since they were already on their way to pick him up. Someone must've tipped them off." Norma paused. "I hope you aren't disappointed in us. I just couldn't harbor a criminal in good conscience."

Tony felt a burden lifted from his soul. With Kevin out of the way, he wouldn't worry so much about Kelli's safety.

Now the ambulance flew along the freeway, and to keep up with it, Tony drove faster than he was comfortable driving. He glanced out the window at the rolling hills, the miles of sagebrush, and the few dry farms just outside of Tremonton. The ambulance turned off at the exit and he started to follow it.

"Good gravy, Tony! That ambulance just exited into Tremonton, didn't it?" Norma said.

"Well, isn't that the nearest hospital?"

"Oh, dear! LaRue would just die if she passed away in Tremonton. Remember, Mabel?"

Tony stifled a laugh, noticing that neither of the women seemed to notice the odd expression.

"Goodness," Mabel exclaimed. "I forgot to warn the ambulance driver. LaRue always said she wouldn't be caught dead dying in Tremonton. So—"

"If she wouldn't be caught dead dying, then she won't die. Mabel, you're a genius. LaRue won't be passing on after all, not today, anyway."

This sounded familiar, but Tony couldn't remember the reason LaRue didn't want to die in Tremonton. "Was it because of the small hospital?"

"Oh, no, sweetie. It has nothing to do with the hospital," Mabel said. "It's just that Tremonton's mortician tried to court her in high school."

It was coming back to Tony now.

"So it's all about dignity, of course," Mabel went on. "She

wouldn't give him the time of day in high school and she certainly doesn't want to give it to him now, you understand. I'm sure he's grown up to be a fine man, but you can see why it would be disconcerting to someone of LaRue's sensibilities—the thought of him putting his hands on her to do what would have to be done just sends LaRue over the edge, always has."

Tony couldn't hide his smile. The things that worried older people often took him by surprise. "He'd be pretty old. Are you sure he's still a practicing mortician?" He couldn't imagine a man that had to be over eighty still working as a mortician.

"Last funeral I attended here, he did. Besides, he's younger than our LaRue by a good six months. No one lays a body out quite like Selmar, although his sons are bound to be as good," Mabel mused. "You know how it is with any successful business, even though I hear it's tough for morticians to plan anything. It's like the saying goes, when it rains it pours. And just like anything else they've got their dry spells."

"Tragedies always happen in threes," Norma put in. "There's no truer saying than that."

"Morticianing is a family affair." Mabel adjusted her seat belt. "I don't know if Selmar actually does much of the bodywork anymore, but he likes to keep his touch on things. I hear tell he's more of a front man for the operation—puts everyone at ease with his stately look, his wavy, silver hair, and that overly sweet way of speaking they all develop to soothe the bereaved. Selmar still puts on a good show, so he's not ready to throw in the towel just yet."

"Well, hopefully she'll be okay and won't be needing Selmar's services yet," Tony said as he pulled in behind the ambulance in front of Bear River Hospital's emergency entrance.

Mabel and Norma followed the emergency workers into the hospital. Tony parked the car and ran to catch up.

LaRue's eyes were closed, but Tony could see the slow rise and fall of the blanket that covered her. The EMTs from Grouse Creek stood back and let the hospital teams take over. Tony recognized the ambulance driver, a rancher he'd seen driving cows to higher pastures.

"Will she make it?" Tony asked.

"Odds aren't too good, but she's as determined and stubborn as they come, so I wouldn't count her out yet." The man took off his cowboy hat and leaned against the wall. "You're the hired hand out at the Box C, right? I'm Tom."

"Tony Stratton."

"How'd things go on your date with the bishop's niece?" Tom scratched his day-old beard.

"Good, I guess," Tony answered, wondering how someone he hadn't met before knew about the date.

Tony ran his fingers through his hair. "Listen, I've got a call to make. It's good to see you."

In the lobby, he called Jamie and apologized for standing her up. Then he told the bishop what he knew about LaRue's condition. Next he tried to call Kelli, but she didn't answer the phone.

Just then Norma approached him, her face fraught with worry.

"Would you give LaRue a blessing? I think she's going to need it."

Thirty-One

NORMA TRIED TO MAKE SMALL TALK ALL THE WAY in from Grouse Creek, but she also said at least a dozen silent prayers, pleading with God to spare LaRue's life. LaRue had spent a lifetime building a fence between them and Norma'd only had a day to tear it down. Surely God wouldn't let LaRue pass on before the sisters finished patching their broken relationship. He wouldn't take LaRue the way He'd taken Norma's husband.

The sisters waited for news in the lobby, and Norma paced back and forth for a while. Then she sat down on a sofa and watched Tony, who leaned against the wall talking on the phone. Norma felt grateful he'd shown up before the ambulance left, as she might not have been up to making the drive in her frenzied state. She certainly couldn't have kept up with the ambulance like Tony did. And he was willing to give LaRue a priesthood blessing, the thought of which gave Norma great comfort.

Mabel stood across the room gazing out the side windows. Norma reached for a magazine and thumbed through it, not even noticing the title. After a few minutes, she realized that she was looking at the magazine upside down.

Tony sat down beside Norma and took her hand. "Everything is going to be okay," he said.

At his sudden kindness, Norma felt tears swim in her eyes. "Of course. Everything will be just as it should be."

Tony put his other hand over hers and leaned back on the sofa.

A doctor emerged from LaRue's room. Norma stood, and as Mabel joined her, the doctor said, "I'm sorry, but LaRue suffered a cerebral hemorrhage. In other words, a blood vessel burst in her brain." The doctor paused, looking between the two women. "The stroke is quite severe. She is conscious, which is a positive sign. At this point, she could improve very slowly or take a turn for the worse. Right now it's hard to tell which way she'll go. If she does recover, it will take a lot of rehabilitative therapy and even then, well, with her age, full recovery is unlikely."

The doctor rested a hand on Norma's arm and one on Mabel's, then nodded toward LaRue's door. "You can go in for a few minutes."

Taking each other's hand, Norma and Mabel walked in and stood at LaRue's bedside. Their sister looked as if she'd aged twenty years in the last few hours. She moved her hand almost imperceptibly.

"The doctor said everything is going to be okay," Norma lied. "You'll be back to your old self in no time at all."

LaRue's eyes darted around and she made indecipherable sounds.

Mabel nodded. "Yes, sweetie, you are in Tremonton. Is that what's bothering you?"

LaRue didn't seem very coherent to Norma, and she guessed LaRue probably didn't even know she was in Tremonton. "Don't worry her needlessly, Mabel," Norma said under her breath.

Mabel took LaRue's hand. "LaRue, we're your sisters and we love you more than anything in the world, and you can rest easy knowing that we will never let Selmar Peterson near you if, by chance, the worst should happen. You are too frail to move, but that doesn't mean he has to be the one. We'll call someone in from the mortuary in Brigham. You can be sure of that."

LaRue made a sound, whereupon Mabel released Norma's hand, touched LaRue's face, and kissed her on the forehead.

Norma couldn't hold back her tears. She wanted to hit Mabel for talking about the mortuary. They couldn't let LaRue think she was dying. It couldn't be true!

"LaRue," Norma finally managed to say, "will you forgive me for everything I've ever said to hurt you?"

LaRue gurgled and then closed her eyes.

"No!" Norma said, certain LaRue was giving up. She looked at Mabel. "Get Tony. He can give her a blessing."

"She wants you to forgive her," Mabel said softly.

"But I already did."

"Then tell her."

"Of course, I forgive you, dear sister. Of course I do." Norma gulped through the tears running down her face. As she looked at her sister's pale face, Norma panicked. Tony had to save her! God had to save her.

Norma ran into the waiting area and called to Tony, who jumped up from the sofa. When Norma explained the situation, Tony discreetly showed her the vial of consecrated oil on his key chain. Within minutes, another priesthood holder—a nurse—had been located, and once that brother acted as voice in anointing LaRue's head with oil, he and Tony put their hands on LaRue's head once more. Tony bowed his head and prayed, "Father in Heaven, through the power of the Melchizedek Priesthood which I hold, I bless LaRue Hansey Mortensen . . ." Tony paused.

Bless her to live, bless her to live! Norma begged silently.

Tony continued, "That she will rest easy, that she will have peace in her heart and know of Thy eternal love for her, that if it be Thy will she will recover, live longer here on the earth, and be a blessing to her sisters, her brother, and her children."

Good, that's right. She needs to be with us. We still need her, Norma thought. *Good, Tony.*

"But if her days on earth are over, take her into Thy presence without undue suffering. And whatever Thy will, let her family accept it and know of Thy love for them. Fill their hearts with understanding and peace. Fill their hearts with the goodness of Thy grace. In the name of Jesus Christ, amen."

After the blessing Norma opened her eyes and looked at LaRue, whose eyes remained closed. Then she noticed LaRue's breathing had stopped. "No!" Norma said aloud, looking at Tony, her eyes pleading for reassurance. He had tears in his eyes.

"I felt it," he whispered, looking stunned. "I felt her spirit leave her body just as soon as I said, 'Take her into Thy presence.'"

"Why?" Norma sobbed. "It's all wrong."

"No, honey, it's not," Mabel soothed. "It's the perfect time. It's just what she wanted, remember? To die at that moment when all was right." Mabel put her arms around Norma, but Norma couldn't reciprocate.

It isn't the perfect time, Norma thought. *The perfect time would be in another fifteen years after we'd taken walks together, talked together, and done everything we could to make up for all the lost years.*

Then Norma wished it again, for the second time that week. She wished it would've been her. She wished she could will death to take her away like it had so mercifully taken LaRue. That way she could be with Wesley, to tell him it didn't matter—none of it mattered anymore.

Thirty-Two

Sam,

I know. Tony is not a jerk. Of course, as usual, I overreacted, but still . . . Sad news. As you probably heard by now, LaRue—that's Norma's sister—passed away. Norma is so, so sad. I didn't think they were that close, but I guess you never know how you feel until someone is gone. How sad. Mabel seems okay. Tony has helped them out so much, but he needs to practice now because his audition is coming up quick.

My job is just a job after all. No magic in counting grouse and wandering in the hills. I'm doing well, but still have my moments—I don't know if you'd call them flashbacks or nightmares or what. But at times I wake up in a panic. And then I'm either back in the car at the moment of impact, or at the funeral, or back on the day

I almost got married. I wake up sweating and can't catch my breath. I know my telling you this will bring you running over here. Don't! I need to figure this out myself. Tony can't do it for me either. And we're still on the awkward side anyway. I'm thinking maybe counseling is the right thing after all. Would you mind checking things out for me over there? I'm over there every other week anyway. I'm sorry! I thought things were going to be great here in GC. But turns out it's just a town after all.

Sam, I'm really missing Mom more than ever!! Why is life so hard sometimes? You're so lucky you have Stacey and soon a baby.

I love you! Kelli

It had almost been a week since LaRue passed away. While Tony felt guilty about not helping Norma and Mabel prepare for the funeral, he secretly felt relieved when Mabel shooed him away, reminding him he only had a few days left to get ready for his audition.

So each night for the past week, he'd slung his guitar over his shoulder and hiked up the canyon behind the Box C, hoping the solitude would eventually mend his heart.

Tony felt he was ready for the audition, but he was more than a little let down that Kelli wouldn't be coming with him. He'd called her every night but she still wouldn't answer the phone. When he stopped by in the evenings, she wouldn't open the door. He decided to try again tonight.

He didn't arrive at the bunkhouse until after dark. The hired hand who'd been his bunkmate had moved to Idaho, so it was just Tony. He changed into his performing clothes: jeans, dress cowboy boots, black felt hat, and a western shirt with pearl snaps. He grabbed his guitar and drove to Kelli's cabin, parking half a block away so she wouldn't hear his truck. His heart pounded. Even though he'd played in front of many large audiences, nothing prepared him for the audience he'd have tonight. He prayed, just like he always did before the start of a concert, that the Lord would bless his performance.

Tony took a few deep breaths, stepped out of his truck, and quietly approached Kelli's cabin. Her light was on, her curtains drawn, but he could see her form on the bed. He sang the first song he'd sung to her back in Montana. It was the Monkees' song "I'm a Believer." He had altered the words then to fit her, and now he changed them again.

It breaks my heart I've hurt the one I love,
Her disappointment haunted all my dreams.
When I saw her face, her pain, her anger,
I knew my life would never be the same.
I've tried to forget her to move on,
What's the use of trying?
All I've done is bring pain,
When she needed sunshine, I brought rain.
When I saw her face, I couldn't bear it.
I'm in love, but I don't deserve her.
I'm in love.
I'm a believer.
I couldn't leave her if I tried.

Kelli came to the window and peeked out of the curtains, her face stoic and unsmiling. She retreated but Tony hoped she was listening. His fingers plucked the guitar strings, his voice floating on the nighttime breeze. He went through a repertoire of five love songs before hearing a door open behind him.

He turned to see Maggie. "You have such a wonderful voice, and the way you play that guitar! If I were fifty years younger, I'd be swooning. And if you want my opinion . . ."

"Yeah?"

Maggie wore a plush terry-cloth robe, and she pulled it tighter around her. "The problem isn't that she doesn't love you—it's that she doesn't love herself. You can sing until you're blue in the face and it won't change that. What she needs is a little more time, a little more prayer, and—I hate to say it—some therapy."

Tony knew Kelli had been to a few counseling sessions, but she'd ended up quitting early to work in Grouse Creek. Everyone had assumed the fresh mountain air would bring her around, but maybe Maggie was right.

"What should I do?" Tony asked softly, his fingers silent on the strings.

"Give her some time, some space. When she learns to love herself again, falling in love will be easy. And if it isn't with you, then accept it."

Tony felt his spirit resonate with the truth of her words. He'd been pushing for something Kelli wasn't ready for, and her being hurt over Jamie and the song didn't necessarily mean Kelli was ready for a relationship with him.

"Thanks, Maggie."

"You want to come in for a minute? I'll fix you a cup of cocoa. Herman's gone to bed."

Tony looked back at Kelli's cabin, then turned and nodded to Maggie.

As Tony sipped his cocoa he thought about how nice it would be to have a grandmother or mother like Maggie, someone to give him advice. Norma had also acted as a sort of surrogate mother to him since he'd come to Grouse Creek. He thought about how many times his own mother had let him down, and he realized he'd spent his whole life angry at her because she hadn't given him the very thing he wanted the most—a father.

However, Tony also knew if she'd been the kind of mother who had encouraged him to try out for sports, or go to Cub Scouts, or do well in school, he might not have turned to his guitar for comfort. And he certainly wouldn't have an opportunity to audition for Buck Branson's group. Life had a funny way of opening doors—of turning something negative into something positive.

"You want one more piece of advice?" Maggie stirred her cocoa. "Don't marry someone you're not in love with and who isn't totally in love with you."

"Huh? I'd never do that."

"Good, but sometimes we do just that. I spent thirty years with a man I didn't love because I thought he would be good for me and good for my image. And all that time, I was in love with someone else."

"Whoa, that would be horrible."

"It wasn't so bad. It just wasn't so good, either." She brought her cup to her lips.

Tony didn't know Maggie well, but he did know she'd only been married to Herman for a couple of years. "So what you're getting at is that I shouldn't marry Jamie or Kelli—Jamie because I'm not in love with her, and Kelli because she isn't in love with me?"

"Now I didn't say that exactly. Jamie might really be the one for you—I could never tell you that for sure. But just make sure you are in love with her and not her qualities, or her looks, or because you think she'd be good for you. If love isn't part of the equation, marrying someone for their qualities is no different than marrying for money."

Tony thought about Jamie, whom he'd seen nearly every day since they'd met, usually at lunch time since he rehearsed at night. They'd gone over to visit Norma and Mabel a few times since LaRue died. Tony had admired Jamie's compassion. "But she's really something. She's funny, she's spiritual, she loves animals and the outdoors, and she's an awesome pianist. I mean, I could go on and on. Besides, she's beautiful." Tony laughed, realizing he'd just named her qualities. "I do like her, though. I can't help it. She's fun to be with. And I think if I can just get Kelli to forgive me for singing that silly song, I'll be able to move on and be able to feel more for Jamie."

"It's quite possible."

"But?"

"No 'but's." Maggie stood and retrieved the pan of hot cocoa, motioning toward Tony's empty mug.

"No, thanks. It's nearly midnight. Sorry to keep you up. I still have one more song to sing."

"Not another love song, I hope."

"No."

Kelli's light was off. Tony hesitated, but then broke out into an altered version of the Beatles' "Uncle Albert."

I'm so sorry, Kelli Carson.
I'm so sorry if I've caused you any pain.
I'm so sorry Kelli Carson,
But I'm the only one to blame.
It's because I'm really lame.
I'm so sorry but I haven't done a thing all day.
I'm so sorry Kelli Car—

The door squeaked opened and Kelli stepped onto porch wearing shorts and a baggy T-shirt.

"What took so long to get to the apology?"

"Oh, well . . ." Tony smiled at her, then noticed the red splotches on her face. "I've tried calling you a thousand times."

"I know, but I was waiting for the song."

"Yeah, well, it's probably lame to show up outside your door with a guitar and a song, but it's all I have to offer. So you liked it?"

"Of course I liked it."

"I've missed you," he said.

"I've missed you, too. And just so you know, I do forgive you, but I still can't be more than friends. I wish I could, but I just can't."

Tony put his guitar back in his case. "I really want you to go to the concert with me. Will you?"

"Tony, it's not that I don't want to, but it's not good for you to keep hanging on to the hope I'll fall in love with you. I'm not sure I can ever feel—"

"That's okay."

"It's okay?"

Tony shuffled his feet and leaned against the building, weary from the long day. "Yeah, it's okay. I'm ready to move on, but I'd like you to share this with me, you know—one last thing." It would be hard for Tony to say, but he knew Maggie was right. He would give Kelli the space, but the concert was too important to share with someone he didn't know and care about.

"But we'll always be friends, right?"

"Sure," Tony said, though he knew it was unlikely.

"How will Jamie feel if you take me?"

"I don't know, but you're the one I want there. Please."

"I don't know. I'll think about it."

"There's something I haven't told you." Tony hesitated. "Remember how I told you my mom said music was in my blood?" He looked away from Kelli. "On my twelfth birthday, when she gave me the guitar, she told me that Buck Branson is my, uh, father."

"Wow, Tony. Really?"

"Yeah." The moonlight shone through a large box elder tree that loomed over the small cabin, creating shadows that danced on the walls. When Tony looked back at Kelli, the shadows had crept over her face, muting her expression so all he could see were her eyes, wide with surprise.

"But how could that be? Why didn't he take care of you? Buck is known for his strong family and Christian values—"

"And I don't doubt he believes that, but he messed up. So what?" Tony turned away, feeling the stab of pain he'd felt so many times since his mother had told him the rest of the story. Basically, he was the product of a mistake.

When he first heard Buck crusade for fidelity, Tony was seventeen years old and a senior in high school. It had never occurred to him that his mother hadn't been married to Buck, and she blamed his absence from Tony's life on his busy career. But then Tony heard Buck on an afternoon talk show, touting fidelity in marriage. The talk show host made it a point to ask Buck if he had ever slept with a woman other than his wife, and he said he'd married his high school sweetheart and they had both been virgins. When Tony asked his mother about it, she'd said, "What did you expect him to say on national television? You're so naïve, kid." She'd ruffled his hair and kissed his forehead.

"No wonder you put his picture on your wall. All this time I thought you were such a nerd." Kelli smiled. "But if he's your dad, then that's so . . . well, I guess it means you're a shoe-in for the band." She touched his shoulders with both hands as if she wanted to hug him, but then she pulled away.

Tony suddenly felt empty. "He doesn't know."

"What?"

"He doesn't know. My mother kept it a secret from him, but she told me so I'd know my potential."

"But you'll tell him—"

"I want to do this on my own. If I get this gig, I want it to be because of ability, not blood."

"But you have both."

"You understand, though, right?"

"Yeah, I guess." Kelli hugged her shoulders and shivered. "But there is something I don't get. I don't get why you're so mad at your mother all the time. It's really hard for me to say this because I think you're the greatest guy in the world, but it bugs me that you still have your mother and yet you talk about her like she's some sleazy night-club—"

"But she is . . ."

"Hear me out. I know your mom gave you your precious guitar. So did you have a lot of money growing up?" Kelli pushed her hair away from her face.

"No, hardly any. Just enough for mom's fancy outfits."

"And your guitar. You said your mom gave you one of the best guitars money could buy. I'm guessing she would've sacrificed just about anything to get that for you. I miss my mom so much, and I can't stand that you have a mom and you don't get along with her.

Tony sighed. "She didn't even come to see me baptized. I might be able to forgive her for everything else, but that was the most important day of my life and she wasn't there."

Kelli touched his arm and shook her head. "Tony, did she know how important it was to you? Did she really know? Think about it. How could she know?"

Tony dropped his gaze from Kelli's. She was right. How could his mother understand how important God had become in his life when He wasn't important in hers? "You're freezing. I'll get going. So you'll come with me this weekend, right?"

Kelli laughed. "Okay, change of subject. Yeah, I'll come. I'll call you tomorrow."

"Great." With a smile, Tony slung his guitar back on his shoulder and walked off into the night.

Thirty-Three

LARUE WOULD'VE LOVED HER FUNERAL, EVEN though Selmar Peterson had been the one to take care of her body. At first Norma protested, telling Mabel they had to follow LaRue's wishes. But the more Norma thought about it, the more she realized it was nonsense. Besides, as the eldest sister now, Mabel had the final word. And when it came right down to it, neither Mabel nor Norma could turn Selmar away.

The normally stoic mortician had shown up at the hospital morgue with tears in his eyes. "She was the dearest soul," he'd said sadly. "You must come by and pick out a casket. We'll certainly be offering the friends-and-family discount." Then he'd touched LaRue's face and gently tugged a smile onto her lips. Already she'd looked better than she had in years.

The funeral itself was an affair worthy of a queen. Just about everyone in Grouse Creek, Montello, and Park Valley attended, along with at least half of Tremonton. At the viewing, the line of mourners wound all the way out the door and down the street.

Soon it was over and life had to go on. But Norma didn't want it to.

In the days that followed Wes's funeral, she had managed to keep going, to put one foot in front of the other. She even forced herself to smile most of the time. But the day after they buried LaRue, she fell apart. Without the bustle of relatives who'd shown up for the funeral, her house felt as cold, empty, and silent as a church. So she stayed in bed, trying to ignore everything.

People flitted in and out of her dreams, or were they dreams? She saw Wes and knew she needed to ask him something—something that nagged at her—but she couldn't remember what it was. She hoped he'd speak to her, but his silence filled the room like his smile. She felt happy to see that his smile, which she had longed to see more of in life, was present after his death.

The day blurred into night and back into day, or was it two days? Dreams played through Norma's mind in a confusing array of colors and sounds, everything jumbled together. For a while she wondered if she was dead. Then she realized if she was dead, she must have gone to hell after all. She heard herself laugh at the thought.

Norma felt someone sit on the side of her bed. Mabel. She stroked Norma's hand and rambled on about the news of the day. Mabel looked like an angel, and Norma knew if Mabel were here, this wasn't hell. Mabel would not be anywhere so cold and dark.

Mabel said something about food. Norma noticed the tray she had brought in and shook her head. She wasn't hungry. Her stomach no longer rumbled for food, but rather felt like a stone had filled up the cavity.

"Here, sweetie. I brought you some peppermint tea and a slice of homemade bread with chokecherry jam. It's from LaRue's. You know her cupboard above the flour bin? It was full of jars of jam. We have enough for years to come. Every day we can spread a little jam and think of LaRue. It's her gift to us, sister."

Mabel lifted Norma's head from the pillow and gave her a sip of tea. Norma felt it dribble out of her mouth onto her chin. Mabel wiped it with a cloth napkin and gave her another sip. Norma let it trickle out too.

"For goodness sake, Norma! You aren't an invalid!"

She'd never heard Mabel talk with such firmness and it surprised her.

"You just can't stay in bed for the rest of your days," Mabel went on. "You just can't."

"Wes was here," Norma managed to squeak out.

"See there, sweetie, you are still in there. I was beginning to wonder. What did he say?"

Mabel gave Norma another sip of tea, and this time Norma swallowed and let the warm liquid flow down her parched throat.

"He didn't say anything. He just smiled."

"Was he humming too? I bet he's humming again."

"I'm not sure." Norma hoped he'd come again so she could notice if he was humming.

"Deloy came over to check on you. He really cares about you. And others came yesterday and today. Herman, Maggie, Bishop Watkins—most everyone in Grouse Creek wanted to make sure you were all right. Tony and Jamie, Kelli, they've all been here."

As Mabel spoke the names, Norma pictured the faces. She felt her dry lips form the hint of a smile. She remembered she wanted to ask something important about Tony. He'd been with her at the time of LaRue's burial, had helped lower the casket into the grave. She'd grown awfully fond of the boy. Then she remembered what she wanted to know.

"Did you say Tony and Jamie? They aren't together, are they?"

"It appears you owe me all the change in the coffee canister."

Oh, dear. Norma frowned. She'd so hoped she was right about Kelli and Tony. For once, she'd been sure Mabel's intuition was wrong and she was right. Could she have mistaken the feelings that sparked between Kelli and Tony? But there was something else she needed to ask. "Did he audition for the band yet?"

"He leaves tomorrow. We're all rooting for him. Since you've been visiting the folks on the other side, see if they can't pull a few strings for him." Mabel chuckled.

"LaRue hasn't come."

"No? Well, I imagine she's busy getting things orderly. You know how she can't stand for anything to be untidy. She's probably reorganizing the clouds and telling God how to make things just a bit nicer. Don't you think? She's probably saying, 'It's unseemly the way you've got that cloud blocking the sun.'"

In spite of herself, Norma laughed.

Mabel stood up, walked to the curtains, and flung them open. The sun streaked in, catching dust particles in its light. Norma squinted from the bright light.

"Now that you're back with the living, I have something else to tell you. Remember Kevin?"

Norma nodded and Mabel gave her more tea. Norma swallowed and scooted up in bed a little, then took the teacup and held it. Her hands trembled, but she managed to bring the cup to her lips and drink on her own.

"Good girl." Mabel smiled. "Jean Brooks has been coming by to see if you're ready to learn to crochet. Looks like you're finally ready for her."

Norma smiled, remembering she didn't know how to crochet, but not why she wanted to learn. "How's Kevin?"

"He's been transferred to the state prison. He pled guilty to most of the charges, so his trial was waived, and he'd rather get on with serving his time anyway. He's finally learning to take responsibility, I think. But Herman is willing to take a chance that Kevin can toss his cattle a bale of hay, so he's offered him a job when he gets out. Herman's slowing down some. Said it'll be nice to train a youngster like Kevin who plans to settle down and raise a family. Said Grouse Creek needs some young blood to keep the school going and such. The judge could've sentenced the boy from now until Armageddon, but as luck would have it, he might be out by next Christmas. By that time the baby will be talking, I expect."

"Baby? Is the baby here?"

"Not yet, but Tony said he needs you to help him find Cadence. He hasn't had time to look yet, actually, but he really wants to start before he leaves tomorrow."

"Cadence." Norma closed her eyes. With a start she remembered one of her dreams. She was riding on a bus packed with everyone she knew and cared about—her family, the sisters from church, the bishop, Tony, Kelli, Kevin, and a dark-haired girl holding a baby. The girl handed her the baby, then got off the bus at the next stop. The baby cried and cried and Norma bounced it, singing, "Hush, little baby, don't you cry."

"Oh, Mabel, I just have to find Cadence and this baby!"

Thirty-Four

Stacey,

Yay, you're finally feeling good! A girl—too cool. I hope Sam doesn't try to make her ride bulls when she grows up, don't you? Send me the names you're thinking of SOON. Tony is so sweet. Have I told you that yet?☺ He came by and serenaded me—an "I'm sorry" song. I think I'm going to have to forgive him. What do you think? Too soon? I would hold out longer, but you should've seen the puppy-dog look on his face. It was Sam all over again, the night he hurt your feelings after the Burley Rodeo. Anyway, I have to say I really hope someday I can find someone just like Tony to marry—but not Tony, if you know what I mean.☺

I had my first counseling session and already feel a bit better. Do me a big favor. Don't get killed in a car accident when your little girl is 14. You have to stick around for her. I don't want my niece to go through anything like that.

Love, Aunt Kelli ☺

TONY STOPPED AT NORMA'S ON HIS WAY OUT OF town. He paused at the door to read a handwritten note taped beneath the triangular window: Please come in. Tony hurried inside and leaped up the stairs, surprised to see Norma sitting on her bed crocheting.

"Hey, you're looking good."

Norma laughed. "I wish I could tell you at what age I went from 'good looking' to 'looking good.' 'Looking good' is what people say when you're still breathing. It's like they're surprised you're still alive."

"No, that's not it. You really do look good. You're smiling, talking, and your face is" —Tony paused, thinking she no longer looked like death, but he could hardly say that— "full of life. Is that crocheting or knitting? I can't remember the difference."

"Crochet. Look!" Norma patted the bed next to her. "These are booties for Cadence's baby."

Tony sat on the edge of the bed and looked at the light green booties. How optimistic of Norma to think they'd find the baby while it could still fit into the tiny slippers. Tony had already made enough phone calls to know it might not be an easy task. "Maybe you ought to make a bigger pair, too, just in case it takes a while."

Norma sat up straighter and set the booties down, her eyes searching the room for a clock. "I'm going to start making phone calls right now. Cadence said she was at a shelter. How many could there be?"

Tony grinned, knowing it would do the older woman some good to help search for Cadence. "Actually, there are quite a few, and most of the time the locations are secret, due to the nature of the issues that cause most women to seek shelter. But we might be able to get in touch with the right people to find some phone numbers. And since I'll be in Salt Lake for a few days, I'll look for her every spare minute I get. Well, I might sleep a little too—and practice the guitar."

When Norma threw back the covers of her bed, Tony noticed she was fully dressed in purple stretch pants and a matching blouse. She set her feet on the wood floor. "I'll need a pen and a notepad to keep track of everything." She rummaged around in a drawer and soon pulled out a notepad and pen. "Can I get your cell phone number?"

"Yes, and if I can't answer, leave a message." Tony took the notepad and wrote it down. "I'll call you as soon as I know anything." He stood to go.

"Wait, one more thing." Norma's eyes grew wide. "Is Kelli going to the concert with you, or is Jamie?"

"Kelli's going to meet me at the concert." Tony sighed. "I hate to disappoint you, but it looks like we're just going to be friends."

"Oh, that's too bad." Norma rummaged through another drawer and pulled out a Salt Lake City phone book. "Well, I've got work to do. Best of luck to you at your audition."

A security guard stood outside a sleek, black, thirty-foot tour bus, which shone in the late afternoon sun. Tony fished his identification out of his wallet, and after glancing at it, the man ushered him through the door. Tony sucked in a breath, sat down, and waited. He hoped Buck would be the one to listen to his audition, but thought that unlikely. Nerves on edge and heart pounding, Tony took another deep breath and gave himself a silent pep-talk.

He glanced around the luxurious bus, breathing in the smell of the chocolate-colored leather upholstery. He craned his neck and looked down the length of the bus to see several people eating at a mini bar. Further back, someone slept sprawled out, his cowboy boots sticking out over the edge of the built-in bed.

"How are you doing?"

Tony jumped as Rowdy Robinson walked up the steps into the bus and put out his hand out. Tony stood up and took his hand. He recognized Rowdy from music videos he'd watched over and over in preparation for the audition. Rowdy wore jeans, boots, and a T-shirt with a band logo. His graying brown hair was cut short, and Tony became conscious of his own longer hair. He probably should've gotten a haircut. Rowdy smiled a welcoming smile that put Tony at ease.

"Nervous?"

"No, I mean, yes. A little."

"Look, just think of me as one of your friends. I bet you play for your friends all the time and it's not a big deal, right?"

"Actually I play for the cows."

"Ah, even better. Just think of me as a big, black Angus cow." Rowdy sat down and motioned for Tony to sit as well.

"I'd rather stand."

"Okay. Anytime you're ready, go ahead."

Tony glanced at the guys at the mini-bar. They laughed and talked, and while they paid no attention to him, they still made him uncomfortable. He bit his lip and held his hands ready to play.

Rowdy turned around. "Hey, guys, go on in the back, would you? Leave us alone."

The laughing stopped and the bus grew quiet as the men stepped out of sight.

With another deep breath, Tony began to sing. He started with “Smooth Talker,” a Buck Branson hit that had topped the country charts for months. At first, Tony’s fingers fumbled on the guitar strings, searching for the right chords and notes, but Rowdy nodded and encouraged him to go on. By the second verse, Tony played confidently, his mellow voice echoing through the bus. Then he sang another Buck Branson song. Soon, a few of the men drifted out from the back, gathering around to listen, and when Tony got to the end of the song, they applauded.

Rowdy leaned back on his chair and kicked his legs out, then smiled and nodded. “Not bad, kid. Before you go on, why don’t you tell me a little about yourself,” Rowdy flipped his hand, motioning to the gathered audience to disperse again.

Tony pulled his resume out from his back pocket and handed it to Rusty. “Well, I grew up in Montana. I graduated from MSU in Bozeman. I’m working for the summer on a cattle ranch up in northwest Utah and trying to learn more about horse training.”

“College-trained cowboy, huh? Buck doesn’t think much of college-trained cowboys, but me, I think that you need to stay up with things if you’re going to make a living at it. ’Course if you’re in our band, you won’t have much time for much of anything else, though eventually you can probably have yourself a little business on the side.”

Tony swallowed hard. He loved music and he loved horses. If he couldn’t figure out a way to do both, he probably couldn’t be happy. But he wanted to focus on this dream right now.

Rowdy smiled. “Well, your résumé looks pretty good, but let’s get back to the tunes. What else have you got? You write any of your own?”

“Yeah.” Tony hadn’t expected that.

"Give me the one the cows like the best, the one you serenade the coyotes with."

Tony grinned, then cleared his throat and sang:

You broke my heart for the last time,
So I take to the hills with nothing but my guitar.
The hills are black, the smell of sagebrush fills
the air,
And I walk until nothing except nothing is there.
It's just me, my heart, and my guitar.
Well, I find me a rock, where I can sit down and
talk.
But instead of talking, I end up singing.
I sing the love songs I wrote for you,
But that was before you told me we were
through.

Tony noticed Rowdy's foot tapping with the rhythm. Tony went on,

So I sing my song out loud and clear as if you
were somehow near.
By the time I reach the chorus, my voice is all
but gone.
I bow my head, with nothing left to sing,
Then the coyotes howl and the cattle gather
round,
They bellow their low, mournful sound.
The night air grows very clear,
Now I wasn't all alone with my heart,
I had cattle, and coyotes, and lizards crawling
at my feet.

Just me, my guitar, and my heart.
Just me, my guitar, and my heart.

When Tony got to the final line, Rowdy grabbed his own guitar and sang along. Tony strummed the last chord and there was a moment of silence before Rowdy smiled wide.

"Welcome to the band."

Thirty-Five

TONY FELT LIKE HE WAS SKYDIVING. IT WAS thrilling, but frightening and unbelievable. “Just like that? What about Buck—what will he say?”

“Actually, I make the decisions around here. Buck just sings. I choose the music. I choose the talent. I’ve been around since the beginning.”

Tony’s mind raced. He wanted to know more about his dad. When would he meet him?

“Why don’t I take you to lunch?” Rowdy asked. “We’ll go over your contract and the tour dates.”

Had he said tour dates? Tony couldn’t believe it. Before he could form any words, he was following Rowdy out the bus door. They walked a few blocks to a café near Temple Square and sat in a booth near the window.

“Order what you want,” Rowdy said. “ It’s on the band.”

When the waitress came to the table, Tony smiled up at her. “I’ll have a chicken fried steak and mashed potatoes with the gravy on the side, and water to drink with no ice.”

Rowdy laughed. "I'll have the same."

"You'll also have the chicken fried steak, with mashed potatoes, sir?"

"Yes, with gravy on the side. And water—no ice. What are the odds?" he winked at Tony. "Ice hurts my teeth."

"Me too."

When their meals arrived, Tony wolfed down his potatoes.

Rowdy took a couple of bites and then looked at Tony. "Okay, tell me a little more about yourself. Are you married?"

"Not yet, but I hope to be someday."

"But I thought from the song that your girl broke your heart for the last time." He winked.

Tony changed the subject. "So tell me about Buck."

"Buck's married. In fact most of the guys in the band are. I'm the odd man out. Danny's wife even tours with us. She helps with all the arrangements, and we couldn't get by without her. You'll like her—she's a real mother hen. Keeps us all in line, and she's pretty nice to look at, too."

"Buck, is he cool? I've loved his music forever."

Tony thought he saw Rowdy's expression change, but in a flash his smile was back. "Buck is a talented musician, and music is first in his life. He's a little hard to get to know. But do yourself a favor. The best way to get along with Buck is to do your job. Don't try to make small talk with him or ask him for advice. He's not into being friendly. He has his own bus and he prefers solitude." Rowdy tipped his head at the waitress, who had just laid down the check.

Tony stuck a toothpick in his mouth and chewed on the end. "But he's so dynamic and outgoing at his concerts. I've never been to one, but I've seen them on TV and on the internet." Tony didn't want to gush about the man, but he couldn't stop thinking about finally meeting his father.

"He's a good actor—a decent guy. Just keep your distance and you'll be okay. And just between you and me, kid, I wrote 'Smooth Talker.'"

"You did? I love the guitar solo on that piece."

"Thanks."

They talked as they finished their meals. Then Rowdy retrieved his cowboy hat from the bench seat next to him and stood up, pocketing the receipt.

"But why didn't you get credit for writing it? I've got the sheet music for it and Buck's name is on it."

"Yeah, well, that's the way it works around here sometimes. Still want in?"

"Of course." Tony decided he could live with Buck taking credit for writing *his* songs, too, since it would be such an honor to have Buck sing them. Wouldn't it?

The rest of the afternoon, Tony hung out with the band members, with the exception of Buck. He'd expected Buck to at least come and meet him, but maybe Rowdy was waiting until after the concert to tell Buck about him. Tony would just have to be patient.

Soon, it was almost time for the concert. When the doors to Energy Solutions Arena opened, Tony took his seat and looked around for Kelli. At ten minutes to show time, the seat next to him was still empty. He'd called Kelli earlier to tell her he made the band. She didn't answer and he assumed she was out working, so he left her a message. He knew she'd planned on leaving Grouse Creek in plenty of time to make it. He craned his neck and searched the faces of people still coming in. *Where is she?* When they announced the band, she still wasn't there. Tony's heart sank.

When Buck appeared on stage, the audience rose to their feet. Cheers, screams, and chants filled the building. Every Buck

Branson show was an event, and this one was no exception. Buck swung in on a trapeze, flipped off, and landed on his feet to sing his first song. Tony watched Buck's every move as he sang. This was his father, and he felt proud. He could see the resemblance and wondered if Buck would ever notice that he looked like him, at least a little bit. They had the same smile, Tony thought. By the time he got to the third song, Tony sang along, stomping his feet. Then Tony felt someone slip into the seat next to him, and he turned his head in anticipation of seeing Kelli, but it wasn't her.

"Mom! What are you doing here?"

She smiled, and Tony had to admit she looked great. Her hair looked softer than the last time he'd seen her. He'd always preferred a more natural look, and his mother had always been just the opposite of that. Now she looked more like a mother and less like a lounge singer.

"Your friend Kelli called me and told me how much it would mean to you to have me here with you. Thanks so much, Tony. I had no idea you wanted me to come. I had to leave early this morning to make it. I'm so sorry I'm late."

Emotions swam through Tony's head. He was disappointed at first, but then his mom grabbed his hand. "This is so exciting," she shouted in his ear. "You made the band, didn't you? I know you did."

Tony wondered why Kelli had sent his mother. Then he remembered telling her how his mother had missed so many important milestones in his life. This was definitely one of those, and Kelli hadn't wanted Tony's mother to miss it. "Yes, I made it."

His mom reached into her purse, pulled out a tissue, and began to cry. Tony was surprised. She had cut hair all day and then left him alone at nights while she sang in bars and nightclubs. She'd usually been too busy or too tired to help him with his homework or to take him to the park to play. But here she was now, and she was crying.

At intermission, they could finally talk. "Make sure you don't say anything to Buck," Tony's mother said. "I mean, you know that's the deal, right? I got you the audition, but you can't ever say anything to him. They don't know you're my son, either. I sent them your audition tape but didn't tell them you're my son. I wanted you to know you got in because of you and not because of me or anyone else. Oh, it's just so great! I knew you could do it. I knew it when you were five years old and could actually carry a tune. Do you know how many five-year-olds can carry a tune? Do you remember when we used to sing together when we'd do the dishes? I always wanted to take you with me to sing in the clubs, but the clubs in town weren't the kind of places for my little boy."

"Yeah." Tony squeezed his mother's hand and gave her a half smile. "Thanks for coming." Tony glanced around at the large audience that was there to see the band he'd be playing in—there to see his dad.

"Darling, is that you?" a deep, mellow voice said from the stage.

Tony looked up to see Rowdy jump off the stage and head toward them. When he reached them, Rowdy grabbed Tony's mother and swung her around in a bear hug, lifting her off the floor. "I can't believe it's you after all these years. What's it been, twenty years now?"

"A few more than that," she said. She wore a black leather jacket, dangly gold earrings, and dark jeans.

"By the way, Tony, remember that song you sang today about your broken heart?"

"Sure."

"Well, this is the woman who broke mine and left me alone

with nothing but my guitar. I tell you, I never got over that." Rowdy's smile faded a bit.

Tony looked at his mother, who suddenly looked like a shy schoolgirl. She hugged Rowdy again. "Of course you got over it. Look at where you are now. We were just a two-pony show back then, and now—it's unbelievable."

"Tony, you wouldn't believe how much talent this woman has," Rowdy put in. "She had everything going for her and then she just up and disappeared one day. She got us our big break singing in Nashville, but then she was gone and we never heard from her again. When I got your audition tape from her, I couldn't believe it." Rowdy turned to look at her. "To hear from you again after all these years . . . and, Tony, I have to say that I knew if Cindy Colter said you were good, then you were good."

"Cindy Colter?" Tony said. His mother's last name was Stratton.

"Oh, you must be married now." Rowdy looked embarrassed. "What is your last name, anyway? I guess that was just a stage name."

"No, I'm not married."

"Mom, why didn't you tell me you're so good?"

"Mom? Did he just call you mom?" Rowdy cocked his head and stared at Tony. "Well, I'll be! No wonder this kid is so talented. He's the son of one of the must underrated singers of our time, Cindy Colter."

If he only knew who my father was, Tony thought, *then he'd* really *be impressed.* Tony still couldn't believe he would be singing and playing in this band. He hoped he wouldn't wake up soon and shatter the dream.

"So, Tony, why didn't you tell me who your mother was?"

Tony shrugged. "I hadn't gotten around to it."

"Cindy, if you're not married anymore, does that mean we

could get together after the show, maybe go out? I'd love to catch up on old times. You look even better than I remembered." Rowdy looked at Tony. "You can't believe how your mother had to fight the men off, especially You Know Who. But your mom wouldn't give him the time of day. When she and I started seeing each other, you should've seen him fume."

"Don't, Rowdy. Please."

Rowdy went on as if she hadn't spoken. "You were the gutsiest gal I ever knew. No woman since you has had the guts to say no to The Man. He's—oh, sorry, Tony." Rowdy looked down and shook his head. "I don't want to taint your image of the almighty king. Really, though, Cindy, I have to hand it to you to quit when you did. It took a lot of courage."

Cindy put her arm around Rowdy's shoulder, and Tony saw tears in her eyes. Maybe she now realized how much she'd given up.

"You're giving me more credit that I deserve," she said. "I didn't quit, Rowdy. Buck fired me."

"He what?" Rowdy stopped talking and took Cindy's hand. "He fired you because he was jealous of me—jealous that you chose me over him! I wish you'd told me. I could've been there, for you. I could've—"

Tears flowed down Cindy's heavily made-up cheeks. "Stop, please. That wasn't it. He fired me because I—I—I was pregnant. He didn't want me ruining the image he was trying to create."

Tony watched Rowdy's face as he looked at Tony, closely scrutinizing him. Now Tony felt ashamed, ashamed to carry the blood of such a hated man, a man who had caused his mother so much grief. And Buck had known Cindy carried his child, and still he threw her out on the street. In fact, he threw her out of the band *because* of the child! What kind of man would do that?

"How will I be able to work with—" Tony started. "I'm not sure I—"

But Rowdy wasn't listening. He reeled back, his tear-filled eyes darting wildly from Tony's mother back to Tony. Tony couldn't imagine the betrayal Rowdy must now feel toward his mother. She had cheated on him with his boss! But then why was Rowdy crying? He should be lashing out at her. She had betrayed him. Buck had betrayed him. Could Rowdy continue to sing with such a man? Could he continue to let Buck take credit for his songs?

"I'm so sorry, Rowdy," Cindy said between sobs. "Do you see how I couldn't tell you? I knew he'd fire you, too. I couldn't let that happen to you. I couldn't let you not have all of this." Tony's mom motioned to the stage, the lights, the people. "You have everything."

"No, Cindy. I don't. You should've asked me what I wanted. I could've had a family. I could've had a son." He looked at Tony again, then shook his head and walked back toward the stage, where the band was starting to take their places again.

"Rowdy!" Cindy shouted, but the swell of excitement for the band drowned her out. She started to sob again, so Tony put his arm around her, not sure what else to do.

The band struck up a tune and Buck came in riding a black horse. Tony tried to smile and enjoy the show, waiting to see Rowdy come back out and play the guitar, but Rowdy didn't return to the stage.

Finally, Tony grabbed his mother's hand. "Let's go find Rowdy. Let's go find my father."

Sam and Stacey,

AMAZING NEWS! Tony made the Buck Branson band. I was supposed to go with him to the concert, but I had an idea. I hope it worked out!!! I still haven't heard. Anyway, I'll let you know when I find out. I'm feeling much better about life. I might even sign up for music lessons when I get back to Burley. I'm going to check to see if that basement apartment is available where I lived when I worked at the bank. Wow, that was forever ago. Do you think you would have fallen in love with each other if it hadn't been for my problems? ☺ *Ha, I like to think I had a small part in it. Stacey, you were right about one thing, but I can't tell you yet.*

Love ya, Aunt Kelli

Thirty-Six

NORMA SIGHED. SHE MUST HAVE CALLED EVERY homeless and women's shelter in the state, but she had gotten absolutely nowhere. Because of privacy and safety issues, no one could tell her if they'd as much as heard of Cadence.

"Well, can you give a message to Cadence if she is there or if she comes in?" Norma had asked in desperation. "Tell her Norma Weaver in Grouse Creek wants her to come live with her. Ask her to please call me as soon as she gets this message." Then Norma would leave her phone number and hang up.

Now she sat waiting, willing Cadence to call. While she waited near the telephone, Norma crocheted, adding to her stash of gifts for the baby. Already she'd crocheted seven pairs of booties, so the baby would have a different color for each day of the week. And when Mabel cleaned out LaRue's closets, she found twenty-three skeins of yarn, mostly light blue, yellow, and green. Norma held the colors together and decided even LaRue would say they didn't look unseemly together, so she started on a baby afghan.

Norma also planned a little dinner celebration for Tony. He had stayed in Salt Lake for a few days after the concert, but she expected him tonight. Tony getting into Buck Branson's band was the most exciting news they'd had in Grouse Creek since Janice and Tom Watkins brought home their adopted baby after ten years of trying to have one of their own. Norma invited Jay and Diane from the Box C, Herman and Maggie, Jean Brooks, the bishop and his wife, plus Kelli, of course. Norma didn't know what to do about Jamie. She couldn't invite her because she planned to invite Kelli, but she didn't see how she could leave Jamie out. While Norma stewed about it, Kelli stopped by to help her decorate and announced she couldn't come to the party. That solved that problem, although not in the way Norma had hoped.

Norma decided it was time to tell the girl just what she thought. "Kelli, I've been thinking about you ever since I took to my bed after LaRue's passing." Tony had come to visit her once when she'd been down. He'd told her about seeing Kelli for the first time, helping her escape from the clutches of a powerful and dangerous cult, and about dancing, hiking, and fishing with her in Montana. Tony also had told Norma about Kelli's brother Sam and how he'd taken care of her all of her life, and how Kelli was searching for someone as heroic and kind as her brother.

"Here." Norma handed Kelli a package of colorful balloons. "Blow these up for me, please. I've been blowing balloons until I nearly passed out. Guess I need someone with extra good lungs."

Kelli sat down on the sofa and began to inflate a blue balloon.

Norma cleared her throat. "You don't know this, but Tony and I have done a lot of talking. Actually, he did the talking and I listened. He's a fine boy. I don't know when I've met a finer or more talented person."

Kelli tied the end of the balloon and set it on the sofa. "I'm not sure what you're getting at."

Norma set down her crocheting and gazed out the window, then looked back at Kelli. "Tell me about Sam, your brother."

"Oh, Sam is the most amazing person in the world! He's smart, strong, and funny, and he's saved my life in more ways than one. No matter what I'm going through in my life, he's there to help."

"Would you call him a hero?"

"He's definitely my hero."

"Now tell me about Tony."

Kelli smiled broadly. "Tony is so cute, sweet, fun to be with, talented, kind-hearted, and . . . "

"Is he heroic?"

"Oh, definitely. He saved my life. Didn't I tell you that? A man tried to kill me, and if it wasn't for Tony's quick thinking—"

"So he's everything your brother is, more or less?"

"Yeah, I guess so." Kelli frowned slightly.

Norma stood up, took the three balloons Kelli had blown up, and taped them to the dining room chairs. Kelli followed her, blowing up a yellow balloon.

"Would you say you'd like to marry someone like your brother?" Norma asked.

"Yes, I would, but more than that I'd like to *deserve* to marry someone like my brother."

Norma put her hand up to stop Kelli from going on. "'Yes' is enough for now. Would you kiss Sam, your brother, on the lips?"

"Eew!" Kelli looked disgusted.

"Would you kiss Tony on the lips?"

Kelli cocked her head as if thinking about it. "Yeah."

"So have you kissed him? I mean really kissed him, not just a peck on the cheek."

"Of course not. I know a lot of girls don't feel this way, but I like the guy to be the one to make that move. Besides, it's not that way between us. Tony's always been like a brother to me."

"Exactly, but you want someone like your brother. See, sweetie, you've got this mixed up in your head. In Montana when you really needed Sam, someone else came to your rescue instead. This time Tony helped you, and your mind told you that only brothers could save you. Because you're mixed up, you think you can't feel romantically for Tony. I've been mixed up before about all kinds of things, so don't be embarrassed about it. Life is about untwisting the twists and fixing the mixes."

"I don't know. How long did it take you to figure this out?"

"A long time. You told me you'd do anything for me, and I've got a big favor to ask." Norma pulled a roll of crepe paper from a grocery bag. "Help me tack this up on the window."

"Of course, but that's not a very big favor." Kelli set the balloon down.

"No, certainly not, dear. That's a little favor. The big favor is that the very next time you see Tony, I want you to grab him, hold him tight, and give him a big kiss, and then call me and tell me if you still think of him as a brother. Because I'd bet money—actually I already have bet money on this—that you and Tony are meant for each other."

Kelli laughed and taped the crepe paper to the edge of the windowsill. "I guess you want this draped across the window."

"Oh, whatever you think. I'll leave you to finish the decorations while I finish the pies." Norma hummed as she cored, peeled, and sliced several large apples.

Mabel busied herself at LaRue's house making cookies. Norma hoped she had convinced her to move into LaRue's house at least temporarily, if not forever.

Norma looked at the clock on the kitchen stove. She had one hour to finish up before Tony's arrival. Norma had told him to stop by her house as soon as he got to Grouse Creek. She'd told him it was important, but she hoped she hadn't given away the secret.

Norma beamed as she checked on the honey-baked ham. Next, she decided to call LaRue to remind her to bring her rolls. No one made rolls like LaRue. Then Norma remembered with a start that LaRue wouldn't be able to make rolls; death had seen to that surely enough. Norma felt a catch in her throat. She glanced at the clock again and saw there was still time to set the table with the finest china. She pulled the plastic cases out of the hutch and unzipped them, then removed the dishes she needed and carried them to the table. One of Norma's mother's nicest lace tablecloths adorned the wooden table. Perhaps by next year, Norma would be good enough at crocheting to make one like it.

"Okay, all done. Anything else I can do before I leave?" Kelli asked as she taped the last balloon to the doorframe.

"I guess that's it. Are you sure you can't come? Tony will be so disappointed."

"Not this time. I don't want to mix the mixes, as you said, and Jamie will be here, so . . . "

"Oh, dear, I'm sorry. I didn't know how to get out of not—"

"It's okay. I've got plenty of time to see Tony again. Besides the last time we parted, things were still a little funny between us. I'd rather see him without an audience, if you know what I mean." Kelli put her hand on the doorknob and glanced around at the decorations.

"Oh, good, then you'll put my experiment to the test. That's wonderful!" Norma beamed, knowing it was just a matter of time before Kelli saw things for what they were.

Kelli blushed. "I didn't mean that. Well, I'll see you later."

After watching Kelli close the door behind her, Norma went upstairs to get dressed for the celebration. She glanced at the baby booties scattered across the bed covers, then gathered them and stuffed them into LaRue's hand basket. After she was ready, she grasped the stair rail and headed back down the stairs.

The smell of burned bread permeated the room. Norma rushed into the kitchen and pulled the forgotten rolls out of the oven. "Oh, dear! Oh, dear! Well, let's see how the ham looks." She lifted the ceramic lid and peered inside. The meat was a nice golden color. The smell wafted in the room as Mabel came in through the back door holding a large tray piled high with an assortment of cookies.

"Is Cadence here yet?"

"Oh, no, I haven't been able to find her yet," Norma said disappointedly.

Mabel set the cookies on the counter. "But you called all those places and left messages. Surely she got your message by now." Norma turned back to the ham and poured some glaze over it. She felt a lump growing in her throat at the thought that neither Cadence nor Kelli would be at this special dinner for Tony.

The doorbell rang.

"Could you get that, Mabel?" Norma said.

"I think you'd better get it." Mabel winked at her.

It was still a little early yet for guests to arrive, but Norma scurried to the door and opened it. But instead of Tony or one of the invited guests, a young woman stood there holding a baby. Her black hair was cut close to her scalp, her pale face drawn and frightened, and she was so thin that she reminded Norma of a Holocaust survivor. She cocked one hip out and held the infant in the crook of her arms. Norma stared at the girl's pixy-like features, and her big brown eyes drew her in.

Norma gasped. "Oh, mercy, it's you!"

Thirty-Seven

CADENCE LOOKED INSIDE THE HOUSE UNCERTAINLY.

"Oh, if only Wes could see you!" Norma said excitedly. "Come in, come in."

Cadence wore an army green T-shirt with the sleeves ripped out. Her shorts were cut-off jeans several sizes too big with a wide belt around her hips. Norma didn't want to frighten the girl, but she moved toward her and carefully embraced her. She felt Cadence step back. The baby squirmed between the two of them. "I'm so glad to see you." Norma felt tears gather in her eyes.

The young woman stepped into the house, then looked around shyly at the decorations and the table set for company. "You're having a party?"

Mabel came in with her tray of cookies. "Yes, of course we're having a party—we've been expecting you." Mabel pushed the cookies toward Cadence. "Here, have one of these while we wait for everyone else to get here. Can we see the little tyke?"

Cadence tossed a blanket onto the floor and set the baby on it. Cadence reached for a cookie, took a bite, smiled, and sat down on the edge of the sofa as if she would spring up and leave at any minute. The baby lay on a blanket, not a soft baby blanket, but an army green wool one. Norma felt her skin itch just at the sight of it. *Oh, dear, all this time I should've been working on the afghan so it would be ready in time.* The baby's jet black hair stood straight out from its head. The baby stared at something on the ceiling.

"What a beautiful baby." Norma felt as if her heart would burst. She couldn't tell if the baby was a boy or a girl by the way it was dressed, so she asked, "What's the baby's name?"

"Wesley," Cadence answered.

Norma eyes filled with tears. "You named him Wesley. That's just lovely."

"Her, I named her Wesley. I wanted to name her after her great-grandpa. And the name fits her, besides."

Norma crouched down to be close to the baby. "Oh, lookie there, sweetie. Just look at you." Wesley grasped Norma's finger. "You're a strong little thing, aren't you? Just like your great-grandpa."

Then Norma managed something she hadn't been able to do in a long time. She sat on the floor and straddled her legs like she used to do when rolling a ball to her toddlers. Norma didn't know how on earth she'd ever get up again, but she wanted to be close to little Wesley.

"By the way dear," Mabel said, sitting down on the sofa, "I'm Mabel, Norma's sister. And she's Norma, your grandmother, on the floor with her great-granddaughter."

Norma couldn't believe it. This was her first great-granddaughter. "Tell me, Cadence—or would you rather be called Katie?—I've been dying to know how you and Kevin got lost from each other."

Cadence ran her fingers through her short hair. "Either one is fine, but most people call me Cadence now. About Kevin, I guess it was all a misunderstanding. That's what Kevin calls it. I stopped and talked to him in the county jail and he encouraged me to come out here. Said you were the most understanding women on the planet. Out at the Sun Tunnels, he was just plain rude, if you know what I mean. I mean, we'd just had this romantic evening and he proposed to me and all. Moon married us, although I'm not sure if that's legal or anything . . ."

"But you can fix all that when he gets out of prison, right?" Mabel asked.

"Uh-uh. We're not back together yet. I mean, it's cool, everything he did for me. Kevin really did help me. I guess you could say he saved my life, and Wesley's, too. But he has yet to come up with a good explanation for what happened out there."

"So what did happen?" Mabel took a bite of a roll she'd snitched from the kitchen, and Norma noticed how hard it was for her to bite through it. It would still take practice for her to be able to bake rolls like LaRue's, though at least she hadn't burned this second batch. Maybe next week she could try again.

Cadence looked over at the table, and Norma realized she must be hungry. "I still don't know what happened for sure. I mean, here we were just married and then I saw him go off with one of Moon's friends, and when I really needed him, I couldn't find him. I thought I was going into labor—turned out to be false—but how was I to know, being my first and all? So I got scared."

Cadence sighed. "I was crying and feeling these pains and they were coming regularly. I didn't have a clock to time them, but they felt like the real thing, so when they got real intense I told Moon he had to take me to the hospital. We looked for Kevin and couldn't find him, but we had to go. When we got halfway there the pains stopped so we drove back to the tunnels and looked for Kevin, but only found Dawdle, Moon's friend. Anyway, Dawdle was asleep in one of the tunnels, but he said Kevin took off and left him, and he was really ticked. Kevin talks like I'm the love of his life, but he ditched me when I really needed him. When I finally did go into labor a few days after that, I got some girl who hung with Moon to take me in. She just dropped me off at the front door of the hospital. Kevin says Dawdle or someone beat him up."

"That's true—we saw him," Mabel said.

Wesley stuck out her lower lip and started to whimper, so Norma scooped her off the floor and held her close. The baby calmed down as Norma rocked back and forth.

"You know, Cadence," Mabel said, "maybe you ought to hear Kevin out. He's made some big mistakes, but it took guts to turn himself in to the police. And getting beat up wasn't exactly his fault."

Cadence smiled and her eyes took on a new brightness. "Yeah, I've kind of been thinking that too. Kevin can be really sweet."

"At times I felt a real connection with that boy," Norma said nostalgically. "That's why I just hated spraying him with pepper spray."

Cadence giggled. "So when are we going to eat? I'm starving."

"I'm so glad to hear it," Norma said. "I mean, because I made all this food." What really made her happy was that Cadence felt comfortable enough in her home to tell her she was starving.

Someone knocked on the door and Norma went to get it, expecting Tony, but instead nearly everyone else she'd invited stood on the porch. She welcomed them in and hoped Tony would arrive soon.

When Tony pulled into Grouse Creek, he noticed a few cars at Norma's house. Even though she'd left him a message that she wanted him to stop by, he didn't want to interrupt her company, so instead he drove to Kelli's cabin. He'd thought about her the entire day and couldn't wait to tell her everything that had happened. He also wanted to thank her for sending his mother to the concert in her place.

His grin grew broader by the second as he knocked on the door. He wished he'd thought to buy flowers. Glancing around, he saw some black-eyed Susans growing along Herman's back fence. He quickly picked a handful, and then ran back to the porch. Maggie would understand, he hoped. By now Kelli had opened the door. She squealed when she saw him and practically jumped into his arms. He dropped the flowers to catch her.

"Ah!" she screamed. "I can't believe it. I can't believe it. It's so totally cool." Kelli planted a kiss on Tony's cheek, then dropped out of his arms and grabbed his hands. "Tell me everything," she said, leading him into the cabin.

Tony sat down in a chair and Kelli plopped herself down on her bed. He grinned and began with the story of his audition. Kelli kept nodding and smiling and clapping her hands with excitement.

"And then the concert, whoa, it was so great. And did you know my mom is a really good singer? I mean really good. She practically ran Buck Branson's band in the beginning. Rowdy said they owe a lot of their success to her."

"Really?"

"Thanks for having her come, Kelli. It was great."

"I'm glad you were cool with her being there. I've been nervous about it, wondering if I did the right thing."

"It could've backfired, you know."

"I know and then you'd end up hating me forever." Kelli

smiled. "So tell me about Buck. What was it like to meet your father?"

Tony swallowed the lump in his throat. "Buck is the biggest fake to ever walk the earth."

"Oh, no. I'm so sorry."

"No, it's okay. I don't care about Buck. I never even got to talk to him."

Kelli looked confused.

"Turns out Buck's not my father. Rowdy is. And Rowdy's great. We're both ticked at my mom right now because she lied to us. She lied to me because she thought I'd really work hard at the guitar if I thought Buck Branson was my father, and she lied to Rowdy so he could go somewhere with his music. But she denied both of us the opportunity to be a family. We're going to try and make up for all that now."

Then Tony started to cry, really cry, like he hadn't done since he was a little boy. If he'd been with anyone else, he would've hidden his tears, but he knew Kelli would understand. When he looked up at her, he saw tears rolling down her face, too. She didn't say anything; she just got off the bed and squeezed into the overstuffed chair next to Tony. His heart raced as she took his hand in hers and leaned her head on his shoulder.

"Guess I should cry more often if it gets this kind of reaction," was all he could think to say as he put his arms around her.

For several minutes, Tony simply enjoyed the feeling of Kelli in his arms. Finally, he said, "I'd like you to meet my mom. You know, I always thought I came second in her life, but it wasn't like that. Buck fired her when she refused to have an abortion and because she wouldn't sleep with him. Can you believe that? The family-values guy himself! My mom, who doesn't believe in any religion, refused to have an abortion. I'm proud of her, and it's a good feeling to be grateful instead of resentful."

"I'd love to meet her. She must be an amazing woman." Kelli suddenly tensed in his arms. "Do you mind if I give you something?"

"Anything you give, is something I want," Tony said with a wink.

"Well, it's sort of from Norma. I mean, she's the one who told me to give this to you. Close your eyes and don't peek."

Tony closed his eyes and waited. He felt Kelli wiggle in the chair, and then he felt her lips on his. She kissed him and he kissed her back, drawing her even closer to him.

When she pulled away, Tony opened his eyes and saw a surprised look on her face. He laughed. "I hope that wasn't from Norma."

Kelli smiled. Tony loved the way her eyes crinkled when she smiled.

"Norma, well, she helped me figure some stuff out," Kelli explained. "She's the one who told me to kiss you."

"Let me get this straight. Norma told you to kiss me like that?"

Kelli raised her eyebrows. "She told me I've got it stuck in my head that you can't be anything but a brotherly type. She said I'm all mixed up because you saved me when I was in trouble, and it's always been my brother that helped me out of a jam. She said my brain told me that only brothers could be all the great things you are, so my brain refused to see it any other way. She asked me if I'd kiss Sam on the lips and when I said of course not, she asked if I'd kiss you and I said I would. She told me to do it, then, not on the cheek, and not a peck, but a full-blown kiss, because she told me that I was in love with you and she knew it."

Tony couldn't believe it. "So what are you going to tell Norma?"

"I'm going to tell her she was right."

"Do me a favor," Tony said happily, squeezing her hand tighter. "Give me another kiss, but this time let it be just you giving it to me and not Norma. Not that she's not a dear—"

Kelli put her finger up to his lips. Then he leaned toward her and they kissed again.

Thirty-Eight

Back in the Saddle

by Grouse Creek Correspondent Norma Weaver

This correspondent apologizes for the lack of news in the past four months. So much has happened! With the death of first Wesley Weaver and then LaRue Hansey Mortenson, the Grouse Creek cemetery has seen a little too much activity for this correspondent's liking. Thus, it is no surprise that Norma has been down and unable to write. But she is back, thanks to the constant care of her loving sister Mabel and a healthy dose of LaRue's famous chokecherry jam, guaranteed to cure the sick and afflicted. And then, dear readers, life just got so full that this column got a little forgotten. But here is a bit about what has happened.

Norma got out of her funk without a moment to spare as Cadence Huff, Wesley and Norma's long-lost grandchild, has come from afar to Grouse Creek to stay until she gets back on her feet, which may be never if Norma has anything to say about it. That is, Norma hopes Cadence gets back on her feet but never leaves. Cadence, also known as Katie, has brought along her spanking-new beautiful baby girl, named Wesley after her grandfather. Even though Wesley is usually a boy's name, it fits this little tyke, who is a Weaver through and through. She has thick black hair that only stays in place with a little hair pomade, a secret her great-grandpa Wes used, and she coos and hums just like her him. Unfortunately, Grandpa Wes passed on before he got to meet his namesake. But fortunately, Norma has learned that Grandpa Wes is as pleased as punch about Cadence and her baby and has taking up humming again on the other side.

A baby shower given by the two Hansey sisters (and attended by all of the women in Grouse Creek, except for Jean Brooks, who is visiting her sister down south) set the young one off on a good foot for at least a year. A favorite gift was hand-crocheted cowboy boots by Jean Brooks, who sent them up with the UPS man. With perfect timing he delivered them before Cadence opened her last gift: a month's supply of diapers, the kind you just toss out with the trash. This correspondent can't imagine such a wonder. If they had been available when she was a young mother, she imagines she might have taken up golf with all her spare time.

The Watkins' family enjoyed a pleasant surprise last Thursday at the sale in Burley, selling their calves for more than they expected. Jed took the whole family out to dinner at Price's Café to celebrate. Ann said she plans to buy a new dress to wear to church as her others are "threadbare and outdated." Jed said, "We're mighty grateful to the Lord for our abundant blessings, and the ban on Canadian beef didn't hurt none, neither." He plans to get the oil changed on his Ford pickup and have the tires rotated.

Unfortunately, in early September the town enjoyed the Labor Day celebration without Norma, but Norma hopes to attend the Deer Hunt celebration at the school and will make cinnamon rolls for the bake sale. Mabel will, as usual, contribute several dozen of her cookies. Last year her cookies sold out before the sale actually began, bought up by the teacher. Norma and Mabel will also contribute a jar of LaRue's chokecherry jam. This should bring quite a nice price, since LaRue is unable to make any more, due to her death. Word has it that Herman Anders plans to get there at the crack of dawn and wait for the sale to start so no one can beat him out of the starting gate to buy the jam. He even threatened to "lasso" the competition. Last year's proceeds from the sale bought two new basketballs and three books for the school library. This year the school hopes to buy a world globe for the big room and a map of the Middle East for the library. "The students need to see what's what and where's where, and that there is a difference between Iran and Iraq," the teacher said. Norma doesn't know how much maps cost, but the jar of jam alone ought to be enough.

Fortunately, Kevin Frazier is expected to get out of jail by Valentine's Day, Kevin is the young man who stole Norma's car last June, but although she never thought she'd say it, she has forgiven him for the crime, since he is paying the time and has said many times how sorry he is. Cadence has been corresponding with Kevin and feels he's made some positive changes in his life. When asked what she thinks of Kevin now, she says, "He's sweet." And indeed he is, writing her love letters from his jail cell nearly every day. They arrive in weekly packets. Cadence looks forward to the day she can see Kevin without barriers.

And, finally, the co-op is running a special on hand-crocheted baby booties. If you hurry you can get a pair for three dollars. Unfortunately, they'll probably only fit preemies and babies up to one month old.

NORMA QUICKLY SCANNED HER ARTICLE. THERE were so many other things she'd wanted to add about the last four months: how nice it was to have Christmas with a baby in the house, how great it was to have Mabel finally move from Montello to LaRue's house in Grouse Creek, how easy is was to love Cadence, and how well Cadence fit into the community, taking over Wes's horses as if she was born to it.

Life felt comfortable, though Norma would always miss LaRue and especially Wes. Cadence and Norma had pored through Wes's letters, journals, photos, and mementos until Cadence felt she knew her grandfather, and until Norma felt she finally knew her husband.

They pasted some loose snapshots in an album Cadence had made. For the cover Cadence hot-glued a piece of LaRue's embroidery onto a binder. The unfinished embroidery, probably meant to become a pillowcase, was of a bluebird. Norma had explained how the mountain bluebirds migrated through Grouse Creek in late spring. Wes loved those birds.

Norma made a second book, wanting to preserve some of Wes's memorabilia for their children. She ordered archive-quality pages and sleeves for the books, so the photos and letters wouldn't deteriorate any more than they already had. Cadence and Norma read Wes's war letters together and slipped them into the preservation envelopes.

Cadence's hair had grown some, but it was still short. Each morning she took Wes's pomade and ran a little through her hair until it stuck up like a porcupine's. On anyone else, the hairstyle would have seemed too masculine, but Cadence was anything but masculine. Her voice sounded like that of a breathless girl who had just been swung around the dance floor. She had unusually large eyes with long eyelashes and full lips. If it hadn't been for her starved look, she could be a Parisian model, although Norma had heard that the starved look was in style and that some were even resorting to surgery to get it.

Norma tried to get Cadence to eat foods high in fat and sugar. Mabel made sure the cookie jar was filled to overflowing so the temptation would always be there. But even with all that, Cadence failed to gain an ounce. Norma, on the other hand, gained a good eight to ten pounds, and one might be forced to describe her as "chubby," although she preferred the term "healthy."

When they finished the scrapbooks, Norma closed the one with the bluebird cover and handed it to Cadence. "What?" Cadence said. "This is yours."

Norma pushed the album back. "I want you to have it. I don't have any need for these things anymore. They've told me all I need to know. There's one for my children and one for you, since you never had the chance to know him in person. And Wesley will need it to get to know her namesake."

"Cool. Thanks." Cadence hugged the book to her chest. "Wait here. I've got something to show you." She disappeared up the stairs. Wesley sat in her high chair tossing blocks onto the kitchen floor and squealing with delight every time she heard one hit the floor.

"Grab your coat. We're going for a quick drive," Cadence said when she returned with a snowsuit for the baby.

As they drove along in the Subaru a few minutes later, Norma couldn't imagine where Cadence was taking her. Soon, however, they passed under the gates at the cemetery.

"Why are we here?" Norma asked, but Cadence just smiled as she parked the car.

Without a word, they trudged through the snow between the rows of headstones to Wes's grave in the far corner. The headstone Norma had ordered had finally been delivered and set in place the month before. She'd seen it, of course, and was pleased with how it turned out; the frieze of horses running across the top was so fitting.

With effort, Norma bent down to brush the snow off the granite stone. She placed her fingers on the engraving and traced the words. "Wonderful husband, father, grandfather, and friend to all."

When she stood back up, Cadence handed her a letter. She unfolded it and recognized Wes's neat handwriting. "I received this in the mail the other day. I couldn't believe it. I guess it's been forwarded several times, but by some kind of miracle it finally found me."

"I didn't think he had a chance to write one before . . ."

"He was planning to write again, you'll see." Cadence set Wesley down at her feet, and the baby played happily in the soft snow. "I wasn't sure you'd want to see it. I was afraid it would hurt you all over again, but I've changed my mind."

"Of course, I want to read it, no matter what," Norma said, tears forming in her eyes. She opened it and began to read aloud.

Dear Cadence,

What a thrill to hear from you. I've often wondered what happened to your mother. I wish I had managed to stay in touch with her. Nothing would please me more than for you to come here to stay. However, I need some time to prepare my good wife. She doesn't know anything about your mother. You must think me a terrible man not to have told her. Believe me, I wanted to numerous times, but I never got the right chance. I mean, I never took the opportunity. Now we are old and I know it's way past time to do that.

I'm a simple man with a simple life. Norma and I have raised five wonderful children. We live in the northwest desert of Utah in a town called Grouse Creek. We used to own a large cattle ranch, but we've given most of that up and now live off what we've accumulated. I do keep a few horses that need to be ridden regularly, and I maintain a small ranch.

You said you've always loved horses even though you grew up in the city. Nothing would please me more than to give you one of my horses. Her name is Junie Moon, since she was born in early June at the full moon. She's a registered sorrel mare and throws fine colts.

I haven't done a lot with my life, but overall, it's been good to me—doing just what I had always dreamed of. Norma is a fine woman. I'm sure she'll be happy to meet you also. She is the light of my life. Forgive me for stalling. You'll hear from me as soon as I've spoken to my sweetheart—I promise.

Norma folded the letter, slipped it into the envelope, and handed it back to Cadence. Norma's heart swelled with joy as if Cadence were her own grandchild, and she'd come to think of her just as much so as any of her own flesh and blood. Wes had been, if not a happy man, at least a satisfied one. He loved his children, his community, his God, and his country. But most especially he loved Norma. There was no longer any doubt about that, and when Norma thought about it, there never really had been.

In her pink snowsuit, Wesley crawled to her great-grandfather's grave and sat on top of it. She giggled and patted the snow, then grabbed some snow and threw it. Cadence bent over to pick her up.

"No, let her stay. Wes would love to have her here. Grandpa Wes is buried here, Wesley." Norma bent over and whispered to the child, hoping to impress on her that this place was special.

Wesley cooed, chattered, and then, as if she understood, began to hum.

Thirty-Nine

Sam and Stacey,

I'm so excited to meet Sammie. I can't believe little Stacey could have a nearly eight-pound baby. Wow! I'll come by after the concert. It's no joke. I really am in love. I'll tell you all about it! You guys are awesome. I can't wait to bring Tony by to meet my niece.

Love, love, love, Aunt Kelli

IT WAS HARD FOR TONY TO FIGURE OUT WHAT WAS a bigger thrill—seeing his mother and father marry in a quiet ceremony back home in Bozeman, Montana, or forming a country-western band with them called Rowdy's Rebels. But undoubtedly the greatest blessing was that Kelli Carson was now a part of his life, not as just a friend, but as his girlfriend. Six months had passed since the night a kiss changed everything.

Many people judged Tony Stratton a fool. He'd given up a sure thing with a top country band in exchange for singing in small venues, roadhouse cafés, theatres, and high school auditoriums. But to Tony, his career had taken a pleasant turn and he couldn't think of anything he'd rather be doing. It didn't matter to him that he'd probably never be famous, as long as he was able to make a decent living and do what he loved. Plus he knew this quieter lifestyle would give him time to work on his other dream, owning a ranch. He'd call it the Rowdy Rebel Ranch, and the brand would be a triple R.

At ten minutes to curtain time, Tony sat down on a metal folding chair backstage and started tuning his guitar.

Rowdy walked by and ruffled his hair. "When you going to get a haircut, kid?"

It was a standing joke between the two of them, and Tony looked up and smiled.

Rowdy went over to make last-minute preparations, testing the sound system. Tony guessed his mother was in the restroom touching up her makeup. Rowdy had no trouble attracting an audience. They'd been playing to packed houses every concert since the split-up had hit the news. At first people came out of curiosity, but word had spread and now they were able to attract an audience because they made good music.

Cindy trained Kelli on the business side of things, and before long Kelli was doing most of the management: setting up interviews, gigs, and recording sessions, and handling publicity. She didn't have to travel with the band because she could do the job from her apartment in Burley, Idaho.

Rowdy pulled up a chair next to Tony. Tony nodded a greeting but kept playing.

"Sure wish I could play like that," Rowdy said. "You play a mean guitar."

Tony laughed, thinking he was joking.

"No, I'm serious. You play better than I ever have—plus you've got the pipes."

"As if you didn't."

The closer they came to curtain time, the more nervous Tony became, because Kelli would be in the audience tonight. Since the band had been touring for a month straight, he hadn't seen her for a couple of weeks. Tonight, they played in Burley. Tony could hear the audience and wondered if she had arrived yet.

"You feeling okay, son?" Rowdy asked. "You look pale."

"I'm okay." Tony licked his lips as his fingers flew along the fret board. *This is ridiculous,* he thought. *Kelli has heard me play before.* He tried to tell himself that tonight was no different than sitting across from her in her cabin back in Grouse Creek or standing outside her door serenading her. "I wrote a song I want to sing tonight. Hope that's okay." Tony heard the quiver in his own voice.

Rowdy's brows furrowed but he nodded his head. "You know you can sing anything you want—this is your band too. I'll never stand in your way. Would you like me to introduce it?"

"Yeah, that would be nice. It's called "Caught between a Dream and a Nightmare," and I either want to do it first or last—whatever you think."

Rowdy scratched his chin and smoothed his graying hair. "Let's do it first."

"Sorry to spring it on you so late in the game. I just wrote it last night, so there wasn't much time to warn you."

"Hey, I've been playing for thirty years for an inflexible man, so it feels good to stretch and bend a little, and do whatever we want." Rowdy adjusted his bolo tie, grabbed his hat, put it on, and asked, "How do I look? It's time."

"Well, Dad, you're looking good and you're good-looking.

There's a difference, you know. My friend Norma told me that."

"Who?"

Tony waved his hand. "Never mind. I'll introduce you to her. I think she's coming tonight."

The curtains rose and Rowdy stepped out onto the high school stage. Tony watched him and wondered if this was difficult for him to do after playing at arenas and football stadiums all over the country, but Rowdy said he'd waited his whole life to do this.

Suddenly, Tony's mother stood next to him. Rowdy introduced her as Cindy Robinson and she walked out on the stage. This wasn't the way they normally did the introductions—usually those came later—but Rowdy had obviously switched things around so Tony could play his song first. Soon, he heard Rowdy begin to introduce him.

"Folks, if you don't mind I'm going to take a minute here to introduce you to one of the finest musicians I know. As you may have heard, I broke from Buck Branson's band last year. I had the pleasure of meeting Tony Stratton and hearing him audition for Buck Branson's band. Tony did an amazing thing—something that gave me the courage to form this band. He turned down an opportunity to sing with the biggest country sensation in the nation—said good-bye to a lot of money and fame to boot, to play with the biggest risk in the business. And I don't mean Cindy. So join me in welcoming Tony Stratton, my son, singing his own song, 'Caught between a Dream and a Nightmare.'"

Rowdy's voice cracked a little on the word "son," and Tony grinned. He cleared his throat, adjusted his cowboy hat, and then stepped out on stage to loud applause.

Tony swallowed, cleared his throat again, and said, "I'd like to dedicate this song to Norma Weaver, whose advice to a friend of mine changed everything." He played the introduction, an instrumental melody, and then began to sing the mellow song.

Dreams have a way of changing
Of disappearing and re-arranging.
I've found myself caught between a dream and
a nightmare . . .
My nightmare changed to a dream
The night a kiss changed everything.
If you hear anything in this song I sing,
Know dreams change and change and change
again.
Folks you thought were strangers turn out
to be family,
Folks you thought were friends turn out to be
lovers,
And folks you thought were enemies turn out to
be friends.
Nothing is sure in the end.
And stuff you thought only happened in dreams
happens for real.
And stuff you thought was real
Turns out to only be a nightmare.
I'll sing this little song, forever the day long,
Trying to make sense of it all.
I'm caught between a dream and a nightmare.

As Tony continued to sing, he tried to squint past the bright lights to find Kelli in the audience. He couldn't see her, and he began to panic as he searched the crowd. Then on the front row, he spotted Cadence and Kevin next to Mabel and Norma. Next to Norma sat Kelli, her face radiant.

Tony went on.

So as I come to the end of this song,
You'll find it isn't the end at all.
And maybe these last words don't quite work,
But they are the ones that I want most to say . . .

Tony said a silent prayer, then stopping singing and jumped off the stage. He walked to where Kelli sat, her eyes wide. He got down on one knee and continued to strum his guitar. "Kelli Carson, will you marry me?" he said it quietly, blocking out the lights and the crowd. It was just Tony, his guitar, and his girl.

"Yes, of course I will. You're my very best friend." Kelli threw her arms around Tony and smothered him with hugs and kisses until he finally just set his guitar down.

When the audience finally realized what was happening, they stood and clapped. Rowdy's Rebels had gotten a few standing ovations before, but this was the first one they'd gotten after the very first song.

Carole Thayne Warburton and her husband Mick taught together in a K-10 two-room school in the remote town of Grouse Creek, Utah, where she acquired much of the material for her novels. Carole graduated from Utah State University with bachelor's degrees in both art education and English literature. She and her husband now live in Avon, Utah, surrounded by the mountains. In addition to writing, Carole enjoys creating unique pieces of pottery. She is an avid lover of the outdoors, where she spends as much time as possible skiing, hiking, riding bikes, and walking.

Sun Tunnels and Secrets is Carole's third published novel. Her blog is www.carolethayne.blogspot.com. She enjoys hearing from her readers and may be contacted at mcwarburton@gmail.com.